Deverell of the Globe

Selected Plays

DEVERELL
of the
GL☉BE

SELECTED PLAYS BY
REX DEVERELL

Edited by Don Perkins

Prairie Play Series: 8
Prairie Play Series General Editor, Diane Bessai

NeWest

Rights to perform or produce the script on stage or in other form are retained by the author. Interested persons are requested to apply for permission and terms to:

Rex Deverell, c/o The Globe Theatre, 1801 Scarth St., Regina, Saskatchewan, S4P 2G9 (306) 525-9553

First Edition

Canadian Cataloguing in Publication Data

Deverell, Rex, 1941-
 Deverell of the Globe

(Prairie Play Series Number 8)

ISBN 0-920897-66-5 (bound). — ISBN 0-920897-64-9 (pbk.)

I. Perkins, Don II. Title III. Series.

PS8557.E877A6 1989 C812'.54 C89-090332-8 PR9199.3.D39A6 1989

Credits

Prairie Play Series General Editor: Diane Bessai
Cover Design: Bob Young
Cover Photos:
 Thomas Hauff, Kevin Bundy, Donna White (*Afternoon of the Big Game*)
 Wendy Van Riesen, William Vickers (*Quartet For Three Actors*)
 François-Regis Klanfer, Susan Kramer (*Boiler Room Suite*)
Printing and Binding: Hignell Printing Limited, Winnipeg

Financial assistance

 Alberta Culture
 The Canada Council
 The Alberta Foundation for the Literary Arts
 The Saskatchewan Arts Board

Printed and Bound in Canada

NeWest Publishers Limited
Suite 310, 10359 - 82 Avenue
Edmonton, AB T6E 1Z9

Every effort has been made to obtain permission for photographs and quoted material. If there is an omission or error the author and publisher would be grateful to be so informed.

Contents

Acknowledgements and Permissions

The publisher and playwright gratefully acknowledge the following for permission to reprint quoted material found within the play *Quartet for Three Actors*:

From *You are My Sunshine* by Jimmy Davis. Copyright 1940 by Peer International Corporation

From *Inka Dinka Doo* by Jimmy Durante and Ben Ryan. Copyright 1933 by Bourne Co., New York. Used by permission of Bourne Music Canada Limited, Toronto, Canada.

From *Those Were The Days* by Gene Raskin. Copyright 1968 by Essex Music, Inc., New York, N.Y.

From *Tip-Toe Thru' The Tulips With Me* by Al Dubin and Joe Burke. Copyright 1929 by Warner Bros. Inc. (renewed). All rights reserved. Used by permission.

From *Cabaret* by John Kander and Fred Ebb. Copyright 1966 by Alley Music Corp. and Trio Music Co., Inc. Used by permission. All rights reserved.

Introduction

The Playwright

It has to be one of the ironies of Canadian theatre that "Saskatche-wan's" Rex Deverell, one of the West's most prolific dramatists, with nearly fifty plays for adults and children, is a transplanted easterner, born in Toronto (more or less by accident, he assures us) and raised in Stephen Leacock country, Orillia, Ontario. The process that turned Deverell into a playwright indelibly identified with the West, and with Regina's Globe Theatre, began by chance and proceeded gradually. The result was a mutually beneficial relationship that has served writer, theatre, and audiences for many years.

Ken Kramer, the Globe's artistic director, records the beginnings of this process this way in the program notes for the original production of *Boiler Room Suite* (1977):

> ... in 1971/72 we engaged an actress named Rita Deverell who brought her husband with her — Rex Deverell. When we discovered he was a writer and read a few of his plays, we ask-ed him if he would be interested in writing for Young People.
>
> The 1972/73 School Tour featured *Shortshrift*, a new play for children by Rex Deverell. 1973/74 — *The Copetown City Kite Crisis*. 1974/75 *Sarah's Play* and *Power Trip* (for High Schools).
>
> By this time our artistic ties were well cemented and both Rex and the Globe wanted a closer relationship. After applying to the Canada Council and the Saskatchewan Arts Board for funds, Rex was appointed writer-in-residence for 1975/76.

Prior to his engagement at the Globe as the first playwright-in-resi-dence in western Canada, Deverell had combined his playwriting with his work as a clergyman. After theological studies that included a Mas-ter's degree in Theatre and Theology, he had been pastor of Edward St. Baptist Church in St. Thomas, from 1967 to 1970. During this period

Rex and Rita Deverell had made a name for themselves performing "put-together" creations around specific themes for churches and various other interest groups in eastern Canada and the U.S.

The decision by the Globe to appoint Deverell began to pay off quickly. In that first year, four new Deverell pieces appeared in the Globe's children's program, while three earlier pieces were reworked for the cultural events of the Montreal Olympic games. In addition, Rex completed a short play called *For Land's Sake* for the Department of the Environment. Furthermore, he was already working on what was to become *Boiler Room Suite*, the piece that would introduce him to Globe's adult audiences and that would prove to be his most widely-performed adult work to date.

More important than the numbers and titles, however, was the process of acclimatization Deverell experienced. In a letter to me dated March 21, 1989, he wrote,

> When I first came to Saskatchewan in 1971, I saw two major differences from the more buffered life of small town Ontario where I grew up. First there was the land, vast and fickle; and second, not unrelated to the first, how close Saskatchewan seemed to the line between survival and destruction. The environment worked on me, got inside, made me a part of it.
>
> My first work for the Globe Theatre was aimed at school age audiences who by far and large lived in rural settings. I set many of these plays in small prairie towns using them as microcosms for serious social issues. I think this was a happy confluence of my questions and aims for theatre and the actual circumstances in which my audiences lived. The result was a series of whimsical issue-related pieces.
>
> When I began to write for the Globe adult audiences I had been writing for their sons and daughters for four or five years. I had become aware of the province as an intensely political place. Its history of democratic socialism and breakthrough co-operative solutions merged with a continuing belligerence against outside exploitation. My agenda changed and I alternated between personal imaginative work like *Boiler Room Suite* and docudramas like *Medicare*. The personal plays took on a political edge and the documentaries no longer used Saskatchewan as a setting but rather as a topic. Each fed into the other. My religious and aesthetic consciousness became linked into the militancy and vigour of the Saskatchewan left/right political dialogue.

I felt there was a pact between the audience and me. If I could reflect both the concerns and the jokes of the community then the community would allow me to share my own particular questions and explorations. I think all in all it was a healthy transaction. Something as important as politics and personal as love came together on a common ground. It was kind of like Ogie's memories of his wife in *Afternoon of the Big Game*: "And this is the point, you see — she turned me towards others."

As the four plays selected for this collection illustrate, the pact Deverell speaks of is a contract in constant renegotiation, taking new forms and striking a new balance with each new play. Sometimes he appears to lean more towards the audience's specific interests or to topical issues, as in *Beyond Batoche*, which was first produced in 1985, one hundred years after the Northwest Rebellion and Riel's trial and execution, and in *Afternoon of the Big Game*, which brings together two of Saskatchewan's abiding passions, politics and the fate of the Roughriders (the third is, of course, the weather — see *Boiler Room Suite*). At other times, as in *Boiler Room Suite* and in *Quartet for Three Actors*, he appears to lean towards his own interests in the role and the effect of theatre in society. However, the scale rarely tips entirely to one side or the other. The essential elements of audience's and playwright's interests are always there, except perhaps in *Quartet*, the only work in this collection not solidly located in the West.

Since 1977, Deverell has written for both Globe's young and its adult audiences. His works for adults have included historical docudramas, work with collectives, "personal" plays, pageants, musicals, and translations. He has also written television and radio scripts. Most recently he has turned to opera with the libretto to *Boiler Room Suite: The Opera*. Always, regardless of form, out from behind the history, the politics, the sociology, the humor, and the meditations on the role of theatre in society, his central driving ideal — turning towards others — emerges as an abiding concern. As he recently admitted in an interview with Doris Hillis, "I have this kind of naive philosophy that suggests doing things together is the best way" (76). His drama, at its best, does not push this philosophy; rather, it illustrates, explores, and explains it, putting a variety of groups to the test of drama.

The Plays

Boiler Room Suite introduced Rex Deverell to the adult audience of the Globe. A piece for high schools, called *Power Trip*, went through considerable revision and has gone on to become Deverell's best-known work. He has recently further reworked it as the libretto of an opera for the music of composer Quenten Doolittle of Calgary. A production, directed by Keith Turnbull, to be mounted by the Banff Centre Music Theatre, has been booked for a tour in Britain. A performance in the Purcell Room of the Royal Festival Hall is planned, at about the same time that this book is scheduled for publication.

In *Boiler Room Suite*, all of the Deverell elements are in place. The lives of the derelicts Aggie Rose and Sprugg are in part a satirical attack on attitudes towards society's outcasts and on the institutions that are supposed to aid them. In the introduction to the Talonbooks edition of the play, Deverell explains that some of the details came from experiences he had and stories he heard as "an optimistic, young theological student," living in a halfway house with a group of alcoholics (7). At the same time, it is a wry commentary on the history of Canadian theatre almost up to the time the play was first produced.

Before they became what they are, Aggie was an aspiring actress who could not find an audience, and Sprugg was a poet who could not make his voice heard. They have been pushed to the fringes of society. Yet, as their improvisations show, their combined talents can still at least temporarily transform even the worst of spaces and most inhospitable of environments, a "thinly disguised metaphor for hell," into an approximation of heaven and an arena of hope and possibility. They can even change the perspective and engage the atrophied imagination of a dour, hostile, prosaic, practical man like Pete — surely the prototypical Canadian audience. They move him so much that he chooses to disobey the rules, so strong is his wish to prolong his contract with this now-fascinating pair and their strange but entrancing power.

Aggie, with her push-pull relationship to an environment she cannot leave and cannot abide, is the vehicle for much of the "western" humor. She went east to try to become an actress, but found it too full of easterners. On the other hand, she has become a drunk to "escape the winter. God, I hate living on the prairies." Her vision of heaven is any place warm, or, at least, not cold.

Beyond Batoche was Deverell's, and the Globe Theatre's, contribution to the 1985 "celebrations" that marked the hundredth anniversary of the Northwest Rebellion. His twin focus on public concerns and personal questioning plays on the various myths that have grown up around Louis Riel, and dramatizes the issues and problems of dramatizing history. In his program notes to the play, Deverell states his hopes "that Batoche in 1885 will lead the viewer to reflect on values current in 1985." Some of the material for the play came from his own experiences producing the script for a five-part CBC radio play, *The Riel Commission*.

Beyond Batoche is about a production team trying to create a script for a made-for-TV movie about Riel. Each member of the team has a favorite vision of the Métis leader, a vision tied in with personal ambitions and self-image. Matt, the playwright, wants a visionary and a prophet, someone who set out to create a new, better kind of world. Shane, the actor, wants a revolutionary hero. He is even momentarily willing to toss over Riel for Gabriel Dumont, when it appears Dumont will play better. Burns, the producer, wants a B-movie western hero, someone who will sell on the international (read U.S.) market. Yvonne, the Métis advisor, wants a Riel who can serve her people as a role model in their continuing struggles for dignity and identity. Typically, the group cannot come together productively until it sheds a major blocking force — the playwright who puts his personal vision and prerogatives ahead of the project itself.

Deverell manages to needle a number of theatrical clichés and techniques of the day. Targets of Deverell's wit include documentary theatre and the influence of money on art. When Burns announces that the eastern interests financing the project forbid any attacks on the reputation of Sir John A. Macdonald, Matt promptly inserts Macdonald's own speeches. Surely the backers cannot argue with "real" history.

Interestingly, Deverell makes the playwright the butt of much of the ironic humor. Matt claims to "be" Riel. After all, as a playwright, he has all of his characters inside him. Matt also holds out for a dramatized history, with created speeches and scenes that convey the greater truths behind the history. To his great shock, he discovers as he creates his artistic version of the truth that he also "contains" Sir John A. Macdonald, more prominently than he does Riel.

Michael Scholar suggests that in the self-reflexive turn at the end, as Matt begins to write the play we have just seen as an exploration and examination of his own shortcomings, Deverell "attempts to capture, or re-define, the mystery of art. For art which has convinced us that art is a lie, has told us truthfully that art is a lie" (338). Deverell also reminds us to consider the motives behind representations of "history," and to watch for the moral or political filters through which both individuals and groups screen their history.

Quartet For Three Actors, the most abstract piece in this collection, is dedicated to actors. Deverell writes in his program note to the Globe production that they are

> that race of people who struggle to bring life to my words. Actors bring light out of darkness each evening. They know the absurdity of their art, a creation that disappears at the end of every performance. When I began this work, my mind went back to the Old Testament story about the prophet who sought meaning on a mountain top: "And a strong wind rent the mountains, but the Lord was not in the wind: and after the wind an earthquake, but the Lord was not in the earthquake: and after the earthquake a fire, but the Lord was not in the fire: and after the fire a still small voice and behold the Lord spoke to Elijah" (From 1 Kings 19). This is what we ask actors to do for us, to create a sound and fury that will lead us to a silence signifying everything.

Mickey, Krull and Fran are brought together by a mysterious "someone" in the control booth so that they can work through personal and professional problems. In part, this play dramatizes the love-hate relationship actors can develop for their work. It is also an extended metaphor for that state actors sometimes experience where they can no longer get off the stage, where they seem trapped in an endless performance. The maze of blocked or lost exits that symbolizes this state took a bizarre turn at one early rehearsal. A Globe building staff member, mindful of some fire regulations, locked a door being used as one of the stage entrances. This gave an audience of production staff pause to ponder the paradoxical dilemma of an actor, playing an actor who could not get offstage, lost for a way back onstage.

Each character tries to save the group through a star turn that features his or her own personal talent in a script that uncannily parallels personal anxieties about career, identity, and purpose. Only by combining efforts in mutually supporting roles in a script that features none of them can they open the doors of the theatre, letting themselves and their audience go — for the moment.

While *Quartet* is obviously not as rooted in the West as the rest of these plays, it is a clear descendant of *Boiler Room Suite*. For example, the mad dance of Aggie and Sprugg becomes the metaphorical "wild dance of freedom and kindness" Fran hopes to arouse her audiences to. Like Aggie, these three actors also tire of "just playing games" and telling stories. And once again, as he does through Pete, Deverell lets the audience reflect on itself. After originally casting them as "not there" in the "empty" theatre Mickey, Krull and Fran enter, Deverell brings the audience into the action as *Quartet* ends. He turns the playgoers' eyes on themselves, to see themselves as the actors see them: a "wonderful looking bunch . . . most of them," transformed, maybe, into "little kings and minor prophets" — if the actors have done their job.

Afternoon of the Big Game brings together in a witty and telling way the two most popular weekend pastimes in Saskatchewan: watching the Riders and arguing politics — not always in that order. This is one of a number of pieces, including the musicals *Mandarin Oranges* and *Resuscitation of a Dying Mouse*, both written with Rob Bryanton, that Deverell wrote in response to Saskatchewan's shift to the political right in the early 1980s. In 1982 voters turned from a party and philosophy that appeared mired in attitudes more appropriate to the Great Depression and chose a party that held out the promise of wealth and growth in the present.

When the Progressive Conservatives took power under Grant Devine, they began to reduce and politically sanitize the civil service and to sell crown corporations to private interests. The process was aided by consultants from Ontario's long-standing Progressive Conservative government — the Big Blue Machine. Deverell capitalizes on this chromatic opportunity when he mirrors the political situation against a football match between the Green and White of the Saskatchewan Roughriders and the Double Blue of the Toronto Argonauts.

The six characters watching the game represent a wide cross-section of Saskatchewan political interests and views. Ogie, the filter through whom we see and hear the action, is the old and not always clear-thinking voice of the Old Left. He still remembers the rhetoric and enthusiasm of his younger days, but is only occasionally in touch with the present. Floyd is the glib young voice of the New Right. Complicating this basic ideological confrontation are women, youth, and a discarded servant of the new order, who has just found himself "returned to the private sector," but who cannot somehow find this cause for celebration — any more than could the many civil servants so returned by the Saskatchewan PC. The six are also a representation in miniature of the Globe audience itself. The stage metaphor, after all, plays with the cliché of the political football, something most of the characters become in the course of the play, and something many in the audience may have felt like at the time.

There is no mistaking where Deverell wants our sympathies to lie. The fortunes of the Roughriders reflect the swings in mood and position in the political argument going on in Bill and Diane's rec room. The last-second, typically melodramatic victory by the underdog Riders follows the rejection of Floyd and his philosophy by everyone else in the room. However, Deverell ends with that characteristic turn. As Ogie reminds us, the game and the play are purely fictional: time now to return to reality. And he — like the party and the co-operative philosophy he represents — is in no shape to compete in that real world against the "me first" attitudes all around. That will take another generation, and a renewed will.

These plays taken collectively and read chronologically exhibit Deverell's developing sense of his audience and of his craft. The combination of his sense of the local, his more general explorations into theatrical metaphor, and his dramatized meditations on the role of theatre in society gives Rex Deverell's drama a rich texture, and a significance that extends into a sphere considerably larger than Regina's Globe.

Don Perkins
University of Alberta
June 1989

Boiler Room Suite

§

First Performance

Boiler Room Suite was first performed at the Globe Theatre in Regina, Saskatchewan, on January 21, 1977, with the following cast:

Aggie Rose — *Sue Kramer*

Sprugg — *François-Regis Klanfer*

Pete — *Stanley Coles*

The production was directed by Kenneth Kramer and designed by Charles Harper. Costumes were designed by Marion Buller.

Characters

Aggie Rose and **Sprugg:** derelicts of indeterminate age

Pete: janitor, middle-aged

Photo Credit: Bob Howard

*Sue Kramer as Aggie, Fran*ç*ois-Regis* Klanfer as Sprugg
Globe Theatre, Regina, 1977.

Act One

The scene is the boiler room of a hotel. We might surmise from the condition of the pipes and ductwork that the hotel is an ancient one, much in need of repair. Sheets of asbestos hang like Spanish moss in a tropical swamp. The room is dank and dirty. Steam and creaking metal are heard, valves shutting on and off automatically, a roaring fire — all combine in an informal cacophony. The boiler room is a fantastic place, a matrix for fantasy, full of dingy concrete, copper, lead, galvanized tin reflecting firelight from a furnace grating.

In one corner of the room, a kind of nest has been built with the aid of an old mattress, dirty blankets, orange crates and cardboard. In another area, a pile of junk forms a kind of staircase up into the shadows overhead.

One or two light bulbs dangle from the ceiling. They are not lit at the opening, but when they are, they will create deep shadows and not much illumination.

At the opening, in the semi-dark, we hear the sound of an old window being pried open. A shaft of outside light projects itself down from high overhead. A large paper bag on a string is lowered into the light. Very slowly, it descends to the floor and makes a gentle landing. Then, the light is blocked out by two hulking shadows. Aggie and Sprugg enter, descending the staircase of junk, out of the overhead ductwork.

These two tramps are not your conventional tramps with the layers of rags and the gloves with the fingers cut out — not at all. These are tramps with airs. Both they and their clothes have seen better days — and the days have been much, much better. How old are they? That is hard to determine with worn battered folk such as they. Sometimes they seem as old as the world, sometimes, not so old.

Aggie climbs up to the light and screws in the bulb. Sprugg, who is caught on the staircase, examines the strange environment revealed by the light. Aggie climbs down and looks enquiringly at Sprugg.

Sprugg: *With a straight face.* Nice place you got here.

After he has spoken, he laughs and laughs — with increasing gusto. His frame becomes contorted with his laughter, and then, with coughing. He produces a ragged handkerchief and mops his face. His eye fastens on an old scrapbook among Aggie's scanty possessions. She rushes to hide it.

Aggie: *Unamused.* It's all right. Take off your coat.

Sprugg: *Taking off his coat.* Thank you.

Aggie: *Removing her own coat.* Look at this, will you! *Looking at her coat, which is wet and covered with slush.* Look at this. The bastards!

Sprugg: What can you do?

Aggie: You see what you have to put up with in this town?

Sprugg: *Shaking his head.* It's like that all over. It's a sad commentary, isn't it?

Aggie: Where do you come from?

Sprugg: *Merrily.* Oh, from going to and fro in the earth, my dear, and walking up and down in it.

Aggie: Walking up and down in it.

Sprugg: *Confidentially.* The Book of Job. That's what Satan says to the Lord. It's in the Bible.

Aggie: Oh. *She is nervous for a moment.* You're not a preacher?

Sprugg: My goodness, no! That's a good one.

Aggie: *Relieved.* You had me wondering.

Sprugg: You won't believe it, but yesterday, I was in Winnipeg. If all this had happened yesterday, I wouldn't have been part of it, would I?

Aggie: I guess not.

Sprugg: It's something to think about.

Aggie: Who are you?

Sprugg: Sprugg.

Aggie: Sprugg?

Sprugg: Yes. It's my first name — Sprugg.

Aggie: Do you have a last name?

Sprugg: Of course.

Aggie: I like to know who I'm drinking with.

Sprugg: Naturally.

Aggie: Sprugg who?

Sprugg: *Annoyed with her.* Just a minute! *He pauses, then becomes annoyed with himself.* This is ridiculous. *There is a long pause, then surprise.* I've forgotten. *Speaking happily.* I have! I've forgotten!

Aggie: *Guffawing.* You've forgotten your last name?

Sprugg: I never liked it anyway. Good riddance. What's yours?

Aggie: Rose.

Sprugg: Rose? But they called you Aggie when they threw the pennies.

Aggie: Aggie Rose.

Sprugg: I see.

Aggie: Did you say they called me Aggie?

Sprugg: Yes.

Aggie: By name?

Sprugg: Go get 'em, Aggie. That's what they said.

Aggie: Bastards.

Sprugg: I know.

Aggie: *Thirstily eyeing the brown paper bag he has placed on the table.* Thanks for the bottle.

She lurches towards the bottle.

Sprugg: My pleasure. . . . I had come into a few dollars, the result of the beneficence of a clergyman in Moosomin. . . .

Aggie begins tearing at the bag.

Sprugg: Wait!

Aggie: What?

Sprugg: *Grabbing the package.* Have you got no patience, no elegance, no *je ne sais quoi?*

Aggie: No!

Sprugg: *Angrily.* You can't just . . . just slosh this down like it was some kind of cheap booze . . . some kind of . . . cheap . . . booze! This is a costly potion full of . . . peculiar properties.

Aggie: *Amazed.* Are you nuts?

Sprugg: I'm disgusted. Were you going to guzzle this down like a common wino?

Aggie: Yes.

Sprugg: *Thundering.* Sit down! I should never have come here.

Aggie is so surprised that she sits down.

Sprugg: This is typical. Typical! We have no civilized drinking habits in our country. You'd think we were a bunch of alcoholics or winos or skid row bums!

Aggie begins to laugh and, after a moment, Sprugg begins to see the humor in what he has said.

Sprugg: We see a bottle of fine wine and what do we do, straight off?

Aggie: Drink it.

Sprugg: Right. No appreciation, no ceremony, no ritual, no damn nothing.

Aggie: Right.

Sprugg And you — you! A few young hooligans throw pennies at you. . . .

Aggie: Bastards.

Sprugg: Just because of a trivial incident like that. . . .

Aggie: I had to go down on my knees in the muck.

Sprugg: You were slightly humiliated. That is still no reason. . . .

Aggie: How did they know my name?

Sprugg: You're known on the streets.

Aggie: Am I?

Sprugg: Probably.

Aggie: Goddammit!

Aggie reaches for the bag in anguish.

Sprugg: No! We'll do this right or we won't do it at all! You don't
turn to the bottle to seek solace, to drown your sorrows!

Aggie: What's it for, then?

There is a long pause.

Sprugg: You're right.

He draws a bottle out of the bag.

Sprugg: A fine vintage, Aggie.

*What we have here is a jug of cheap port. Sprugg unscrews the cap
and sniffs it as he would a cork. Aggie reaches for the jug.*

Aggie: Come on. . . .

Sprugg: No, no, no.

He goes to his coat and produces two very large wine glasses.

Aggie: I'll be damned.

Sprugg: I'm never without them.

*He pours the wine and they raise the glasses to one another, tasting the
wine elegantly.*

Sprugg: An elixir, Aggie. An elixir of solace.

Aggie: Sure.

Sprugg: I don't know if you're known in the streets, Aggie. How
would I know that? I haven't been in this city for years. The last
time I was here, I stayed up there.

He indicates the hotel overhead.

Aggie: No kidding.

Sprugg: Yes, I remember being awakened at one in the morning,
when the tap room let out. There were drunks shouting in the
street. That was a long time ago. Now look at me.

Aggie: I never stayed here.

Sprugg: You do now.

Aggie: *Happier.* That's true. *There is a pause.* Thanks, Sprugg.

Sprugg: For what?

Aggie: For helping me out of the slush.

Sprugg: A damsel in distress.

Aggie: They laughed at me . . . and I crawled in the gutter . . . and for what?

Sprugg: Three cents.

Aggie: I thought they were dimes. Three lousy cents . . . and they knew my name, the bastards!

Sprugg: Forget about them, Aggie, forget about them. We shall sweep ourselves away from all of that. This is no ordinary wine. In this bottle, my dear, there is a strange elixir known only to me and the Liquor Board. We . . . we shall conjure up reality, my dear . . . conjure it up! *He drinks some wine.* Ah, in wine is truth. *In vino veritas est.* That's Latin.

Aggie: Latin? You're a queer old duck.

Sprugg: What's wrong with Latin? There's nothing wrong with Latin. People don't learn it anymore. That's the only thing wrong with Latin. *In vino veritas est.*

Aggie: I'll drink to that.

Sprugg: *Non solum veritas sed veritas ut opportat.* Not only truth, but truth as it ought to be.

Aggie: Here's to it. Amen.

Sprugg: *Intoning.* Amen.

There is a great blast of steam from one of the boilers.

Sprugg: Lord, how did you ever find your way down here?

Aggie: The back alleys are main street for the likes of us. I shop for holes in the walls . . . wherever I can crawl in out of the cold. I didn't know this was The Provincial.

Sprugg: No?

Aggie: Not at first. Old Blinks MacPherson saw me climbing out of here one time. "Hey," he says, "Aggie, I see you got a room at The

Provincial." He thought it was a big joke. Blinks. We call him Blinks because he blinks all the time, you know? God, it was cold today.

Sprugg: Aggie, you must have been a good looking woman in your time.

Aggie looks up at him in surprise.

Aggie: Maybe.

Sprugg: I mean, you still are.

Aggie: Hmph.

Sprugg: But I bet you were a real looker in your prime.

Aggie: They used to say. . . .

Sprugg: What?

Aggie: That I was, I guess.

Sprugg: Have you kept pictures?

Aggie: No.

Her glance betrays her lie.

Aggie: I never show them to anybody. I don't look at them myself anymore.

Sprugg: Why not?

Aggie: Why?

Sprugg has no answer, so he nods wisely.

Aggie: Look up there.

Sprugg: *Looking up.* Yes.

Aggie: All those pipes.

Sprugg: There are probably two or three hundred rooms up there.

Aggie: And pipes to every one of them. . . .

Sprugg: Yep.

Aggie: Sometimes — not all the time, mind you — but sometimes I look up there and I think I can see through the ceiling.

Sprugg: *Astonished.* Through the ceiling.

Aggie: It's a trick of the imagination.

Sprugg: No, no. The imagination doesn't play tricks.

Aggie: It's like an X-ray.

Sprugg: *Delighted.* And you can see into the lobby?

Aggie: Into the lobby and right up through the ceiling of the lobby.

Sprugg: Amazing.

Aggie: And right up through the ceiling of the second floor and on up through the rooms — one room after another, on and on. You know something?

Sprugg: What?

Aggie: This hotel must weigh a considerable weight.

Sprugg: I suppose so.

Aggie: Yes.

Sprugg: An enormous avoirdupois.

Aggie: Enormous. A what?

Sprugg: Avoirdupois.

Aggie: Yes.

Sprugg: Extreme weight.

Aggie: Yeah. . . .

There is a pause.

Aggie: It'd be awful if it all came down on us.

They contemplate the prospect for a time.

Sprugg: It would be.

Aggie: *Hiking up her skirt.* Look . . . I have sores on my legs.

Sprugg: That's too bad.

Aggie: Ulcers.

Sprugg: Ulcers?

Aggie: That's what they told me.

Sprugg: Who told you ulcers?

Aggie: At the clinic.

Sprugg: You get ulcers in the stomach.

Aggie: So I got them on my legs . . . from worrying too much.

Sprugg: What about?

Aggie: Stupid things. Like this building falling in on me. I worry about that.

Sprugg: If it falls — it falls.

Aggie: But I might be drunk or asleep and I'd have the whole she-bang down on me and there I'd be: people crawling all over me in their nightshirts, bell boys trying to have their way with me, salesmen trying to sell me stuff, waitresses trying to take my order, desk clerks trying to write down my name . . . managers trying to charge me for the room . . . it's a nightmare.

Sprugg: Yes, indeed.

Aggie: I break out in a cold sweat just thinking about it . . . all those inmates trying to find their suitcases.

Sprugg: Aggie, right now! Who do you see up there?

Aggie: *Becoming calmer.* Yeah, who do I see? *She begins to laugh.* I see an old woman up there. . . .

Sprugg: Go on. . . .

Aggie: With tears in her eyes.

Sprugg: That's not amusing.

Aggie: She doesn't have any pants on.

Sprugg: *With a snort.* Oh! Why is she crying?

Aggie: I don't know. I think she is, somehow.

Sprugg: Drink up, Aggie. Details like that interest me.

Aggie: *Waking up.* It was only some kind of dream . . . a daydream or some other kind of dream.

Sprugg: *Annoyed with her.* Only a dream?

Aggie: Yes.

Sprugg: Only?

Aggie: Yes.

Sprugg: Only! I will not have this . . . this dismissing of the truth. This demeaning of an absolutely valid perception. You see an old lady up there. . . .

Aggie: No, I don't.

Sprugg: Nonsense, you do!

Aggie: You're crazy.

Sprugg: Drink up! No, no, no! The whole purpose of my life has suddenly taken focus. Suddenly, the purpose of my life has become that of making things possible — show me her face — to . . . to twist things . . . yes, twist things so that life is not life per usual — *show me her face* — going on as it always goes on, you understand? So I will not permit you to sabotage the whole purpose of my life as it has recently . . . become . . . and that is final.

Aggie: You *are* crazy!

Sprugg: That has nothing to do with it. Show me her face!

Aggie: Whose face?

Sprugg: *Exasperated with her.* The old woman. You see her. What does she look like?

Aggie: Sprugg, I haven't really got X-ray eyes. I was just pretending. For all I know, there might not even be an old lady.

Sprugg: Show me her face!

Aggie grunts in disgust and screws up her face.

Aggie: There, like that.

Sprugg: *Delighted.* Again.

Aggie: You want a performance. All right, I'll give you a performance.

More determined, she begins to contort her face and her body into those of a proud old dowager, who is full of sadness and rage.

Aggie: Like this. How's that?

Her voice changes to suit the character.

Aggie: Yes, like this. Now, you old man, are you satisfied?

Sprugg: *Laughing triumphantly.* Yes, yes indeed! I knew you could bring her down here!

He escorts her to the centre of an imaginary stage.

Sprugg: And now, Ladies and Gentlemen: The Story of the Old Lady without Pants.

Aggie and Sprugg become like children playing a game. They step in and out of character quite freely and it is apparent how much they enjoy putting the characters through whatever ordeals they can contrive. Various pieces of junk in the boiler room become props or costumes.

Aggie: *Suddenly inspired.* This old lady has not left her room in a very long time.

Sprugg: Ah.

Aggie: Several years, in fact. She is old, but she is also rich ... very rich. It used to be her habit to clothe herself in brocade and adorn her bosom with glittering cascades of jewellery. One everning, clad in a gown of gold brocade with banners and roses imprinted thereon, a diamond diadem upon her head and great carbuncular rings upon her fingers. . . .

Sprugg: I like that.

Aggie: Don't interrupt.

The lights seem to have changed. Aggie seems to have taken on the whole character of the woman she is describing. From bits of debris, a costume has come. We know we are still in the boiler room, and yet, we are somewhere else. The illusion is fragmented and in that incompleteness is the magic.

Aggie: Thus encrusted, one evening, I say, she descended in the elevator ... to the mezzanine. From the mezzanine, she proceeded down the grand staircase, all eyes upon her, to the main dining room. . . .

Sprugg: The Cadillac Room.

Aggie: Of course, the Cadillac Room ... and there, in the Cadillac Room. . . .

Sprugg now moves into the performance, becoming a series of supporting characters, improvising whatever the story needs to keep it going.

Sprugg: *As the Maitre d'.* The usual table for Madame?

Aggie: Of course, you fool. What would I want with an unusual table. Unusual tables are for fools and wastrels. Lead me to my usual table and be quick about it.

Sprugg: Yes, Madame. Immediately.... Shall we give this lady a name?

Aggie: She has a name.

Sprugg: Yes.

Aggie: Her name is Mrs. Avoirdupois. Her husband was a baron.

Sprugg: A baron?

Aggie: Yes, a railroad baron.

Sprugg: Oh.

Aggie: From Moose Jaw.

Sprugg: I see.

Aggie: Long since dead.

Sprugg: Yes.

Aggie: Which is why she is living in The Provincial.

Sprugg: *As the Maitre d'.* Come this way, Mrs. Avoirdupois.... Does that have to be her name?

Aggie: Yes, that one raised on the little dais. It allows me to survey the other diners, one by one. I want to know what they are eating and I want to disapprove of some and, perhaps, in a mild fashion, without excess enthusiasm, approve of others. *She has been seated.* Thank you, garçon.

Sprugg: An aperitif before dinner, Madame?

Aggie: I believe I shall. What shall it be? Something light, delicate. I do not believe persons of authority should drink indelicately.

Sprugg: No, Madame.

Sprugg pours her some more wine from the jug.

Aggie: Thank you. That will do beautifully.

Sprugg: Menu, Madame?

Aggie: I do not need a menu. Menus are for those who do not know what they want. I know what I want. I always know what I want;

therefore, I do not need a menu. I shall have what I usually have — the baked peasant under glass.

Sprugg: Peasant, Madame?

Aggie: Whatever.

Sprugg hurries off and leaves Aggie augustly surveying the dining room. She frowns at some of the diners and nods curtly once or twice at others. Finally, she sees someone she knows

Aggie: How do you do. Indeed.

She continues her survey of the room.

Aggie: Good evening.

Sprugg: *As a politician.* How are you, Mrs. Avoirdupois?

Aggie: Fine, thank you, Mr. Mayor. Fine, thank you. Essential services, Mr. Mayor — remember, essential services. That's the word for the day.

Sprugg: And a good word it is, Mrs. Avoirdupois. I promise to keep it in mind.

Aggie: You do that.

Sprugg: Enjoy your meal.

Aggie: Thank you. Good evening.

Sprugg: Evening.

He changes character into a sycophantic little man.

Sprugg: Ah, Mrs. Avoirdupois, it's so nice to see you again, and you're looking so well, too.

Aggie: Yes, I am. Who are you?

Sprugg: Bowens, ma'am. The general manager from down at the yard, ma'am, in Moose Jaw.

Aggie: I seem to recall you. Of course, I was never able to keep track of the workers. I left that sort of thing to my husband . . . my poor, dear husband.

Sprugg: He was a great man, Mrs. Avoirdupois. I don't mind saying so. We'll never see his likes again.

Aggie: Behind every great man, Bowen, there lies a greater woman.

Sprugg: We all knew that, ma'am. You were the power behind the throne, so to speak, and a very fine power you were — and still are — very fine, ma'am.

Aggie: Yet he was a man of quality in his own right.

Sprugg: Oh yes, oh yes! No doubt about that!

Aggie: However, I shall never forgive him for dying. It was most inconsiderate. I had a great deal to do that day. In many ways, he was a very annoying man.

Sprugg: Yes, of course.

Aggie: I beg your pardon?

Sprugg: I'm sure he was. . . .

Aggie: Was what?

Sprugg: Annoying.

Aggie: Is that an aspersion?

Sprugg: No! No, it isn't.

Aggie: *In a majestic fury.* I will not listen to such slander! Never, n ver, do you hear me, never let anyone cast the least shadow upon the absolute integrity, *integrity*, of my dear but departed husband. I shall not stand for it, do you understand? I shall not and I will not. Waiter!

Sprugg: Yes, Madame.

Aggie: I no longer find this a desirable place to dine, garçon. I shall have my peasant sent up to my room.

Sprugg: Very good, Madame.

Aggie: *Resuming the narration.* She stood to leave. The eye of every diner was upon her; her rage had not gone unnoticed. She stepped down from the dais and stalked away. But her gown did not accompany her. It had caught on the corner of the table and there remained. Never had brocade torn so easily. Never had the Cadillac Room of The Provincial Hotel been so silent. Never had there been such complete suspension of all movement.

Sprugg: Roast Rock Cornish hen lay untouched on the plate. Beef Wellington cooled in the paralyzed jowls of the Mayor. Steak Diane hung, helplessly impaled on the tines of a silver fork, as all gazed aghast at the retreating Mrs. Avoirdupois.

Aggie: And for an amazing reason. The railroad baroness, caught up in the exultation of dressing herself for dinner, had omitted the precaution of underpants.

Sprugg: She clutched the shreds of her dignity around her and raced for the elevator.

Aggie: She spotted a potted palm tree in the vestibule and tried to tear the leaves off . . . but the tree was artificial, the leaves would not come away! Picking up the entire plant, she held it before her, entered the elevator and rose to her room.

Sprugg: No one had offered her a coat or even a hat to cover the shame of her nakedness.

Aggie: She collapsed in tears on her bed . . . and there she stayed. . . . To this day, she has never gone forth from that room. The maid cleans every morning with averted eyes. Her meals are left outside the door. She has never spoken another word to anyone.

Sprugg: So that is why she sits for hours on end before her mirror. . . .

Aggie: Trying on one piece of jewellery after another. . . and weeping.

There is a long pause. Aggie, Sprugg, and the boiler room return to themselves.

Sprugg: That was very good.

Aggie: Yes.

Sprugg: It was my peculiar power that made it happen.

Aggie: I thought it was my acting.

Sprugg: No, I tell you I can make things happen. Around me, strange things happen all the time.

Aggie: Oh.

Sprugg: Yes.

Aggie: I was . . . at one time . . . on the stage.

Sprugg: Really!

Aggie: I didn't do very well. But I could have. Things did not work out.

Sprugg: I, too, had a grand aspiration.

Aggie: What was it?

Sprugg: It was not the theatre.

Aggie: There was no theatre.

Sprugg: Mine was the world of literature.

Aggie: Do you know what it's like to be a talented actress in a country where there is no theatre.

Sprugg: I had no opportunity, you see. If I had had the opportunity, I would have been a poet.

For Sprugg, the words have a sacred romance about them. For Aggie, the words are full of grievance.

Aggie: There were only touring companies from the United States and Great Britain.

Sprugg: People didn't understand the potency that was in my verse.

Aggie: I didn't stand a chance.

Sprugg: I was years ahead of my time.

Aggie: Who could?

Sprugg: They were cretins! Bloody cretins and Philistines! I was thirty or forty years ahead of my time.

Aggie: I played Lady Macbeth one time. I was brilliant. "Come to my woman's breast, all ye angels and ministers of grace — take my milk for gall!"

Sprugg: What?

Aggie: "The quality of mercy is not strained, but it pattereth down like a gentle rain. This bond doth give thee here no jot of blood. Take then thy bond, take thy pound of flesh, but in the cutting of it, thou art mad to say it . . . who would have thought the old man had so much blood in him."

Sprugg: Magnificent.

Aggie: "What's done cannot be undone. To bed, to bed, to bed."

Sprugg: Oh, I've given that up.

Aggie: That is in the play.

Sprugg: Of course.

Aggie: Have you?

Sprugg: Given it up?

She nods.

Sprugg: The spirit is willing. . . . *Regretfully.* But the flesh is weak.

Aggie: Anyway, it was an amateur company and didn't get reviewed by anybody who knew anything.

Sprugg: If people could read my work today, they might think more of it . . . but it's all gone. I lost it all. One moves so much. I couldn't keep it with me.

Aggie: There might have been a theatre somewhere in this country . . . but if there was, I didn't find it.

Sprugg: Why didn't you go to the States?

Aggie: I should have. I went East, one time.

Sprugg: Yeah?

Aggie: Sure. I got a few bucks together and I took the Greyhound bus to Toronto. When we got there I was fit to be tied. I never saw so many houses in one spot . . . and Easterners living in every one of them. Sent shivers up my spine. I had to come back. I thought about going to the States, but I hear it's worse.

There is a sudden great burst of laughter, offstage.

Aggie: Shhhh!

Sprugg: *Who will not be silenced before saying anything.* I thought we were alone.

Aggie: Shhhh! . . . No.

The sound of the grate opening is heard. The stage is lit by the furnace for a few moments. The grate closes.

Aggie: It's the janitor.

Sprugg: Does he know you're here?

Aggie: Sometimes I think he does and sometimes I think he doesn't.

The sound of footsteps retreating up metal stairs is heard.

Aggie: He sneaks up on me sometimes. Catches me by surprise. But

I'm usually very quiet. I sing to myself sometimes. . . but in a whisper. No. He may not know I'm here. If he knew, he'd kick me out, wouldn't he? He'd send me into the snow, the bastard.

Sprugg: He may know you live here and not be a bastard. If he does know, he's not a bastard. If he doesn't know, he may be or he may not be.

This is logical although Sprugg may not be sure that it is logical.

Aggie: *Logic aside.* They're all bastards.

Sprugg: If he's one, why doesn't he kick you out into the snow?

Aggie: Because he doesn't know I'm here!

Sprugg: Huh.

End of argument.

Aggie pours herself another drink.

Aggie: There was a time in my life, I drank bathtub gin.

Sprugg: They don't make it anymore. They make bathtubs. . . but they don't make bathtub gin. They use the tubs for baths.

There is a pause.

Sprugg: I'm worried.

Aggie: Why?

Sprugg: I can't think of anything to say.

Aggie: Nothing to worry about.

Sprugg: It is. If I don't say anything, then nothing will be said.

Aggie: Leastways, nothing foolish.

Sprugg: Pardon?

Aggie: What were you saying?

Sprugg: If nothing is said, this basement will descend into silence.

Aggie: Let it.

Sprugg: It's against my nature. It's a sin.

Aggie: Yeah?

Sprugg: By nature, I am compelled to fill every corner of life with sound and fury! With vivid coloration. The more the better! *He pauses.* But sometimes I can't think of anything.

A light bulb goes out.

Sprugg: Aggie?

Aggie: Yeah?

Sprugg: Did the light just go out?

Aggie: Yep.

Sprugg: *Relieved.* Oh, good. I thought it might be the booze.

There is a pause.

Sprugg: So, silence has set in and the lights have gone out.

Aggie: And you're getting weirder all the time.

Sprugg: *Rapidly.* I come from humble origins. My father and mother were simple, uneducated folk. I wish I could remember their names. Their last name — and my last name, of course — sounded like some sort of vegetable.

The light comes back on.

Aggie: There. It comes on and off like that.

The light goes off again.

Sprugg: My father dug ditches for a living. My chief memory of him is of a man down in a hole. One day, when I was only a small tot, I was watching him at work . . . down in a hole. After a time, I picked up a large rock which he himself had excavated. It was probably a very heavy rock, although I remember it as being very light. Memory takes the weight out of things. I carried the rock over to the edge of the ditch. My father dug away, unsuspectingly, far below. I took careful aim and let the rock fall.

Aggie: Did you kill him?

Sprugg: I missed.

Aggie: That's quite a vicious streak.

Sprugg: I have since gotten over my need for patricide. I deal with harsh realities in other ways.

Aggie: *Nervously.* Like what?

There is another blast of steam from one of the boilers.

Sprugg: Magic.

Aggie: Oh.

The light dims up hopefully, but fails and goes out.

Sprugg: There must be a failure in the power system.

Aggie: Must be.

Sprugg: What would you do if you had unlimited power?

Aggie: Fix the light.

Sprugg: Seriously. Do you know?

Aggie: Oh, I know, all right. First off, I'd show those punks up there — the bastards who threw the pennies — I'd show them a thing or two.

Sprugg: And then?

Aggie: I'd mop up the floor with Pilkington, the scum.

Sprugg: Pilkington?

Aggie: Down at the Welfare. And after I'd cleaned up on the bastards in this world . . . I would then order up an unlimited supply of booze and drink the whole thing.

Sprugg: *Disappointed.* You have a limited supply of imagination.

Aggie: I'm past insults.

Sprugg: Look at them, up there, Aggie: a thousand people . . . just a few hundred feet away . . . all kinds of people . . . people who make decisions . . . people who carry out decisions — people with power! There they are, stacked one above the other — tinker, tailor, soldier, sailor. . . . Pick one, Aggie!

Aggie: Prime Minister.

Sprugg: All right . . . Prime Minister!

The sound of a buzzer is heard. Light comes on. Sprugg sits behind a box and looks like a bureaucrat sitting at his desk.

Aggie: *As a voice on an intercom.* Mr. Pilkington, sir?

Sprugg: What is it, Miss Winthrop?

Aggie: Aggie Rose to see you, Mr. Pilkington.

Sprugg: *With patronizing amusement.* What a pleasant surprise. Can you get rid of her?

Aggie: She's becoming a little abusive, sir.

Sprugg: We can't have that, can we? Send her in, Miss Winthrop.

Aggie enters, as herself.

Sprugg: Ah, hello, Aggie! What brings us here today, eh?

Aggie: *Mimicking him.* What brings us here today, eh? You know damn well what brings us here today, eh!

Sprugg: Well, sit down. Let's discuss it, shall we?

Aggie: I'm giving you one last chance, Pilkington.

Sprugg: Mr. Pilkington, Aggie.

Aggie: And you wonder why I think you're a pig's ass.

Sprugg: No need for crudity, Aggie. . . .

Aggie: Shut up. Now, do I get it or don't I?

Sprugg: Get what?

Aggie: Welfare, you idiot! You're the welfare officer aren't you? I want to know if I'm going to get welfare.

Sprugg: You mean social assistance. —

Aggie: I mean the dole, dammit! Yes or no?

Sprugg: Yes or no?

Aggie: Yes.

Sprugg: No.

Aggie: No?

Sprugg: No.

Aggie: No what?

Sprugg: No . . . you do not receive social assistance.

Aggie: Why not?

Sprugg: There are many reasons.

Aggie: Name one.

Sprugg: Let me put this as delicately as possible. *He pauses.* Aggie . . . you're a common drunk.

Aggie: Hah!

Sprugg: And you're obnoxious.

Obviously, they both have had frequent encounters with the Pilkingtons of this world. They enjoy this scene mightily.

Sprugg: Now, we've offered to cure you, Aggie. We've offered to send you to a rehabilitation centre where you could get yourself dried out and return as a more responsible member of society. Then, perhaps, we could consider giving you a certain amount of social assistance until you find your feet again. We've made that offer to you many times, Aggie, many times. We don't owe you a living, Aggie . . . but that offer — that very generous offer — is still open.

Aggie: *Setting him up.* And that is your last word, Mr. Pilkington?

Sprugg: That's it.

Aggie: *Pitifully.* Even though I'm starving, Mr. Pilkington?

Sprugg: You find enough to buy booze, don't you?

Aggie: Even though it's thirty below out there and I don't have a roof over my head, Mr. Pilkington?

Sprugg: It's all up to you, Aggie. Yes, that is my last word.

Aggie: Good!

Sprugg: What?

Aggie: Because I don't need your filthy social assistance.

Sprugg: *Shocked to the bone.* Of course you do. You have to need it. You're down and out. You're starving to death. You don't have adequate shelter. You obviously need our assistance.

Aggie: Then give it to me.

Sprugg: No, we won't!

Aggie: Fine, because I just happen to have become the Prime Minister of Canada — Le Premier Ministre du Canada — and I just happen to get more welfare than you get salary.

Sprugg: *Regaining his composure.* Hahaha, alcohol does strange things to the mind, Aggie.

Aggie: Listen to this then, you fool! *Addressing Parliament.* Mr. Speaker.

Sprugg: *As the Speaker.* The Prime Minister.

Aggie: *An example of oratorical pyrotechnics.* Mr. Speaker, it has come to my attention that certain social workers and glorified welfare officers are using their office to maintain an egotistical and sadistic power over their clients. This is a sad state of affairs in any state and I am of the opinion that it needs to be changed. It is undemocratic, fascistic, and not nice!

There is applause. The Prime Minister takes the opportunity to drink from a glass of wine near at hand.

Aggie: The poor unfortunates who fall under their evil machinations have enough to put up with without that. These are the sorry souls, burdened with our society's financial degradation. These are the sensitive souls who cannot bear the pain and injustice of life and so have turned to alcohol. Some of these are simply the essential group of unemployed. . . . I say essential, because, if there were no unemployed, where would you find anyone to employ?

There is more applause.

Aggie: Why should these poor little people bear the wild Machiavellian cruelty of power-hungry mandarins?

There is prolonged applause. The Prime Minister takes some more wine.

Aggie: *Coming down to the finish line.* Gaze within your hearts and put the question. Surely the heart, if it contains one tiny element of human warmth or kindness, will utter a cry of no! no! no! This cannot be; this shall not be! Therefore, as of this moment, I declare the slaves to be free!

Triumphant music begins to swell.

Aggie: Pilkington is out!

A tumultuous explosion is heard — the cheering of the Canadian masses — then there is music. The Prime Minister takes a final victorious glass of wine.

Sprugg: *As Pilkington, down on his knees.* Oh please, please, Madame Prime Minister, don't do this to me!

Aggie: Our mind is set. The course is irrevocable.

Sprugg: But I didn't mean it. I didn't know what I was doing. I was just following orders. (I know that's no excuse, but I'm trying everything I can think of!) I have a family to worry about! My wife doesn't work. . . . I have a small baby and there's another one in the oven. . . .

Aggie: A child?

Sprugg: I mean, my wife is pregnant. So please don't fire me, sir — I mean, Madame — please don't. . . .

Aggie: You have a child?

Sprugg: I'm a career civil servant. I have to have two children. I don't know how to survive out there. I wouldn't know how to make out on social assistance.

Aggie: You have a child, Pilkington.

Sprugg: Yes, but I'll give it away if you'll let me keep my job. . . .

Aggie starts to cry.

Sprugg: What is it, Aggie?

Aggie: I had a child once.

We are back in the boiler room.

Aggie: I had a child. . . .

Sprugg: *His own voice.* Once?

Aggie: He was a beautiful boy.

Sprugg: Where is he?

Aggie: I don't know. Do you?

Sprugg: Was I the father?

She shakes her head.

Aggie: That's true, we met only today.

Sprugg: No, I'm not the father . . . we just met.

Aggie: I must have left him with his father.

Sprugg: When you're on the move, it's hard to keep things with you.

Aggie: He was five years old. *Angrily.* A woman has to make a life for herself, doesn't she?

There is a long moment. Aggie begins to weep again, but silently this time. Sprugg offers her his handkerchief. To accept it would be to admit weakness, but finally she does accept it.

Sprugg: I was married once. I know what it's like.

Aggie: Did you have any children?

Sprugg: No. Being a parent is an awesome responsibility. Children can hold it against you all their lives.

Aggie: So what did you do?

Sprugg: We smoked a lot. We'd borrow each other's cigarettes until neither of us had any left. Then we'd search through the house . . . trying to find old bent ones we'd misplaced in a sock or somewhere. Finally, one of us would have to go out into the night to find a store still open and often there wasn't.

Aggie: All to keep from having children?

Sprugg: Eh?

Aggie: I find it hard to believe.

Sprugg: Oh, yes, I had such a relationship.

Aggie: You used cigarettes?

Sprugg: I don't understand why you are so amused. I don't find that amusing. Well, it is funny, I guess, being so desperate to get a cigarette. . . . If we'd had the foresight to stock up on weekends. . . .

Both Aggie and Sprugg are totally confused.

Aggie: I think we could probably figure this out.

Sprugg: Ah, forget it. People should be more content with not being able to understand things.

Aggie: More and more I understand less and less.

Sprugg: I'm the same way. It's old age.

Aggie: Maybe it's the booze. Down at the clinic they told me the booze was making my brain go soft. They said if I don't stop, my brain would turn to mush.

Sprugg: Who needs a hard brain?

Aggie: I'm having the D.T.'s. I thought it was real for a while, there.

Sprugg: What?

Aggie: Pilkington, the Prime Minister, all that.

Sprugg: It was.

Aggie: It was? No, it wasn't.

Sprugg: Yes! *He taps his head.* What's real is what's in here. That's what's real. All the rest doesn't count. That's why I drink — to lubricate the inside of my head. The inside of my head is the most important thing I got.

Aggie: Won't change a damn thing though.

Sprugg: Yeah?

Aggie: We can sit here making up fancy stories till we're blue in the face — and it won't change a damn thing up there. The bastards'll still do us in. Want a cigarette?

She rummages around in the junk until she finds a couple of carefully preserved cigarettes.

Aggie: And the weather'll still be freezing cold to boot.

Another great burst of laughter is heard offstage.

Sprugg: He's listening.

Aggie: No . . . he just laughs like that sometimes. . . for no reason at all.

Sprugg: No reason?

Aggie: No.

Sprugg: Maybe he remembers a joke.

Aggie: Maybe.

Sprugg: One about stoking furnaces, maybe.

Aggie: I don't know that one.

Neither does Sprugg.

Sprugg: You know what this place is, don't you?

Aggie: Sure.

Sprugg: It's a thinly disguised metaphor for hell.

Aggie: *Shocked.* It is not!

Sprugg: Look at it — furnace, fire, demonic keeper with demonic laugh, infernal light, heat, it's all here. It's a symbol of hell, Aggie.

Aggie: Who says?

Sprugg: I do.

Aggie: You think you can just call this a symbol of hell and all of a sudden it's a symbol of hell?

Sprugg: Yes.

Aggie: You're a pain in the ass.

Sprugg: I have every right. I can call this hell if I want to.

Aggie: What about me then?

Sprugg: I don't care. Do whatever you like.

Aggie: Okay, then . . . this place is no longer a symbol of hell . . . it is a symbol of. . . .

Sprugg: Wait a minute. . . .

Aggie: A symbol of heaven. There.

Sprugg: You can't do that.

Aggie: I just did.

Sprugg: A symbol has got to bear some relationship to the thing it symbolizes, damn it all! A boiler room hasn't got anything to do with heaven.

Aggie: Yes, it has. It has!

Sprugg: What, then?

Aggie: It's nice and warm down here.

Sprugg: Heaven isn't warm!

Aggie: I suppose it's freezing cold all the time.

Sprugg: No, but it isn't warm.

Aggie: In that case, I'd sooner be in hell.

Sprugg: Bodily comforts! Is that all you think of?

Aggie: My feet are always too cold. When I first came here, I thought this was a godsend.

Sprugg: Heaven is a place that is absolutely perfect.

Aggie: Do you believe in heaven?

Sprugg takes a long drink of wine. He does not answer her.

Aggie: When I was a little girl, I believed in heaven. I became very religious. *She indicates her scrapbook.* There's a picture of me in there in my confirmation dress. I think there is. There used to be. Anyway, I went to church, religiously. I wanted to become an altar boy. When they called for new altar boys, I turned up at the meeting. The priest said, "But you're a girl, Aggie, you're a girl." Then he began to laugh. Me too. I laughed too. And I ran out of the church. I lost my faith because I was embarrassed.

Sprugg: You lost your faith because you lost your face.

Aggie: I never looked back. From then on, I was an atheist.

Sprugg: Are you really an atheist?

Aggie takes a long drink of wine. She does not answer him.

Sprugg: Our generation does not answer questions like that quickly.

Aggie: Are you?

Sprugg: *Quickly.* No. No, I'm not. The universe, my dear, operates with the precision and the order of a divinely ordained dial-the-time-lady service.

Aggie: Dial-the-time-lady?

Sprugg: Indeed. If you were out for a stroll in the woods and you came across a woman talking into a telephone saying, "The time is . . ." *He pauses.* " . . . two forty-five and ten seconds. The time is . . . two forty-five and twenty seconds. The time is . . . eight forty-eight . . . " and so on. Now, if you came across such a lady in the middle of a forest, would you suppose . . . would it be logical to assume that nobody had put her there? That she was there merely by chance? Of course not! That is why I am a believer.

Aggie: I never looked at it that way before.

Sprugg: No. And another thing, you see . . . the time-lady is a real person — not just an impersonal chronometric machine. That is why I not only believe in God, but I believe in a personal God.

Aggie: I can't argue with that.

Sprugg: And another thing: *Speaking intensely.* I believe that I *am* the time-lady.

Aggie: No!

Sprugg: Yep. I and the time-lady are one.

Aggie: I wouldn't give you the time of day.

Sprugg: Neither of us?

Aggie: I hate time. Time is terrible. It carries you on its back like a slow old monster. You don't know where it's taking you and it laughs at you every step of the way. I'd rather get there and be done with it, Sprugg. The going is awful.

Sprugg: Ah, I understand what you mean.

Aggie: Is God time?

Sprugg: God is eternal.

Aggie: Maybe that's why he doesn't speed things up.

Sprugg pours Aggie more wine.

Sprugg: Then you've abandoned all hope.

Aggie: Once I thought politics might be the answer. I joined a party. Then . . . I don't know. . . .

Sprugg: You became disillusioned?

Aggie: I figured out that politics couldn't change the weather. The blizzard is always going to come.

Sprugg: You gave up politics because of the weather?

Aggie: Yep.

Sprugg: That's disgusting.

Without warning, Aggie flies into a rage.

Aggie: Don't you judge me! What right have you got to judge me, you stupid, miserable, broken down excuse for a half-assed wino pile of garbage. Don't go. Conjure up something else.

Sprugg: I try to bring a little warmth, a little human kindness into your tired existence . . . and this is how you repay me.

Aggie: You called me disgusting. C'mon. . . .

Sprugg: Stupid, am I?

Aggie: No, I'm sorry. C'mon, Sprugg.

Sprugg: I can't think of a thing.

Aggie: Sure you can.

Sprugg: Do it by yourself.

Aggie: I can't. It takes genius, Sprugg.

Sprugg: Well then. . . .

Aggie: Okay?

Sprugg: Cast your eyes aloft once more, Aggie. . . .

Aggie: Cast my eyes aloft?

Sprugg: And choose. Who do you want to be?

Aggie: Hmmm. . . . What about God Himself? Hell, eh? I've been everything else!

Sprugg: This is a little delicate. People aren't actually supposed to be God . . . I mean, there is a long tradition of His not approving of it.

Aggie: I thought you could do anything.

Sprugg: Yes, of course . . . maybe. We can give it a shot, I guess. I'm not promising anything though.

Aggie: *Waving her glass in the air.* Giver yer best!

Sprugg: Okeydoke. Aggie Rose you are now . . . God the Omnipotent.

Aggie: Right.

Sprugg: *Singing.* "God the Omnipotent! King, who ordainest Great winds Thy clarions, lightnings Thy sword: Show forth Thy pity on high where Thou reignest. Give to us" . . .uh . . . "Give to us everything we've got coming, oh Lord."

This hymn is accompanied by great winds, lightning flashes and the boiler spouting steam and sparks.

Aggie: Yahoo!!! Listen to me, this is Aggie Rose, Lord of Heaven and Earth; listen to me, all ye starry hosts and shut up. I shall now reorganize the geography of the earth. First of all, Hawaii — palm trees, hot surf, all of it — pick yourself up and plunk yourself down, smack dab in the middle of the prairies!

This is accomplished with a mighty movement of lands.

Aggie: Down with the mountains. That's the next item of business. . . . I never liked them — nasty jagged things. God-like splendor be damned. Flatten them right out.

The mountains are levelled.

Aggie: Also, may all the roses in the rose garden wilt on the arbor. Up with tooth and fang! Reveal yourself for what you are, you cruel old ball of dirt. Flood the rivers with fire! I'm sick of it all. Stop praying, mankind. Stop singing your joyful hymns of praise. I'm sick of all the drivel. Blink out, sun and moon and stars of heaven — snuff out your silly light. I'm bringing the world to an end!

The basement descends into darkness brighter than we have ever seen and silence louder than all the noise.

Aggie: *In a small voice.* Because Aggie is tired and sick and she doesn't understand how she got to be like this.

There is a long pause.

Sprugg: Aggie. . . .

The lights rise slowly. Aggie can't stop shivering.

Aggie: I . . . maybe I wasn't ready for that. . . .

Sprugg: Now you know what it's like.

Aggie: It's lonely.

Sprugg: Aggie . . . you're cold.

Aggie: I'm all right.

Sprugg: Here . . . let me put my arm around you.

Aggie: Go away. Ah, you stink.

Sprugg: So do you. It's not an insurmountable problem.

Aggie: Get away!

Aggie is suffering too much to be bothered with Sprugg's ministrations.

Sprugg: People have got to hold onto one another sometimes.

Aggie! *Yelling.* We are all we've got! *Taking another approach.* Aggie, you're a.... Let me tell you....

Aggie: You're a drunk.

Sprugg: You are a beautiful and enchanting lady.

Aggie: You're a bum.

Sprugg: We admire one another, don't we?

Aggie is trying not to be interested.

Sprugg: Upstairs, in the Stardust Ballroom, there is a magnificent party taking place. It's . . . it's a wedding reception and the wine — the champagne — is flowing like a river. The tables have been pushed back and the band is playing. And you and I, Aggie, are there.

Aggie: I wouldn't go to a bowling alley with you.

She is weakening.

Sprugg: Oh, but this is a wedding and even God goes to weddings. Listen, they're playing our song!

Aggie: What song is that?

Sprugg: "Memories."

He hums the tune.

Aggie: That's not "Memories," you fool.

Sprugg: What is it then?

Aggie: "Fascination!"

Sprugg: That's our song!

He begins to dance.

Aggie: Oh my God.

Sprugg: And the lights are down low . . . and mirrors refract rays of red and blue hither and thither. . . .

Aggie: Hither and thither?

Sprugg: Around the room.

Aggie: Now, wait a minute. Wait. This is not going to work, not this time. I'm not playing. Not this time. And you can't get me into anything I don't want to get into. That's one of the rules of hypnotism. Do you think you're a bloody hypnotist?

Suddenly, a band is playing "Fascination."

Aggie: Sprugg?

He is very pleased with himself.

Aggie: Where's that music coming from?

Sprugg: From your deepest desires, my dear.

Aggie: Not my deepest desires. Shut it off!

Sprugg: Do you think it's a radio or something? I can't shut it off, willy-nilly. It took a great deal of psychic energy just to turn it on. Besides, it's coming from up there. It's seeping through the floorboards.

Aggie: Like an overflow in the upstairs toilet.

Sprugg: Aggie, how can you resist it, Aggie? You're such a beautiful woman. Your body was made for dancing.

Aggie: I was. Not exactly beautiful ... my mouth is too big for that ... but attractive in a sensual kind of way. ...

The music begins to change to a more haunting and less recognizable melody which takes possession of Aggie. The lights have begun to change as well.

Aggie: I wasn't a tramp.

Sprugg: No.

Aggie: But I slept with everybody.

Almost absentmindedly, she begins to dance with Sprugg.

Aggie: I believed that for any relationship to be meaningful, it had to be physical. I had convictions that way.

Sprugg: It's a lovely sentiment. Sometimes I feel, maybe, under the right circumstances, once again the old. ...

Aggie: No, thank you, Sprugg.

Sprugg: Ah well, I have enough ecstasy in my life as it is. Besides, you're all skin and bones.

Aggie: I diet. Hell, what are we doing?

Sprugg: Dancing to the mellifluous music of Mac Daniels and his

Band. Happy New Year's and the Wrinkled Canadians. Sprinkled Sprugg and his Swinging Sweethearts.

Aggie: Make up your mind.

Sprugg: Just dance and relax and I'll take care of you. . . . That's too relaxed.

Aggie: I used to see my whole life as one mad wild dance from pillar to bedpost.

Sprugg: Pillar to bedpost. Delightful figure of speech. Life is a kind of dance, isn't it? Of course, that's not original with me.

Aggie: But what have I got to show for it?

Sprugg: Just the dancing, Aggie.

The music has begun to speed up. They have to shout over it.

Aggie: It caused my downfall!

Sprugg: Pardon?

Aggie: It caused my downfall! I didn't know what to do, so I did everything! I'm a fallen woman!

Sprugg: Aggie, we live in a puritan country. We're the product of many generations of self-righteous livers. They want us to feel guilty!

They are now doing a kind of parody of a wild dance.

Aggie: Who does?

Sprugg: They do! They all do! But who cares, eh?

Aggie: Right! Who cares? I sure as hell don't!

Sprugg: Did you enjoy falling?

Aggie: Sure!

Sprugg: Every minute of it?

Aggie: Every damn minute.

Sprugg: Wonderful!

Aggie: What?

Sprugg: I said wonderful! Aggie . . . I . . . I can't keep up with you.

Aggie: What?

Sprugg: Stop for a while ... I can't keep up.

Aggie: I can't hear you.

The music reaches a climax.

Sprugg: *Screaming.* I can't keep up!

He collapses. The music stops. Aggie is left suspended in motion.

Aggie: *After a moment.* Are you all right?

Sprugg: For ... for ... Oh, Lord.

Aggie: What is it, Sprugg?

Sprugg: For an old woman with ulcers on her legs you do pretty well.

Aggie: Thanks. ... You're just out of breath.

Sprugg: Out of practically everything.

Aggie: You'll be all right.

Sprugg: It doesn't matter anyway. Oh, God, I can't breathe.

Aggie: You're out of breath. Of course you can't breathe.

Sprugg: Damn it! Why doesn't the body do what the mind does?

Aggie: *Unfolding a tissue.* You want this?

Sprugg: What have you got there?

Aggie: An aspirin.

Sprugg: One aspirin?

Aggie: I've been saving it.

Sprugg: Forever.

Aggie: I was trying to be helpful, you know.

Sprugg: I need a more drastic cure than that.

Aggie: That's all I have to give you. Agh ... you're all right.

Sprugg: No, I'm not, Aggie. I'm an ill man.

Aggie: Ill in the head.

Sprugg: Probably.

Aggie: Nah ... I'm kidding. You're out of breath.

Sprugg: Let me tell you a secret. I hang on to reality by a very thin thread, Aggie. Everywhere around me, things tremble and heave up. The world is constantly melting away, reforming itself into new and strange shapes, hideous configurations. One day, I am in charge. You understand. You've seen me in charge. The world is mine because I made it. I am all there is. I snap my fingers and there is light. I snap them again and there is a table, a chair, a bottle of wine. . . . But then, the very next moment, I hang from a thread over the surface of the sun.

Aggie: At least you won't get cold feet. Take me . . . my feet are always cold. I mean lately . . . they always seem cold.

Sprugg: Hold on to me, Aggie.

Aggie: A lot of good that would do either of us.

A great janitorial guffaw is heard offstage. Aggie and Sprugg are paralyzed by the sound.

Sprugg: *After a long period of total immobility.* I'm getting a cramp.

Aggie: Did he leave? I don't think he left. I think he's still there.

Sprugg: *Whispering.* I'm getting a cramp.

Aggie: Shut up.

Another great laugh is heard, offstage. A pile of garbage cans falls over by itself. Aggie screams.

Pete: *Offstage, the source of the laughter.* Funnier that hell. . . . You fellows are funnier than hell!

Aggie: *To Sprugg.* Did you say that?

Pete: *Offstage.* I never believed a coupla drunks'd be such an entertainment!

Aggie: *Annoyed with Sprugg.* Are you doing that?

Sprugg: Of course, it isn't me. What do you think I am, a ventriloquist? No, it's somebody else, entirely.

Pete, the janitor, enters. He is a surprising character in many ways. By now we have accepted Aggie and Sprugg as the standard of normalcy. Pete, a middle-aged working man, is hardly the demonic figure we might have expected from his laughter. Yet he is shockingly different from the other two. He could be a member of the audience. He is not well educated, conservative by nature, yet more volatile than one

*might expect. Merriment and anger are close to the surface and close
to one another. At any rate, he is a serious intruder in the strange
world Aggie and Sprugg have created for themselves, and he threatens
to change everything.*

Pete: The name's Pete. I guess I know who you are.

Sprugg: *After a long pause.* Have a drink?

Pete: Nope, nope. Not while I'm working . . . never touch it while
I'm working. I got a lot of responsibility down here, y'see. A terrible lot. So I never touch the stuff while I'm working . . . and to
tell you the truth, I don't much care for it when I'm not.

Sprugg: Good for you. Bad habit to get into.

Pete: Boy, you fellows are sure good for a laugh. It's too bad I gotta
get you out of here.

Sprugg: Wait a minute, Aggie. Let me handle this. *To Pete.* You
intend to eject this lady from her only place of habitation? To cast
her out, homeless, into the cruel ravages of the winter, to expose
her to the bitter wind seeping across the plains, rendering all
before it frozen and lifeless?

Pete: I gotta do it.

Aggie: The hell you do!

Pete: I gotta! It's my duty. It's my responsibility to keep this hotel
decent . . . and look at this — look at it. It's a mess. No, no . . . I
held off as long as I could . . . but you gotta go.

Aggie: *To Sprugg.* This is your fault.

Sprugg: My fault? I didn't do anything.

Aggie: He heard you yapping; I should never have let you come
down here!

Sprugg: *Injured.* But I brought the booze.

Aggie: That doesn't excuse everything. Booze or no booze — I'm
going to lose the roof over my head. All because of you.

Sprugg: After all we've been through together. . . .

Aggie: Shut up.

Pete: Well, I hate to do it, you know. But this is no place to live, eh?

Aggie: Beats many.

Sprugg: She's right.

Aggie: Let me stay, will you? Least until I find some place else, right?

Pete: It's a rat's nest.

Aggie: Yeah, but I call it home.

Pete: Oh, geez, I dunno. People aren't supposed to live down here.

Sprugg: It's a hotel, isn't it?

Pete: Up there, it's a hotel. Down here, it's a boiler room.

Sprugg: Jesus was born in a stable.

Pete: *Startled, turning to Aggie.* You're not pregnant, are you?

Aggie: Yeah.

Pete: Geez.

Sprugg breaks up laughing.

Aggie: What are you laughing at?

She has to laugh too.

Pete: *Angrily.* Don't fool with me.

They sober up immediately.

Pete: Pack up your stuff.

Aggie: He really is, he's going to kick me out.

Sprugg: Once again, no room at the inn.

Aggie: Give up, Sprugg. It's no use — the story of my life — kicked out, kicked down, kicked around, nobody showing the least kindness. . . . *She begins to cry, somewhat theatrically.* Life is so cruel. . . .

Pete: Sure, sure. I know you people . . . you bring it on yourselves.

There is immediate hostility to his remark.

Pete: You heard me. You bring it on yourselves, you alkies. You don't have no will power!

Sprugg: What do you know about it?

Pete: I got eyes, ain't I? I see you people lying around in doorways, dead drunk. Why do you always lie in the doorways?

Aggie: Because you bastards won't open the bloody doors, that's why!

Pete: Hey, hey! There's no call for language like that, now.

Sprugg: Take it easy, Aggie.

Aggie: I told you he was a bastard, didn't I? I knew it before he even walked in here. I knew it!

Pete: I don't need to stand for this kinda talk.

Sprugg: Now, wait a minute, don't be hasty, Mr., er . . . sir. . . .

Pete: Pete.

Sprugg: Pete. Now, you've raised a good question here, about drinking, you see. Now I've given the whole subject a lot of study, you see — a lot of thought. Now, if you're interested, we could discuss it for a while — you know, before we actually make our . . . uh, departure.

Pete: Well, I'll be hanged. All right. . . . You're the limit . . . I've gotta say that.

Sprugg: Yes, well . . . you're interested in why people like us drink?

Pete: Sure. I'll listen to your side of it. I'm fair minded.

He sits down.

Sprugg: Responsibility!

Aggie: Hah!

Sprugg: Yes, responsibility. The alcoholic, Pete, is one who feels acutely responsible for everything that happens. He knows himself to be a very powerful man. He knows that anything he does, any decision he makes, will make a difference in the way the universe operates.

Pete: Sounds like this here alkie has got too big an opinion of his self.

Sprugg: No, no. Everything we do is part of a divinely ordained pattern. Good Lord, man, you can't let the universe down, can you?

Pete: So why does he drink himself stupid?

Sprugg: Oh, the alcohol. Well, this is the fine point, you see. The alcohol helps relieve the anxiety over the responsibility. You see, the anxiety is the killer. You gotta get rid of that!

Pete: You're an educated man.

Sprugg: Thank you.

Pete: But you're crazy.

Aggie: Hee-hee.

Pete: So what about you?

Aggie: Me?

Pete: How come you're a drunk?

Aggie: To escape the winter. God, I hate living on the prairies.

Pete: It's good for you. Healthiest climate in the world.

Aggie: Some people fly south. Same thing.

Pete: What a sad kettle of fish. It all boils down to one thing. You guys can't face things the way they are. That's how it looks to me.

Sprugg: Nonsense. I make things the way they are. You, for instance . . . all you are is a figment of my imagination.

Pete: Is that so?

Sprugg: That's right.

Pete: That's all right . . . but I'm still going to kick you out of here, the two of you.

Sprugg: No, you can't do it.

Pete: I can't?

Aggie: Sprugg, you're getting carried away.

Sprugg: I shall demonstrate.

He walks over to Pete and gives him a feeble shove.

Pete: I'll be damned!

He gives him another shove.

Pete: *Irritated.* Hey.

Aggie: Careful, Sprugg.

Sprugg: You see? I can put you out of our lives, just like that.

He pushes him one more time. Pete retaliates by throwing him across the room.

Pete: *Roaring at him.* Who the hell do you think you are? Your party's over . . . now get yourselves out of here.

Aggie: *To Sprugg.* Well?

Sprugg: Some things are fixed in my mind more solidly than other things.

Pete is enraged. He rushes Sprugg.

Pete: Get out!

Sprugg: *As if attempting to perform an exorcism.* In the name of the Father and the Son and the Holy Ghost, and all the whole holy hierarchy of angels and principalities of the heavens, I banish thee, I cast thee out, into outer darkness, into the shadows from whence thou hast come!

Pete: Cast out, eh? You'll see who's gonna be cast out in a minute or two.

Pete hauls Sprugg to his feet.

Sprugg: I exorcise thee, I castigate thee, I relegate thee to the bottomless pit. . . .

Pete: Shut your mouth or I'll shut it for you. . . .

Aggie: Leave him alone. . . . What's he done to you?

She tries to pull them apart. Failing that, she breaks an old chair over Pete's head. He falls down unconscious.

Sprugg: There, you see? *Looking at him after a moment.* Is he dead?

Aggie shakes her head.

Sprugg: Good, I didn't want to kill him.

Aggie: I thought he was going to kill *you*!

Sprugg: Yes, even figments of the imagination can become quite dangerous. I had to take strong measures.

Aggie: Sprugg . . . I was the one who took the measures.

Sprugg: Not me? Well, in a manner of speaking. . . .

Aggie: I saved you, you old fool.

Sprugg: I'm sure it seemed that way to you. . . .

Aggie: I saved you!

Sprugg: All right, all right.

Aggie: I picked up that chair and dealt with him. I solved the problem. Me, myself. I never saved anybody before in my life. It's got me thinking. Look at this place. This is no place for a person with self respect. I deserve better.

Sprugg: No question.

Aggie: I don't like the view.

Sprugg: It is a little cluttered.

Aggie: I ought to move to a higher floor.

Sprugg: A higher floor, yes.

Aggie: The top floor, Sprugg! A room with a view out onto the prairie . . . and a bath! Definitely, a bath!

Sprugg: My goodness.

Aggie: I'm going to show the bastards a thing or two. I'm going to check in.

Sprugg: Check in?

Aggie: That's right. Check in.

Sprugg: At the desk?

Aggie: No, at the men's washroom. Of course, at the desk.

Sprugg: With all due respect, Aggie, you don't look respectable.

Aggie: Piffle. You forget I am an actress of consummate artistry.

She has located a few remnants of respectability in a shopping bag. She transforms herself on the principle that it is not what you wear, but how you wear it that counts.

Aggie: Come on . . . come on, Sprugg! It's time we saw the light of day!

They scramble up and out of the boiler room as the lights go down.

END OF ACT I

Act Two

The scene is the same as at the end of Act One. Nothing seems to have changed. Pete lies in the same position on the floor. Gradually, he begins to stir. The boiler lets off a blast of steam as he comes to.

Pete: *Groaning.* Oh, hellfire and damnation!

He sits up, looking round, blinks, looks at his fingers, blinks, touches his head, grimaces, looks at his fingers and blinks.

Pete: Blood! Hellfire and damnation! Something happened to me. What happened to me? *It gradually dawns on him.* They. . . they tried to . . . kill me! *He begins to laugh.* I wouldn't a thought they had it in them. *He has a sudden spasm of pain.* Ooooh. . . . *A sudden thought.* Maybe they succeeded. Oh, hellfire and damnation, I hope they didn't. I couldn't take it . . . being dead. What am I saying? I'm not dead. I couldn't be. *Another pain.* Oh, if this is hell, Lord God Almighty, get me out of it. *His eyes focus.* Thank you. That's better. That's better. I'm still here, eh? Good. I'm glad. Holy Hannah, that's a relief. *There is a pause.* All right, come out here now. The both of ya . . . get your hides out here. Don't worry . . . I won't do anything to you . . . much. Leastways, not until I get my hands around your necks. Come out here. I see you . . . I know you're there, skulking in the dark. I'll give you three to get out here and then I'll come back there after you. One. . . . Two. . . . Now, don't make me do anything you'll regret. Two. . . . You're making me mad. . . . Two. . . . I've got a fearful temper. . . . All right, this is it. . . . Three! Maybe they're not here. Cowards. Chicken livers. Club me over the head.with an axe or something and then run out on me. Shoulda expected it. *There is a pause and then he remembers something.* I never did see a pair of drunks carry on like that. Yep, that was somethin' very amazing. *He sighs and gets up.* Back to work. Another day, another dollar. At least I can get this place cleaned up. That's one good thing, ain't it? *He resumes speaking.* Good riddance. They were getting under my skin. Silly galoots. Drinkin' themselves stupid. Never had any use for it. Makes me mad. Living off the taxpayer. Makes me damn mad.

He begins sweeping now, making up a little chant as he sweeps.

Pete:

A coupla bums, a coupla bums
Down in a hole, down in a hole.
Hmmmm hmmmmm.
I snift them out, with my snout
And gave them the boot, right out
Of the hole.
Hmmm, hmmm hmmmmmmm.
Yeah, yeah, yeah.
And I don't care
Where they went from there.
I don't care,
No no no,
Yeah, yeah, yeah.

He is sweeping Aggie's stuff across the floor towards the furnace.

Pete: What's this? Disgusting. Lives like a pig. Shoulda got her outa here long time ago. *He finds Aggie's scrapbook.* Some kinda book? Scrapbook. *He puts down the broom and stands under the light. He has to put on a pair of glasses to read.* "To Agatha Rose ... " Agatha Rose. Hmph. "On the occasion of her graduation from High School." ... There you are. Both of them got an education and look what they did with it. It's a crime. "All of the very best wishes for a lovely and sweet young lady. Please use this scrapbook for your theatrical notices. We are all sure that they will be rave reviews, Miss Halverson, Grade Twelve English." Hah! *He turns the page and there is a photograph of a young Aggie. He is startled.* My gosh. Look at her. She is lovely — no.... *He is moved.* ... very ... lovely ain't the word for it. A fella could break his heart over a girl like that. It's a crime. It is. It's a crime. *He looks through more of the book.* Damn her. Damn her, anyway.

Disgusted at himself, he throws the scrapbook into the pile of rubbish. He then sets about dismantling the staircase of crates and boxes that Aggie uses for access to the boiler room.

Pete: Get rid of it all. It's high time.

Finally, after he has gathered everything together, he begins to incinerate it. He pauses over the scrapbook. Suddenly, Aggie's large purse is thrown down from overhead. He walks away from the furnace towards the spot where the two must descend.

Pete: You coming back? You've got a nerve . . . half killing me and then coming back. All right, get down here. C'mon, get down here and fight like a man, both of you.

At this point, Aggie and Sprugg drop from the ceiling. They miss the staircase which has been removed, and fall on Pete. All three lie in a heap on the floor.

Pete: Get offa me!

Aggie and Sprugg climb off him. They seem emptier, more frightened and more desperate than before.

Sprugg: *To Aggie.* I forgot about him.

Pete: I could have you up on assault, you know!

Aggie: So did I.

At an impasse.

Aggie: *Wearily.* What do we do now?

Sprugg: I don't know. How should I know?

Pete: Well, you could start by apologizing.

Aggie: *Shrugging.* Sure. Why did you take the stairway away?

Pete: What stairway? Those crates? Because I'm cleaning up down here, that's why. Where were you?

Aggie: It hardly seems like the same place.

Sprugg: Maybe it isn't.

Pete: Oh, you're starting your nonsense again?

Aggie: That would be a good one.

Pete: You conked me on the head and you're gonna pay for it!

Aggie: I never did anything of the sort. I don't even know you. You're somebody else again. *To Sprugg.* How's that?

Sprugg: I don't know if you're going to get away with it.

Pete: You darn near gave me a concussion.

Aggie: Not me.

Pete: I'm not a tolerant man. Now, own up to it and apologize.

Aggie: Do you know what he's talking about?

Sprugg: I'm trying to figure it out.

Pete: All right then. *Handing Aggie the scrapbook.* Who is this?

He feels as if he has pulled off a coup, outwitting Aggie on her own ground.

Pete: Now tell me you never been here.

Aggie stares at the scrapbook for a long time. She does not open it.

Aggie: No, I don't know anything about this.

Pete: *Failing to understand her.* What? Open it.

Aggie: No, it's none of my business.

Pete: *Opening it for her.* There . . . "To Agatha Rose on the occasion of . . . ". Now, that's you . . . so stop playing your silly games with me, you understand? *To Sprugg.* Look here, have you ever seen a prettier sight?

Sprugg: *Awestruck.* Oh, Aggie.

There is a moment.

Aggie: Who is this?

Pete: You, damn it!

Aggie: No.

Pete is about to explode.

Sprugg: *Quickly.* Maybe I can explain this, Mister. You have to understand the complexities of Aggie's thinking, she has a very subtle intellect.

Pete: If you ask me, her intellect is all in her head.

Sprugg: No, no . . . she's putting the past behind her, don't you see?

Aggie: Look, this guy says I hit him over the head. I say I didn't. I say I wasn't even here. Ever. I deny knowing this man, I deny being in the vicinity, I deny knowing this woman, I deny everything.

Sprugg: She denies everything.

Pete: I'm stymied. You can't talk sensible to drunks. This ain't yours?

Aggie: No.

Sprugg How could an ineffable creature like that do violence to another human being?

Pete: Then you won't mind if I get rid of it.

Aggie: What do you want from me?

Pete: *Puzzled.* I don't know.

Sprugg: Well, there we are.

Pete: I think you owe me something, or I owe you something, or something. . . .

Sprugg: *Finding the bottle again.* Have a drink.

Pete: *Taking a drink.* Thanks.

Aggie: *To Pete.* So now what are you going to do?

Pete: I should get you out of here. If the boss ever finds out. . . .

Aggie: It doesn't matter . . . we've found another place.

Pete: You have?

Aggie: Yep, eh, Sprugg?

Sprugg: Sure we have.

Aggie: We sure have.

Sprugg: Sure we have!

Pete: Well, there . . . that solves the problem, don't it? You do admit that you walloped me over the head. . . .

Aggie: I'm guilty.

Pete: Yeah. Well, that's in your favor. I'm glad you owned up to it.

Aggie: It gets easier all the time.

Pete: *Taking another drink.* I think this is helping out my head.

Sprugg: Take a little wine for thy noggin's sake. That's in the Bible.

Aggie: It is not.

Sprugg: It is so.

Pete: Seems to be helping.

Drinks are poured all around.

Aggie: I just came back for my things.

Pete: You know, you're probably not bad people, under it all ... you've just gotten a little foolish, eh? And you've got your drinking problem. Have you ever tried A.A., eh?

There is no answer.

Pete: And there's some kinda medicine you can take ... so whenever you take a drink it makes you sick. Have you ever tried anything like that? Well, you should, you know? It might cure you, you see? Where are you moving to?

Aggie: Upstairs.

Pete: *Dumbfounded.* Upstairs?

Sprugg: Yep, we've taken a suite.

Pete: You can't do that! How can you do that?

Aggie: We just checked in.

Sprugg: At the desk.

Pete: Oh, you did, did you? And how was the service?

Aggie: Wonderful. You should go up there sometime.

Sprugg: Exquisite service in an exquisite setting. Retaining a flavor of old world charm with up to the minute conveniences.

Pete: Oh, for sure! That's fancy.

Aggie: I'd like to add a word of appreciation. Both the men at the desk and the bell boy were very courteous.

Pete: Were they?

Aggie: *Confidentially.* You know neither of us are looking our best these days. . . .

Sprugg: How can you say that?

Aggie: It's about time you faced it, Sprugg. It's true. Nevertheless, dressed as we are, bearing certain marks of hard times ... these people showed us as much respect as if we were visiting royalty.

Pete: I can't believe it.

Sprugg: It is hard to believe, in this day and age.

Aggie: And they put us on the top floor. What do you think of that?

Pete: Oh, boy.

Aggie: When we get back they're going to have our dinner waiting in the room.

Pete: Are they?

Aggie: Yes, we have already given them our orders. Sprugg is going to have whole roast duckling a l'orange and I . . . I shall have sole in cognac preceded by an appetizer of escargots and followed by ice-cream baked in Alaska.

Sprugg: I don't think they actually bake it in Alaska, Aggie.

Aggie: I believe they do.

Sprugg: Then they do. My goodness, it will be nice to take a bath again.

Aggie: The decor is very special in the deluxe suites.

Sprugg: Decorations.

Pete: Oh, decorations.

Aggie: There are beautiful paintings by prairie artists.

Sprugg: Grain elevators and such.

Aggie: Draped horizontally across the landscape, with white horses running up railroad tracks and things.

Sprugg: It must have cost a fortune. I mean, grain elevators standing straight up are expensive enough . . . but lying on their side. . . .

Pete: Maybe the picture's hung crooked.

Aggie: You know nothing about art.

Pete: I know what I like.

Sprugg: What do you like?

Pete: Grain elevators in the sunset. Straight up.

Aggie: That's the view out the window.

Pete: What?

Sprugg: A prairie sunset. I mean at sunset, that's what the view will be ... the sun, setting purple and crimson across a vast vista of rippling wheat. ...

Pete: It's winter.

Sprugg: ... In the fall ... and blue-white snow in the winter ... as it is now, right, Aggie?

Aggie: Exactly.

Pete: I'm in trouble now. I can't let you stay up there either.

Aggie: Why not? We're official guests.

Pete: No, you're not.

Aggie: We are until they ask us for the money ... and then that's our problem, it isn't your problem.

Sprugg: *Gaily.* And until then we are going to have the biggest blowout bash of our lives — the best food, the best liquor — the best of everything. Right, Aggie?

Aggie: Right, Sprugg. They send us to jail, I'll go to jail happy.

Pete: Shut your mouths. Shut up! It's not like that, and you know it.

Aggie: You shut up. It's like that if we say it is!

Sprugg picks up a length of pipe.

Pete: It is not!

Sprugg: *Advancing.* We got an investment here, so shut your own mouth.

Pete: *Wheeling around on him.* Now don't tell me to. ... I'd put that down.

Aggie arms herself with Pete's broom.

Aggie: This is a kind of war, Pete. It's us against the bastards. You know what they do to traitors.

Sprugg: In times of war, treason is a capital offence.

This is getting kind of scary.

Pete: Look, you ... you're getting all crazy again.

Aggie: You've judged yourself, Pete.

Pete: Look ... I don't think my skull could take another bruisin'. ...

Sprugg: Probably couldn't.

Aggie: Get him, Sprugg!

Pete: Wait!

Sprugg: What?

Pete: Somebody'll come looking for me.

Aggie: Who?

Pete: When I don't come home. . . .

Sprugg: You don't live down here?

Pete: Of course I don't live down here. Who'd want to live? . . .

Sprugg: Imagine that, Aggie.

Pete: I have a room.

Aggie: And a family?

Pete: Just a room.

Sprugg has dropped his guard. Pete grabs the pipe away from him.

Pete: There. And I was startin' to feel friendly with you sonsa . . . guns. Now tell me what really went on upstairs or I'll beat you to a pulp.

Sprugg: Go ahead.

Pete: Well?

Sprugg: Why's this so important to you?

Pete: Why are you trying to put this fancy story over on me when I know the truth?

Aggie: What truth?

Pete: The truth!!!

Aggie: We went up there like we said, and they took us to a room high up above the city. And they said we could start all over again up there because once you are in a new room you are a new person with new opportunities.

Sprugg: That's God's truth.

Aggie: The past is behind us. We've been elevated. Like the Pope.

Pete: Behind you, eh? So you won't have any need of this again.

He begins to pick up Aggie's bedding and other things and throws them into the furnace.

Sprugg: Hey!

Aggie: Let it go . . . it's infested.

Sprugg: Are you sure?

Aggie: Lousy.

Pete: And this stuff?

He throws some other odds and ends, some garbage, a small mirror, some magazines and some pictures into the furnace.

Aggie: Who wants it?

Sprugg: *Trying to look at the covers of the magazines.* Anything interesting?

Aggie: Junk.

Pete: *Grimly and angrily.* Away with it.

Sprugg: I haven't read a thing in years. My eyes aren't up to it.

Pete finally gets to the scrapbook.

Sprugg: Sometimes when I'm half asleep, I see printed pages on the inside of my eyelids. Stuff I've already read. There's never anything new.

Pete: And this?

Aggie: You are a bastard.

Sprugg: Still, I'm a reading fiend. I read the inside of my eyelids for hours on end.

Pete: It's a crime what you've done to yourself.

Aggie: So, it's a crime.

Pete: *Ripping pages out of the scrapbook.* The beautiful little girl. Agatha Rose.

Sprugg: The words float by, like leaves in a stream.

Pete: I didn't have an easy life either, you know. I don't have anybody.

He is ripping the scrapbook methodically now. Each page causes a searing agony for Aggie.

Pete: But I faced it. I didn't run away. I didn't try to kill myself with booze. *He comes to the picture of young Aggie.* If I had found somebody like this, eh — when I was that age — things might've been good.

Sprugg: My favorites are the classics of English Literature. But there are certain modern authors I enjoy.

Pete: Who's this?

Aggie: My little boy.

Pete: Oh, he must be proud of his mother . . . real proud. Why weren't you just an ordinary person, eh? Like the rest of us? You could have been happy. Are you happy now? The theatre . . . more make believe. Politics. More still. What's this?

He finds an old leaf pasted to a page.

Aggie: A souvenir. Somebody who made love to me once.

With a great roar, he casts the whole thing into the fire. He then collapses, exhausted.

Aggie: *In a strange new tone of voice.* The truth? The truth is we went up there . . . around to the street side of the hotel. I hadn't been around to that side for a long time. The sun surprised me. It filled the air with bright silver, shafting off the snow and the windows . . . the light seemed so harsh, cold — judging almost. Not at all warm. My eyes couldn't get used to it. We tried the main doors. They wouldn't open. They were locked. Sprugg said . . . what did you say, Sprugg?

Sprugg: You're a cruel man, Pete.

Aggie: What did you say, Sprugg?

Sprugg: I said they must have been expecting us.

Aggie: We had a good laugh about that. Finally we pried plywood off one of the windows in the little alleyway. We got in that way. The lobby was empty.

Sprugg: And dusty.

Aggie: Full of dust. Nobody rushed up to take our luggage — we didn't have any luggage, but nobody rushed to take it. There was a bell on the desk and we rang it but nobody came. We weren't impatient. We waited a long time but nobody came. We climbed the grand staircase and then several more that weren't so grand.

Sprugg: I had to stop on the stairs many times.

Aggie: We walked through corridor after corridor. We could have had any room we wanted. They were all available. The windows were boarded up on the lower floors. There was not a sound in the whole building except for our footsteps padding along the carpet.

Sprugg: A dreadful silence.

Aggie: And it was cold. Your furnace isn't doing its job, Pete. Every floor was colder than the one below it and the top floor was freezing. The hallway there was painted white, like a hospital, and all the doors were closed against us. Far down the main corridor there was a window that let in light.

Pete: And from there you looked across the city and out onto the prairie?

Aggie: No. What was the use? We came back.

Sprugg: And there you have the truth. Satisfied?

Aggie and Sprugg take a drink. The bottle is getting very low now.

Sprugg: Truth can be very deceiving at times. I'm not fond of it.

Pete: I should have told you. I didn't know you were going up there, you know.

Sprugg: It was her idea. When she knocked you out with the chair . . . she thought the world was her oyster.

Pete: Oyster?

Aggie: I was carried away with a sense of my own power.

Pete: So what does it matter, eh? It doesn't make any difference, eh? So the hotel's empty . . . so what? Don't hold it against me.

Aggie: If you can't have what you want, then you can pretend. But if you can't pretend either, what is there?

Sprugg: The idea of a hotel full of characters was an inspiration to me . . . it got my creative juices flowing. That's gone now.

Aggie: I used to look up at the ceiling and think there's a bunch of bastards up there and they don't know I'm down here — people never know who they're sleeping on top of. I got a lot of satisfaction out of thinking: someday I'll go up there with them and we'll get a good look at each other. Finally I did, didn't I? And it took a lot, believe me, to actually go up there. So I went, and what did I find? The bastards had left!

Sprugg: It would have been better to go on, imagining The Provincial Hotel as it used to be. We could have gone on like that.

Pete: It's better to face the facts.

Aggie: Big bloody deal.

Pete: I can't understand you people. I can't. You let me throw your whole life story in the furnace instead of facing the facts.

Aggie: Yeah.

Pete: I'm sorry I did that. I don't know why I blew up like that. Maybe I see you people are kinda dangerous or something. Like you're human, but you've gone rotten. I figure I might get infected. Same as I see a person who's double jointed, you know . . . like he can bend his arm backward, eh? Geez, it makes me sick to see something like that. But I'm sorry I did that.

Aggie: What's done is done.

Pete: But you made me mad.

Aggie: Who are you? I don't have to talk to you. You want us out of here? Kick us out. Don't talk to me, that's all.

Sprugg: You shouldn't be so unkind to her.

Pete: I'm not . . . am I? Well, look at her. You saw her in the book. . . . She didn't have to let herself go like she is now.

Sprugg: She had no choice.

Pete: You people are always making up excuses. Sure, she had a choice. You've got only yourselves to blame. . . . Life can be hard but. . . .

Sprugg: I had a friend, once. He was much older than I . . . good fellow, never had a vice that I knew of. Last time I saw him, he was in a nursing home for the aged. I found him watching a hockey game on television. The old guy had soiled himself. He was reeking. I asked him why he hadn't gone to the toilet. He said he couldn't get out of the bleachers in time. See, he was senile. He couldn't remember whether he was in the arena watching a hockey game or in front of a TV set. Never touched a drop of booze in his life — just old — like you'll be sometime.

Pete: I'd kill myself before I got like that. . . .

Aggie: Good.

Sprugg: No, you won't. Now, this same man used to do magic shows in my town when I was a kid. He used to entertain all of the children in the neighbourhood. His hands were faster than the twinkle in his eye and when he laughed at his own jokes, we all had to laugh with him . . . and we all knew that he knew we'd figure out the tricks one day, because we were so clever he couldn't put one over on us forever. . . . Pete, I've lost the point.

Pete: This man changed into a different person when he got senile, right?

Sprugg: *Triumphantly.* No, no! It was the same person!

Pete: Oh.

Sprugg: And a different person. *Joyfully.* His whole life had all happened and you couldn't take one part away from him — or away from us. You don't grasp my meaning?

Pete: I can't say I do.

Sprugg: *At a loss.* I'm sure it's very important . . . but it keeps slipping away from me.

Aggie: It's simple. Whatever happens . . . happens. That's all.

Sprugg: Is that all I was saying?

Aggie: Yes.

Sprugg: There are a few things that don't happen, that also happen.

Pete: You're beyond me.

Aggie: He's beyond himself. Look . . . we don't understand how we got this way. Maybe it was because we weren't strong enough.

Sprugg: Strong enough for what?

Aggie: For what we wanted to be . . . for what we wanted to do . . . when there was nobody around to be interested. We were ahead of our time. . . . People should be sympathetic to people who want to do the impossible.

Sprugg: That's a very profound analysis.

Pete: It's a lot of hogwash. Still, I'm sorry about the scrapbook.

Aggie: What do you want me to do about it?

Pete: I don't know . . . say you didn't want it anyway. Why didn't you stop me?

Aggie: You want me to forgive you?

Pete: I guess so.

Aggie: I can't get up the energy.

Sprugg: *Looking at the bottle.* Not much left.

Aggie: And it doesn't come easily.

Pete: I was tired of the playacting. Instead of doing something about yourselves, you just make up stories, don't you see.

Aggie: Wasn't doing you any harm.

Pete: You listen to enough stuff like that, you go crazy yourself. I got enough to put up with in this job, being by myself all the time . . . *There is a blast of steam from one of the boilers.* . . . having to listen to the steam firing off all the time . . . checking the furnace all the time. It's not easy, you know. System gets too much pressure and the place'd go sky high. A man could go batty just from working in a job like this.

Sprugg: Why do it?

Pete: It's gotta be done.

Aggie: Yeah, why's it gotta be done?

Pete: It's gotta.

Sprugg: Nobody in the building, except you . . . and us.

Pete: I don't know. The boss would know. They say a building begins to fall apart once the heat's turned off.

Sprugg: We have much the same vocation, Pete.

Pete: You and me? Hah!

Aggie: That's a joke.

Sprugg: No, we have to keep up hope . . . the two of us. When things start to fall into despair, we take it upon ourselves to provide a little warmth, you know what I mean? You understand, Aggie, don't you?

Aggie: No, no . . . we've been brought down to earth, Sprugg, good and proper.

Sprugg: *Looking at the bottle again.* Not much left, Aggie.

Aggie: No, Sprugg, I couldn't go on another one of your . . . your. . . .

Sprugg: Voyages of discovery! Ah, they will say of us, how brave, how adventuresome . . . to launch off on a brand new voyage of discovery at a time when things are at their lowest. At a time when most would have given up, disillusioned, embittered, we set forth once more like little children treading on spring grass, hand in hand. . . .

Pete: You're still at it, aren't you?

Sprugg: Of course I am . . . because I have the power.

Aggie: *Wistfully.* Have you still?

Sprugg: Still. *To Pete.* And you will come with us on our adventure.

Pete: Not on your life.

Sprugg: You owe us that much.

Pete: Nobody owes you anything.

Sprugg: After taking away one romance, after destroying one dream . . . you will help us create another.

Pete: I'm leaving.

Sprugg: No, you're not.

Pete: I have duties. I have to check the pressure.

Sprugg: It will keep. Aggie. . . .

Aggie: No, Sprugg. It's no use.

Sprugg: Pick a story — any story.

Aggie: *Rocking back and forth.* No, Sprugg. . . .

Sprugg: We've lost our palace of characters. Go beyond this place, beyond this time. Where do you want to go?

Aggie: Down a river — a long river in the summer time — on a barge.

Pete: On a barge. Lovely.

Aggie: *Beginning to dream.* Like Cleopatra's barge, with slaves and attendants fanning me with great golden ostrich plumes . . . a river like the South Saskatchewan, flowing through valleys further away from the plains towards the Arctic Ocean. But then it would be cold, wouldn't it? Another river in another place then, carrying me to some tropical paradise.

Sprugg: And I shall be the boatman. . . . *Quietly.* You trust me because only I know where we are going or how to get there.

Pete: And I'm leaving.

Sprugg: No, please. We need you.

Pete: Not me . . . you don't need me.

Aggie: It's only a story. It won't hurt you.

Sprugg: Just here, Pete, the river passes into another country. . . .

We hear soft, haunting music rising under the fantasy.

Sprugg: And it is your office, Pete, to stand on the great bluff towering above the river. What do you see?

Pete: *Spellbound.* Some kinda. . . . Looks like something out of a fairy tale.

Sprugg: And you question her, Pete. You question the fabulous woman on the royal barge.

Pete: You there . . . in the boat. . . . Who are you?

Aggie: I'm Aggie Rose and I'm passing on to better things. Let me continue. Don't stop me.

Sprugg: And you tell her, Pete. . . .

Pete: Aggie, I wish I could do something for you, but downstream there aren't any better things. You have to stay in your own land, Aggie Rose.

Sprugg: The man cares.

Aggie: It's so beautiful, drifting downstream, with the warm sun beating on my face. . . .

Pete: No, no. . . . You have to turn back.

Sprugg: Then sleep, Princess, sleep. *To Pete.* There's no turning back, Pete. It's a pity to end it here. *He drinks the last of the wine.* Out.

Pete: She looks more like her picture now.

Sprugg: *Knowingly.* You're imagining things. She'll never look like her picture again.

Pete: If I don't tell my boss, she can probably stay here as long as she likes.

Sprugg: Very generous. Look, now that you've taken away our grand staircase to the stars, would you be so kind as to show me how to get out of here?

He gathers his wine glasses.

Pete: Where are you going?

Sprugg: Somewhere, I suppose. I'm a restless sort of person. I keep on the move. I wasn't here yesterday, you know.

Pete: Do you have to go? Right now, I mean?

Sprugg: Why not?

Pete: You must be hungry.

Sprugg: I hadn't thought.

Pete: *Rushing off.* I usually eat about this time.

Sprugg: Yes, well. . . .

Pete: *Offstage.* I mean, I have more than I need. Pressure's okay. *He re-enters with his lunch bag.* Look. *There is a loaf of bread and some fruit in the bag.* Would you like to . . . I mean. . . . Stay and have some, will you?

Sprugg: *Looking at Pete.* So. *After a moment.* Very well. *He joins him.* It's very good. Mmmm, fresh! Aggie? Aggie?

Aggie turns in her sleep.

Pete: She's sound asleep.

Sprugg: Let her sleep. When she wakes, she'll find the world has turned kind. It does sometimes. But it takes so much work. I exhaust myself with the task.

The lights fade on Sprugg and Pete sharing Pete's bread. Aggie continues to sleep.

THE END

Beyond Batoche

§

First Performance

Beyond Batoche was first presented by Regina's Globe Theatre April 10, 1985, with the following cast:

Matt — *David McCulley*

Burns — *James Timmins*

Shane — *Mark Wilson*

Tour Guide/Father André — *Stephen Fielden*

Yvonne — *Tantoo (Martin) Cardinal*

Kelly — *Anne Wessels*

The production was directed by Kenneth Kramer, with stage design by Marion Buller and with Marrilee Houston as stage manager. It toured to several Saskatchewan centres and to the National Arts Centre, Ottawa.

Characters *(in order of appearance)*

Matthew: a screen writer

Burns: an independent film producer

Shane: an actor

Tour Guide

Yvonne: a teacher and a Métis

Kelly: a researcher, married to Matthew

Father André: Riel's confessor

Note on staging **Beyond Batoche.**

The original production of **Beyond Batoche** *was presented in-the-round. In Act I, Matt's library occupied the centre of the stage, surrounded by the Batoche tour sites. At times, the guide would lead his tour through the central area ignoring the set and its occupants. The library set was very detailed (although without walls) while Batoche was just the bare stage periphery.*

In Act II, the library was moved off centre, leaving a good part of the stage to function as a movie studio. Riel's witness stand and gaol cell were impressionistic and quite obviously movie set pieces.

Through Act II, the historical Riel scenes should carry the sense of a film getting closer and closer to actual production. Bits of the costumes appear, the set is used — perhaps technicians appear in the studio and lights are set. We hear part of the sound track (The voice of the Judge) on tape and we see Shane in rehearsal. The final scenes, of course, are very realistic. This is for the camera — but it should come as a bit of a shock when we are returned to reality.

Photo Credit: *Richard Gustin Photography Inc.*

David McCulley as Matt, Mark Wilson as Shane, Tantoo Martin as Yvonne
Globe Theatre, Regina, 1985.

Act One

As the lights slowly rise.

Shane as Riel: The Spirit of God made me see how arrogant England is, and how she behaves when she does not want to accede to a request. She does everything possible to assure victory over those she does not like; and when she has the upper hand she cries out in rage, "I won't do it." Oh my God! Do not let England get the better of me. For she would annihilate me together with my nation. Save me from her power for the sake of Your Son, for the sake of the glorious Virgin Mary, for the sake of Saint Joseph. *Shane is having more and more difficulty with the speech.*

Lights rise on Matt's library. It is a malleable space that can be transformed into other places — cosy and intimate at one moment and yet at other times seeming vast. It is late at night. We have caught Matt, Burns, and Shane with scripts, notebooks, pens and pencils in hand. They are stuck on a creative problem. Matt and Burns are in their late thirties and are a contrast in sensitivities. Shane is younger. Having just read Riel's speech, he is in despair. All three are very tired and very disturbed. Sometimes one or another will spring into animated fury, but at other points it is hard to tell whether they are still thinking about the problem or falling asleep. Creative agony is in the air. The evidence of a long work session is strewn about the library. It is a very long time before anyone speaks, but the body language and the groans are eloquent.

Matt: *With the weariness of existence.* All I'm trying to say is . . .

Burns: I know what you're . . .

Matt: Listen, okay? All I'm trying to say here is if you want me to write the thing, don't tie me down . . .

Burns: I'm not . . .

Matt: Don't tie my hands before we even get going. I've gotta have room to breathe here.

Burns: Don't tie . . .

Matt: I mean there's no joy in that . . . if you can't . . . if you can't get to the point where the . . . you know . . . where the character and your own . . . your own guts talk to one another . . .

Shane: *To Matt.* But that's . . .

Matt: Then don't start. Don't even start because you'll hate doing it . . . you'll hate every minute of it. You probably won't finish and if you do finish it'll be horse manure.

Shane: That's what I'm saying. I'm saying the same thing. Don't you hear me saying the same thing? Don't screw me up here before we even bloody start. What am I going to do here? What am I going to do if we go ahead with the project and the writing's got an image of the guy that I can't play? I can play it . . . but I won't play it. I won't play it. *Matt is so hostile.* I won't.

Burns: Look, we gotta tape this damn thing. I'll sell it . . . I'll sell it. And after I sell it you guys can fiddle around with your creativity, your artistic pretensions all you want, but all we want here is a ten minute pilot tape. Is that too much to ask? *He is up and on his way to a coffee pot.* Just to give the idea that we're offering a quality product here, give a sense of what a wonderful actor we got here . . . what a wonderful writer we got here . . . what a wonderful producer we got here . . .

Shane: Yeah, sure.

Burns: I'm going to sell Riel and somebody's going to buy him . . . but first you gotta give me ten minutes of what they most want to see.

Matt slumps back.

Matt: That's what I'm giving you.

Burns: Why am I drinking this stuff? It makes me tireder.

Burns goes back to his place as before.

Matt: Sorry.

Burns: Adventure. That's what they want. *To Matt.* What for?

Long pause full of suffering. Finally:

Shane: I can't say it. It's not going to work.

Burns: *Annoyed.* Of course it won't work.

Matt: This is crazy. Why won't it work? It'll work!

Shane: I can't say it.

Matt: You're an actor. Act it.

Shane: I can't act it if. . . . *Holding back.* What do you know about acting? It's not credible.

Matt: It's what he said . . . it's what he said. If you can't act what the guy said how can you act anything?

Burns: Hold on, hold on . . . look, the kid's got a problem. I've got a problem. Just explain the problem, Shane. Use words.

Shane: I think it's "God. . . . " *Assuming same character inflections we heard at the beginning.* "Save me from her power for the sake of Your Son, for the sake of the glorious Virgin Mary, for the sake of Saint Joseph. Oh my God! Hasten to help me." Jesus, Joseph and Mary. This isn't the heart of the thing. Not this. Go write commercials for the Catholic Information Centre.

Matt: "The Spirit of God made me see how arrogant England is, and how she behaves when she does not want to accede to a request." He's having a vision.

Shane: But that's what I won't be able to play. I mean I can play the anger against England. . . . I can play the revolutionary . . . but how am I going to play bloody mysticism?

Matt: It's prophetic. Look at it that way . . . he's calling down the wrath of God against his enemies. Back off.

Burns: He's right, Matt. I can't sell that. It's a turnoff. I'm gonna have to sell this in Toronto, for crying out loud. . . . You don't go to Toronto with a bunch of Bible Belt stuff.

Matt: You gotta paint him the way he was!

Shane: I know what he was. He was a revolutionary. He was the first Canadian Socialist political leader.

The other two speak together.

Burns: Ah, c'mon. I can't sell that either.

Matt: That's overstating the case a little. . . .

Shane: No it isn't. . . . Look. . . . It starts with the buffalo hunt.

Burns: Don't. Don't get into the buffalo hunt, Boyo. Not this late.

Shane: They organized a government every time they went on a buffalo hunt. A *gouvernment provisoire*. And the principle was share and share alike. . . .

Burns: I can't do anything here anymore tonight. I'm going home. I can't even see straight . . . I'm that tired.

Matt: We know all that, Shane.

Shane: And Riel just based his idea on the buffalo hunt. . . .

Burns: *To Shane.* Wanna ride?

Shane: Government when necessary but not necessarily government!

Burns: Do you want a ride?

Shane: Sure.

Lights down as they start to put on their coats. Lights up on Tour Guide in Batoche, wearing regulation Parks Canada attire.

Tour Guide: Welcome to Batoche National Historic Site. My name is Bertram . . .

Matt: First thing tomorrow?

Tour Guide: . . . and it will my privilege to be your tour guide while you're here on site.

Shane: Give me a break.

Tour Guide: What I would like to do first of all is explain the main theme of the museum. . . .

Burns: Make it around eleven. . . .

Tour Guide: The main theme of the museum is the tragedy of Batoche . . .

Burns: I've got appointments.

Burns and Shane leave. We remain vaguely aware of Matt in his library as we watch what happens at Batoche. Tour Guide advances. In the group are Kelly and Yvonne. Kelly is beautiful, stylish, intelligent, but has found it useful to assume a naive innocence of approach and this is how she approaches Yvonne, wandering up to her casually.

Yvonne is probably about the same age, she looks naive and has that preoccupied air of someone seeking answers for herself.

Tour Guide: . . . being a conflict of cultures. The conflict being between the white culture and the Métis culture and to a lesser extent the Indian culture . . .

Kelly: Hi.

Yvonne nods and tries to put some distance between them.

Kelly: *Persistent.* Are you enjoying this? It's interesting, isn't it?

Yvonne: Yes.

Kelly: I love history, don't you?

Yvonne: Some of it.

Kelly: And getting out here, you know, where it actually happened . . . it really makes it come alive, doesn't it?

Yvonne: Yeah, it does that.

Kelly: Do you live around here?

Yvonne: No. Vancouver.

Kelly: Where do you live?

Yvonne: Vancouver.

Kelly: I love Vancouver. What do you do there?

Yvonne: I teach.

Kelly: Yeah?

Yvonne: Yep.

Kelly: That must be interesting. I admire teachers. I could never do it . . . control a bunch of little brats all day . . . think up things for them to do all the time. . . .

Yvonne: High school.

Kelly: You teach high school? *Yvonne nods.* That might not be so bad. In Vancouver. *Shy.* Are you a Nootka?

Yvonne: A what?

Kelly: A Nootka?

Yvonne: I don't think so. *Grins suddenly.* No I'm not. What are you?

Kelly: I'm a research assistant. Am I being nosy? I am. I'm sorry. I do this. It's a bad habit I've got. I treat people like exhibits. I'm really interested and everything but I get carried away. . . . I'm sorry. . . . It's a kind of mode of thinking, do you know what I mean? It's like a research mode of thinking. . . . It's like going through life as a tourist, you know what I mean?

Yvonne: Yeah, I've seen it in people.

Kelly: My name's Kelly. I'm sorry.

Yvonne: My name's Yvonne. It's all right.

Yvonne exits with tour but Kelly turns towards Matt and starts to clean up the debris from the night before.

Matt: Listen to this, Kelly, I like to think this, okay? I like to think this. Louis Riel has just led the Red River Rebellion . . . which everybody knows wasn't actually a rebellion, it was just a provisional government, you know, that brings Manitoba into Canada and . . . you know the history, right . . . because you're such a buff . . . and he gets elected to Parliament, even though the Orangemen of Ontario have put a price on his head because he executed Thomas Scott and we have that whole scene about how he sneaks into Parliament and signs the role and then escapes and all of his wanderings and then we get to this all important letter from Bishop Bourget. . . . Are you listening?

Kelly: Yes, Dear.

Matt: Right . . . so he tells him he's got a mission and Riel writes back saying, right, I've got a mission, and then he's in church in Washington and this is sort of based on his description of his experience. . . .

"Joy came suddenly. It swept through me like laughing fire. I would have laughed out loud and — oh I knew I had to hide my smile from my neighbours — they might have thought I was laughing at them. I took out my handkerchief and put it over my mouth and still a little boy, looking every which way but at the altar — noticed me and he grinned at me. Maybe he was about ten years old, this boy.

"I felt such consolation, such consolation. But then after only about two minutes I was struck by an immense sadness of spirit. And if it had not been for the great efforts I made to restrain my sighs, my tears and cries would have made a terrible noise within the church. But that great pain, as great as my joy, passed away in just as short a time and it left me with this thought: On this earth man's joys and pains are brief. Not long afterwards, only a few days, people began to treat me like a madman."

Do you like that?

Kelly: Yeah.

Matt: So do I. So do I. It really catches the man, doesn't it? Well, he actually said something close to that . . . only in French . . . but I find it very moving, and you know . . . like the fine line between ecstasy and religious understanding . . . and the inner world . . . where some people call you insane because they can't understand why you're laughing or crying and there's no way to explain. . . . But I'm not going to be able to sell Shane or Burns on it. Burns: "I gotta go to Toronto with this thing." *Disgusted.* Toronto.

Kelly: *Still cleaning up.* Is that what all this was about?

Matt: Was it ever. On and on. Me trying to write the mystic, Shane insisting on the revolutionary, Burns. . . . Burns wants to make a cowboy movie. But this . . . this has to be where it's at. *Pause.* What do you think?

Kelly: Matthew?

Matt: What?

Kelly: Have you ever met a Métis?

The tour guide enters and takes us away from the library. Kelly is caught between the two scenes.

Tour Guide: We're standing on the site of the village of Batoche, which is located on a river flat along the Eastern bank of the South Saskatchewan River . . .

Kelly: Have you?

Tour Guide: . . . approximately three quarters of a mile northwest of the rectory and the church . . .

Matt: Sure . . .

Tour Guide: . . . which formed the parish of St. Anthony of Padua. . . .

Matt: I must have . . .

Tour Guide: The village itself was more or less founded by Xavier Letendre . . .

Matt: . . . once or twice . . .

Tour Guide: . . . or Batoche as he is known as. He was the first merchant to settle in the immediate area.

Matt: . . . one time or another.

Tour Guide: The location itself of the village was brought about . . .

Matt: Why?

Tour Guide: . . . because of the fact that the Humbolt and the Carlton trails joined at this particular site.

Kelly: I met one . . .

Yvonne catches up to the guide.

Tour Guide: Xavier Letendre, besides occupying the first store . . .

Matt: You?

Tour Guide: . . . in the area, owned and operated the first ferry, which the people used to cross the South Saskatchewan River . . .

Yvonne: *Picking up something from the ground.* What's this?

Kelly: *To Matt.* Last summer. *To Yvonne.* Piece of glass. *To Matt.* Doing the research. *To Yvonne.* People just leave broken glass around . . . people just leave it around . . . they don't care, eh?

Tour Guide: . . . when they were travelling either to Duck Lake or to Fort Carlton or to Prince Albert.

Yvonne: It looks old. Do you think it's old?

Kelly: It does, kind of.

Tour Guide: The Village of Batoche itself is composed of two parts. *Noting that he has lost part of his audience.* What have you got there?

Yvonne: Nothing. Just some trash.

Tour Guide: Let's see? *Taking the glass.* Ah. The moles push things up, you see. This may have come from the cellars of Phillipe Garneau's Hotel, you see. It could have been an old wine bottle once.

Yvonne: Really?

Tour Guide: Yes indeed. It even looks like it has wine stains on it. See? Impossible to tell, of course . . . but. . . .

Yvonne: May I keep it?

Tour Guide: I'm sorry. No artifacts may be taken away from the site.

Kelly: It's just a piece of broken glass.

Tour Guide: Madam, that is not just a piece of broken glass. It is a piece of history.

Yvonne: Yeah, mine.

Tour Guide: Yes, a piece of Canada's history.

Kelly: Your history?

Yvonne: Yeah.

Kelly: Are you . . . are you a Métis?

Yvonne nods.

Tour Guide: Would you mind . . . ?

Kelly: Wait a minute. *To Yvonne.* I didn't think there were any of those left.

Tour Guide: If you'll give that back, please.

Yvonne: There are.

Kelly: Well then it belongs to you. *To Tour Guide.* It belongs to her.

Tour Guide: It belongs to Parks Canada. If you don't give it to me I'll have to ask you to leave the site.

Yvonne: Oh, well, in that case . . . *Gives it to him.*

Tour Guide: Thank you. Now, this may not mean anything to you, but do you know how many people we get through here every summer?

Yvonne: No.

Kelly: How many?

Tour Guide: A great many. And if every tourist picked up an artifact, no matter how trivial, do you know how long this site would last?

Yvonne: How long?

Tour Guide: Thank-you. *Resuming.* The Village of Batoche itself is composed of two parts: the East Village where we are standing right now . . .

Kelly: There's not much left of it, is there?

Yvonne: Not much.

Tour Guide: . . . and then the West Village, which is located on the West shore of the South Saskatchewan river.

Kelly: Are you really?

Yvonne: Really?

Kelly: A Métis?

Yvonne: No, I'm a Nootka.

Tour Guide: The village itself was not all that large. The buildings that were found in the village itself were Xavier Letendre's store, a small house owned by Garneau, and Boyer's store and also Fischer's store, along with a small blacksmith's shop which was also owned by Xavier Letendre. . . .

Kelly and Yvonne fall behind the tour.

Kelly: You're teasing me.

Yvonne: Really I'm Métis.

Kelly: I didn't know what a Métis would look like if I met one.

Yvonne: What did you expect?

Kelly: I didn't know. I never thought I would meet one.

Yvonne: Well you have . . .

Kelly: I thought it was all history.

Yvonne: So what do you think?

Kelly: What do I think? I'm a real bozo, aren't I? I told you, it's the tourist. . . . I mean . . . because you look Indian. . . . Is this racist? Am I being racist?

Yvonne: Not really.

Kelly: Thank goodness.

Yvonne: Just silly.

Kelly: Oh.

Yvonne: I've got just the same amount of European in me as Indian. Some of us come out blond hair, blue eyed. . . . But I turned out looking Indian. *Pause.* It was good. It made it harder to stay away. . . .

Kelly: From here?

Yvonne: I guess so. Yeah, here.

Kelly: Did you grow up in Vancouver?

Yvonne: Is this research?

Kelly: No, come on. Well, maybe. Who knows? Where did you grow up?

Yvonne: Here and there. A bunch of places. I don't know all the places.

Kelly: How come?

Yvonne: Foster homes.

Back in the study, Shane enters.

Kelly: Where were your parents?

Shane: Matt?

Yvonne: I don't know. I'm trying to find them.

Shane: I let myself in.

Matt: Just a sec. . . . *He's working.*

Kelly: *After a moment.* I guess some people are lucky and some people aren't so lucky.

Yvonne: What are you?

Matt: *To Shane as he continues to write.* Did you look at the scene with the buffalo hunt?

Kelly: I'm sort of lucky. My husband, . . . he's really lucky.

Shane: Where's the book with the paintings?

Yvonne: Oh?

Matt: *Indicating.* Paul Kane.

Shane settles down with the book.

Kelly: You wouldn't believe it. Anything he puts his hand to, it turns out great. As soon as he got out of university, he set up a little consulting business and it went great, but he got tired of it so then he invented this game . . . have you ever heard of Scrabble?

Yvonne: Your husband invented Scrabble?

Kelly: No, but he invented a game where you have to put words together, only they have to make some kind of poetic sense. It's called "Bard"? Anyway, he sold it right off to Parker Brothers . . . and then he didn't want to do that sort of thing any more, so he tried writing and he sold his very first book, and now he's started to write screenplays.

Yvonne: I'd like to do that.

Shane: What's with the music, Matt?

Kelly: Really?

Yvonne: Yeah, I like movies and I used to try to write things.

Matt: Helps me to concentrate.

Kelly: You should have kept it up.

Yvonne: No. It all came out sounding. . . .

Kelly: What?

Yvonne: Not to be offensive or anything . . . but it came out sounding white.

Yvonne and Kelly leave. We begin to hear the chamber music Matt has been playing as he works. Shane continues to look at the book.

Shane: This could be fantastic.

Matt: I'm not convinced.

Burns: *Entering and hanging up coat.* Break out the cognac, gentlemen! We have something going here, something going! Well, don't just stand there . . . bring on the snifters. We are going to have ourselves a little toast.

Matt: Tell us.

Burns: Where's the booze.

Shane: Come on, you bastard.

Matt: *Pouring cognac.* All right . . .

Shane: Just a beer for me, Matt. . . .

Burns: *Disgusted.* A beer, a beer!

Matt: *Exits.* All right, all right.

Burns: This is no time for. . . .

Shane: Cognac is classist. It makes me puke.

Matt: *Returning with beer.* A Remy Martin, and a Bohemian. All right, Burns, what's the story?

Burns: VistaComNet!

Blank stares from Matt and Shane.

Burns: VistaComNet. What is this? Is everybody deaf? Vista. . . .

Shane: Yeah, yeah . . . VistaComNet.

Matt: What's VistaComNet?

Burns: Pay TV.

Shane: Are they buying?

Burns: Are they buying? Yes, they are buying. They're in it hook, line, and sinker. I go to Toronto this aft. I bring back the contracts. It's in the bag. . . .

Great joy all around.

Burns: If we can get something like the CBC to come in on the deal.

Less joy.

Matt: Substantially?

Burns: Well, enough to be serious. Yeah, substantially.

Joy greatly diminished.

Shane: You've gotta be kidding.

Matt: They don't have any money. They've been cut back. . . .

Shane: They've done their own Riel . . . they're not going to finance another. . . .

Burns: Sure you're right. Why didn't I see it before. I just can't believe how fast you guys think. Me, I've been stewing over this for ... oh ... about three months now, and I thought maybe I was beginning to come up with maybe answers, but you fellows, you just go straight to the heart of the thing. . . .

Matt: Okay, tell us the rest.

Burns: I've got connections. I use my connections. Maybe we get the CBC in on it ... maybe we don't ... but I've got parties ... Eastern parties ... big Eastern parties who want to invest in the arts. We might have to make a few adjustments ... here and there. . . .

Matt: What kind of adjustments?

Burns: Who knows? I've got to talk to my people in Ontario. I'm just warning you, we might have to be a little flexible. If we're going to get off the ground we might have to be willing to compromise here and there. . . .

Shane: What's it going to be about then, Laura Secord?

Burns: No, no. It's going to stay about the whole of the Batoche thing — the battle of and everything. All I'm asking for is room to manoeuver. Will you give me that? Will you give me room to manoeuver?

Focus shifts to the Tour Guide who is standing on a raised level. He is joined by Yvonne and Kelly.

Tour Guide: We are standing in the cemetery.

Burns: Listen, fellahs, I'm talking big money here.

Tour Guide: The cemetery is still owned and operated by the parish of St. Anthony of Padua ...

Burns: I'm talking about a mini series on the networks ...

Tour Guide: ... but they have given us permission to conduct people through it ...

Burns: ... and a major feature ...

Tour Guide: ... as there is some historical significance to the cemetery itself.

Burns: ... a major feature on Pay TV.

Tour Guide: At the present time we are standing by a fence which marks the site of the mass grave.

Burns: So do I have room to manoeuvre?

Tour Guide: May the 12th, after the last shot was fired, the Métis dead were brought here to the cemetery . . .

Shane: Sure.

Tour Guide: . . . each cross representing one person who was buried in the grave.

Burns: *Glances at watch and then to Shane.* You going to drive me to the airport?

Tour Guide: If you'll follow me . . .

Shane: Sure.

Shane and Burns leave. Music fades out.

Kelly: *After they contemplate the grave for a while.* It's sad, isn't it?

Yvonne: I thought it would be.

Kelly: It is.

Yvonne: I don't know. There's something strong here. I thought it would be like . . . you know . . . defeat and tragedy . . . and all of that . . . but there's . . .there's the sound of ghosts here. . . .

Kelly: What?

Yvonne: It's like . . . those old guys under the ground are saying, "Hey. . . . we fought back. . . . You can fight back too." Something like that.

Kelly: You're weird.

Yvonne: Me?

Kelly: This was the end of it, Yvonne.

Yvonne: No it wasn't. Look at me.

Kelly: I'm looking.

Yvonne: Take my hand. Take it. Do you feel it?

Kelly: Yes . . .

Yvonne: Am I here, Kelly? Am I with you?

Kelly can only nod. Yvonne squeezes her hand until she winces.

Kelly: Ow.

Yvonne: You aren't dreaming?

Kelly: You're here, Yvonne.

Yvonne: Yeah, I'm here. We're still here. We survived Batoche. There were half-breeds all over the Northwest. Back in the bush there were whole villages of Métis people — there still are. I was born in one of them. Here . . . the day the battle ended the women hid themselves along the water and the men fled to the hills and we survived. The soldiers ran wild . . .they looted Batoche. They took everything. They burnt the farms. But we survived. After it was all over we gathered in the ruins . . . shivering in the cold . . . trying to keep our babies warm . . . and we had nothing to feed them. But all across the Northwest the Métis gathered among the ashes of La Nation Métisse. It was cold and bitter that year and the next year and it is still. But we survived. Keep your mind straight about that.

Kelly: You sound as if you were there.

Yvonne: All my relatives were.

Kelly: *She knows there is more to this.* Oh. And it's still cold? How do you mean?

Yvonne: What do you want? Do you want a lesson in Métis realities?

Kelly: I think so.

Yvonne: Really?

Kelly: Yeah.

Yvonne: All right. *Deep breath and plunge.* The first thing you have to understand is that in the eyes of the government and a lot of people who make decisions, we're not Indian and we're not white.

Kelly: But you're both. . . .

Yvonne: Yeah, both! Or neither. We don't fit into the white system — not easily, anyway, unless we look white and act white and forget that we're Métis. And we don't fit into the Indian system. We've been the poorest people in the North. We haven't had land. . . . Many of our people were just squatting in tar paper shacks on land that nobody else claimed . . . road allowance land . . . park land if nobody kicked us off. *And we've been kicked off reserves, kicked out of Indian schools because we weren't Indian. . . .* We've been oppressed and we've been colonized . . . and for five generations we've been told that we're inferior. And our people are killing themselves fast and slow, and that's why. And our families are being torn apart, and that's why . . .

Kelly: But you . . . you're a high school teacher.

Yvonne: Yeah.

Kelly: How do you explain that?

Yvonne: Luck, I guess. I was the only one.

Kelly: What? . . .

Yvonne: In my family. I was the lucky one.

Kelly: What happened to the others?

Yvonne: I'll tell you sometime. Okay. If we keep knowing each other.

Kelly: That's not likely, eh? *Intrigued.* Do you think we will?

Focus shifts to to the library. The room is in shadows. Matt is partly lit by his desk lamp.

Matt: How do I picture you, Louis? I want you to be a prophet for me . . . but you're not speaking to me. You're not leading me, Louis, and I have so much invested in you. Listen . . . I feel like that young man you stole from Prince Albert . . . that Protestant Henry Jackson. You made him secretary of your council. He was your go-between with the English settlers when you were trying to help them with their grievances. He fell in love with the ideal of community, Jackson. Changed his name so it sounded more French — Joseph Honoré Jaxon. Converted, too . . . became a Catholic. That's 'cause he believed in you, Louis. He knew things couldn't stay the same. He knew you were the only open . . . the only radical clear break with the process. Hah. . . . Maybe Shane's right . . . you were a revolutionary. But I can't believe that. You wanted to put pressure on the government . . . fair enough. Fair enough. But why did you want blood, Louis? Did the Lord command you to lead his people down into the valley of the shadow of death?

Shane as Riel: *Moving into the light as Riel.* We were a council. I did nothing on my own. We did it together. . . .

Matt: But the eyewitnesses . . . they said you flew into rages. You were going to put your cousin to death because he was backing down. . . . You saw traitors behind every tree. . . .

Shane as Riel: Do they say that?

Matt: They give the impression.

Shane: *Breaking with the character.* You want to make him over in your own image?

Matt: No. We think alike. That's why I admire him. Don't stop now. This is very helpful. I think we can make a scene out of this. . . .

Shane: Do you think alike?

Matt: Of course. He's the mystic who wanted to better the lot of his people. He dreamed the voice of God and acted on it. I'm an author who dreams stories and I want to change the lot of my people.

Shane: To change the lot of your people?

Matt: I've got a social conscience.

Shane: Do you want to change the system?

Matt: I don't know about that. Maybe just raise people's awareness level.

Shane: Riel was a careful political strategist. He wanted to take power.

Matt: That's the distortion that Eastern Canada . . .

Shane: When he was in exile in Montana he would call leaders of the Métis and the Indians together and plan how a general revolt could succeed. He was *conspiring*, Matt.

Matt: Well, more power to him.

Shane: He was trying to set up a system of his own . . .

Matt: Yes, but what a system where all the peoples of the world could live. . . . Okay. . . . Under a theocracy . . . with Bishop

Bourget as the Pope. Okay it sounds crazy . . . but what a fantastic dream. And what's wrong with a theocracy, with all people living under the rule of God . . . ?

Shane: You are getting religious in your old age . . .

Matt: Oh, I'm going around and around it. I want to know how such a good man could become involved in so much bloodshed.

Shane: Is that it?

Matt: Yeah.

Shane: Do you think he was wrong?

Matt: Well I know you don't . . . but you're a radical.

Shane: Write it for us.

Matt: Will you do it?

Shane: If it works.

Matt: Of course it will work. Try it. *Hands him page.*

Shane as Riel: I kept myself in control most of the time until the memory of outrages made against me took possession and I in turn became outraged or enragé . . . how do you say? Fifteen years ago, in 1870, in Manitoba, we were not a rebellion. We were the only government there was. The Hudson's Bay Company was selling the Northwest to Canada . . . they couldn't govern it themselves. The clown McDougall, would-be Lieutenant-Governor, had not even the legal right . . . the deed hadn't been signed. And all of it as if we didn't exist . . . we who lived on the land . . . who had the right to the land. It was ludicrous. But I kept myself in control. We merely set up a provisional government, and we negotiated . . . not whether we would enter Canada . . . but on what terms. They called us ignorant half-breed savages but we counted among us some of the best educated men in the settlement. We went to Ottawa and we got what we wanted . . . except for me. For me it was persecution and exile. I was hunted like an elk! And when I came back I came back as an angry man. You wonder how I could call myself a Catholic, a Christian, and have led my people to revolt. I will tell you I risked hell for my people. We know how England acts. When she is asked for anything she becomes insane. And to negotiate with her is to enter into insanity. But I was willing to go that far for my people. *Pause — Shane puts down the script.* How far are you willing to go?

Matt: For the production?

Shane: Naw . . . for your people . . . for "the Country."

Matt: This is a different day and age.

Shane: How far?

Matt: Revolut . . . ? C'mon. That's a little out of style, isn't it? The country is doing the best it can for the greatest number of people, eh? Sure there are problems . . . but we can work things out. There's no need to get uncivilized.

The tour sweeps through the library and the focus changes to Batoche.

Tour Guide: This is the church of St. Antoine de Padoue and next to it is the rectory. If you look up there to the second story of the rectory you can still see the bullet holes made by the Gatling in 1885, the Gatling being an early form of machine gun, built by the Gatling Company of New Jersey and being tested here under battle conditions for the first time.

Kelly: Are you going to stay long?

Yvonne: Here?

Tour Guide: During the Battle this area changed hands every day. . . .

Kelly: I mean in the province.

Yvonne: As long as it takes.

Kelly: As long as what takes?

Tour Guide: But at night he retreated to the zareba, the site of which you may have observed on the road as you drove up.

Yvonne: I've kind of given myself some time. . . . I might not go back to work this fall. You know, to find some . . .

Tour Guide: When General Middleton withdrew . . .

Kelly: Roots?

Yvonne: I guess.

Kelly: Here. *Giving Yvonne her address.* It's my husband's card. Will you come and see us? I'd really like you to.

Tour Guide: . . . the Métis fighters under Gabriel Dumont — Gabriel Dumont being Louis Riel's military comander — were left in possession of the church, the priests and nuns taking care of the wounded.

Kelly: Excuse me?

Tour Guide: Yes.

Kelly: What is a . . . a zare . . . the thing that General Middleton went back to?

Tour Guide: Zareba.

Kelly: What is that?

Tour Guide: A zareba.

Kelly: What is it?

Tour Guide: A zareba is a temporary fortified encampment. The zareba in this instance was a rectangle about a hundred meters around with supply wagons and horses on the perimeter, surrounded by trenches dug to one meter in depth, with the dirt taken from the trench heaped on the outside. Above this were placed two logs, one above the other, somewhat separated to permit rifle fire. Now if you will follow me . . .

Kelly: How can I get in touch with you?

Tour Guide, Kelly and Yvonne leave. Burns enters waving contracts.

Burns: *Triumphantly.* Got 'em!

Matt and Shane spring up.

Shane: Good man!

Matt: Let's see them!

Burns spreads the contracts out on the desk and Shane and Matt pore over them.

Shane: What does this mean? What does this mean? Where's the part about me?

Burns: You're in there. Page five of this one and this one . . . page seven of this one. We're all in there. We agreed. That's part of the deal. Besides, they think you're the greatest thing since sliced . . . er . . .

Matt: Bread?

Burns: Yeah, bread. No problem.

Shane: And the money?

Burns: Good money. Great money.

Matt: And the artistic freedom?

Burns: Good artistic freedom. Great. Where's your pen? Hey . . . we need a witness. Get the little woman in here.

Matt: *Calling.* Kelly! *To Burns.* How'd you do it, Burns?

Burns: Regionalism.

Shane: Come on.

Burns: No, really . . . I did it. I said, "Look it's time you three piece suits in Ontari-ario stop screwing around with the rest of us in the rest of the country . . . in the big . . . very big . . . very angry . . . very political rest of the country. This is our hero, this Riel . . . our hero, you understand. Don't make another one of your twiddly oh, so artsy Toronto based disasters about this man who stood for everything you fellows are against . . . like giving us our share of the natural resources, of the oil revenues, giving us the Crow Rate, giving us just as much right and investment . . . you hear that *investment* . . . in being Canadians as you have had for two centuries.

Shane: And it worked?

Burns: The evidence is lying there before you. Sign right there . . . beside your name.

Matt: Kelly!

Kelly: *Off.* I'm on my way.

Matt: So now we can start . . . in earnest.

Burns: In earnest.

Matt: No restrictions.

Burns: None.

Matt: Terrific.

Burns: To speak of.

Matt freezes, his pen in midair.

Matt: To speak of?

Burns: Nothing really. Sign there.

Matt: What restrictions, Burns?

Burns: You can't criticize John A. Macdonald. Sign there.

Shane: What?

Burns: It's a little compromise, really. Some of the funding depends on it. You know, political sensitivities. . . . Sign there.

Kelly enters.

Shane: But he was the villain.

Kelly: Who was?

Matt: He caused the uprising! Not Riel . . . it was Macdonald! How can you write about 1885 and not paste him to the wall?

Shane: You gotta just blast him!

Burns: Well he was the father of Confederation, and our first Prime Minister . . . builder of the CPR . . .

Matt: He was deceitful, he was manipulative, he was unprincipled, he was a white supremacist . . .

Shane: He was a Tory.

Matt: He was a drunk.

Burns: You gotta admire a man like that.

Matt: Come on. Just listen to the words that came out of his mouth. Read his speeches in parliament . . . read his correspondence. He set the Métis up!

Kelly: What did you guys want?

Shane: You're kidding us aren't you, Burns?

Burns: Would you witness our signatures?

Kelly: I don't see any signatures.

Matt: Answer the man, Burns. It is a joke, right?

Burns: No. It's serious. We gotta go easy on Macdonald. Certain people are tired of seeing Macdonald get the short end of the stick whenever the subject of Louis Riel comes up.

Matt: I can't believe this.

Burns: Stranger things have happened. People get sensitive.

Kelly: What signatures?

Matt: *Wearily.* There aren't going to be any signatures.

Shane: Right.

Burns: All because of this Macdonald thing?

Shane: Sorry Burns. This is the end of the road.

Burns: Look. How be we work out a compromise.

Shane: Forget it.

Matt: Not on this one, Burns.

Burns: No, no, no. Hear me out. Just a little compromise. I'll go back and tell them. . . . What? I'll tell them . . .

Matt: We can't do it.

Burns: No, no. I'll say we'll play it like it was. We won't go out of our way to put Sir John A. in a bad light . . . we'll just let him quote himself. Let the chips fall wherever.

Matt: You'll do that?

Burns: Matt, we've gone too far to stop now.

Matt: Listen to this!

Matt rummages through documents and produces a photocopied sheet. Matt playacts character of Macdonald. There is a subtle light change and the present is altered.

Matt: Feb. 23, 1870: To the Honourable Sir John Rose: "Everything looks well for a delegation coming to Ottawa including the redoubtable Riel. If we once get him here, as you must know by this time, he is a gone coon. There is no place for him in the ministry next to Howe, but perhaps we may make him a senator for the Territory! I received yesterday your cable to the effect that Her Majesty's Government will co-operate in the expedition. These impulsive half-breeds have got spoilt by this émeute, this riot, and must be kept down by a strong hand until they are swamped by the influx of settlers."

Leaving character. That was Red River, and this was after Batoche. *He passes one page to Shane and reads from the other as Macdonald.* John A. Macdonald to Lord Lansdowne, Governor General of Canada, August 28, 1885: "This Northwest outbreak was a mere domestic trouble, and ought not to be elevated to the rank of a rebellion. The offences of Riel were riot and murder of such an extensive nature as to make them technically amount to treason."

Shane (as Lansdowne):   Lansdowne to the Prime Minister of Canada. "The outbreak was, no doubt, confined to our own territory and may therefore properly be described as a domestic trouble, but I am afraid we have all of us been doing what we could to elevate it to the rank of a rebellion, and with so much success that we cannot now reduce it to the rank of a common riot."

Matt (as Macdonald):   Macdonald to Lansdowne: "I fear you have me with respect to the character given to the outbreak. We have certainly made it assume large proportions in the public eye. This has been done however for our own purposes, and, I think, wisely done."

Lights return to the present.

Shane: Will they accept that?

Burns: They'll have to.

Matt: So I'll put in that Macdonald couldn't get the money to finish the Canadian Pacific Railway unless the public thought there was a full scale revolution going on?

Burns: Did Macdonald say that?

Matt: What else was he referring to?

Burns: Did he say it?

Matt: Not in so many words.

Burns: Just put in what he said.

Shane: That'll be enough.

Matt: All right.

General jubilation.

Shane: Let's go for it.

Burns: I'm a genius.

Matt: As you have always said.

Burns: Have I?

Shane: A humble genius.

Kelly: *Putting her arm appreciatively around Matt's.* You guys have been working so hard. It would be awful if it all collapsed now.

Shane: *To Burns.* What made you think we'd go along with that?

Burns: I told them there'd be trouble. I told them. Sign already.

They start to sign.

Kelly: What about the consultant?

Matt: That doesn't have to go in these . . .

Burns: Consultant?

Matt: Yeah, I want a consultant in on this. *This is the first the others have heard of this.* But that doesn't have anything to do with these contracts . . . that's something we can decide between ourselves.

Kelly: You said you wouldn't go ahead without . . .

Shane: What kind of a consultant?

Kelly: A native.

Burns: A native consultant? What's a native consultant?

Kelly: *To Matt.* You said you'd make it a condition . . .

Matt: I know.

Shane: What's going on, Matt.

Matt: I thought this could wait . . . but this is as good a time as any . . .

Burns: *Incredulous.* You want to change the agreement?

Matt: Kelly and I got talking about the project the other night and she brought up something . . . and I thought about it and I got to thinking that she was right . . . there's been something missing in all of this that we have been missing in all of this.

Shane: What?

Matt: I'm getting to it. We need a Métis in on the project.

Shane and Burns look at each other as if Matt has been speaking a foreign language. They are very confused.

Kelly: A Métis.

Shane: I don't get it.

Burns: We got all kinds of Métis in the show. It's about Métis for the sake of almighty God in Heaven.

Matt: I mean a real one.

Burns: Aw for. . . . Where are you gonna find a Métis at this late date?

Shane: And even if you could find one, what is he going to know about film?

Kelly: They don't all live in the back woods, you know.

Matt: It's right, it's right. Trust me.

Burns: It's an extra expense, Matt.

Matt: No, it should have been in the budget. Kelly brought up the point . . . and I agree with her now — after we discussed it a bit — that we're developing this show in a vacuum. We forgot that the Métis people weren't obliterated at Batoche . . . that there's an ongoing reality here, see what I mean?

Burns: No.

Matt: We can't just speculate about these people . . . or depend on the research. We should have a kind of partner from the Métis community working with us day by day as we develop the screenplay . . .

Shane: I guess it can't hurt.

Matt: It'll help. It'll give us some first hand experience . . . we'll be able to get the flavor, the texture of Métis life . . . you understand what I'm saying.

Shane: *Not really enthusiastic.* Yeah.

Matt: What's wrong?

Shane: How much influence would this guy have? I mean we don't want to get too many in on the act.

Burns: It's a point, Matt.

Shane: We've been a kind of tight functioning group, right. We've had our problems but we've overcome them, right? We've produced some good stuff together.

Burns: Damn good stuff. It's been hell, but the process works, eh? It works.

Matt: Well, we'll set up so the process isn't disturbed too much.

Kelly: That makes me sick.

Matt: Honey.

Kelly: No, I'm sorry, it does. Either you want somebody to come in on this or you don't.

Matt: Well we want somebody but ... you have to understand creative process.

Kelly: What are you going to do? Invite somebody in on this and say, "We'd like you to tell us all about being a Métis but don't expect us to change anything."

Burns: *Abruptly.* It's all academic, anyway. We're never going to be able to find anybody.

Kelly: She'd never stand for it.

Matt: *To Burns.* Why not?

Kelly: I bet she won't even come and talk ...

Burns: We don't have any contacts. Do you know any Indians?

Shane: You have somebody already.

Matt: Kelly met somebody who could. ... I don't know ... we might see her.

The light crossfades, taking us away from the library to the Tour Guide in isolation.

Tour Guide: If you'll follow me down towards the river we'll pass by one of the Métis rifle pits. As opposed to Middleton's army of a thousand, there were only one hundred and seventy five Métis farmers and their Indian allies defending Batoche; however, they made their force seem larger by rushing from rifle pit to rifle pit and also with the use of straw dummies. General Middleton was convinced he was up against a larger force than was actually the case. Nor did he have any idea of how desperate they actually were. General Middleton may have been misrepresented by many as an incompetent General. However it seems as if he was working on a kind of seige of the village with the intention of winning the battle with the least number of casualties on either side. Nevertheless, on the final day, May 12, 1885, an impatient and impetuous officer led his men on a charge down the hills towards the village. The Métis fighters, reduced to using pebbles as ammunition in their muzzleloading rifles, could not sustain such a determined rush, and broke. The Canadians pushed through to the village itself, and took it. The Métis made one last attempt to rally and retake the village, but this proved to be in vain. Dumont fled to the United States. Riel surrendered to General Middleton. Middleton's troops put farms to the torch for miles around Batoche.

END OF ACT I

Act Two

Lights up on the library. Kelly, Matt, Burns and Shane are sitting about in various stages of rapt attention. Yvonne is sitting in a central position reading from Dumont's account.

Yvonne: "The fourth day, May 12, at about two o'clock, on exact information from those who betrayed us, that we had no more ammunition, the troops advanced and our men came out of their trenches. Then were killed José Ouellet, 93 years of age; José Vandal, who had both arms broken first and was finished off with a bayonet, 75 years old; Donald Ross, first fatally wounded and speared with a bayonet, also very old; Isidore Boyer, also an old man; Michel Trottier, André Batoche, Calixte Tourond, Elzéar Tourond, John Swan and Damase Carriere, who first had his leg broken and whom the English then dragged with a rope around his neck tied to the tail of a horse. . . . "

Burns: I never heard about that.

Yvonne: "And there were two Sioux killed."

Burns: Where did you get that?

Yvonne: It's Gabriel Dumont.

Kelly: That's awful.

Shane: Maybe I should play Dumont.

Yvonne: So what I'm saying is we weren't the ones who committed the atrocities.

Shane: I'd make a better guerilla fighter than a politician.

Matt: But what about Frog Lake?

Shane: Don't be a bleeding heart, Matt.

Matt: Bleeding heart? Come on. Bleeding heart? There are two sides to every story, Shane. Frog Lake's the other side. Let's have a balanced perspective on this, eh?

Shane: Why?

Matt: For the sake of credibility.

Burns: What happened at Frog Lake?

Shane: You're supposed to know all this, Burns.

Kelly: The Cree killed the priests and the Indian Agent and . . .

Shane: They were driven to it. They were starving.

Burns: But priests, Shane. God . . .

Shane: You can only drive people so far, and then they strike out . . .

Yvonne: Do you want to hear what I think?

Everyone turns to Yvonne.

Shane: Yeah. What do you think?

Yvonne: It wasn't pretty . . . but what was happening to them wasn't either. I'm not apologizing for them but . . .

Matt: We're not asking you to do that, Yvonne.

Yvonne: I mean how would you like it if somebody came in here . . . into your own house, and told you where to sit, what to think, how to believe . . .

Shane: Right.

Matt: Exactly. Well?

Yvonne: Well?

Matt: Are you going to join us? We need you.

Shane: Dumont. What do you say, Burns?

Yvonne: *To Matt.* I'm going to have to think it over.

Burns: *To Shane.* What?

Shane: Dumont.

Matt: *To Yvonne.* Of course.

Shane: *To Burns.* It makes a lot more sense.

Kelly: ·I hope you'll say yes.

Shane: With Riel ... I don't see my way clear. You know, all I ask is, "Give me an emotion ...

Matt: I don't want to rush you ...

Shane: ... or tell me what to play and I'll play it."

Matt: ... but we're getting close to our deadline ...

Burns: Yeah.

Yvonne: Okay.

Shane: Dumont is straightforward like that. I can do that. But with Riel ... half the time I don't get it.

Burns: We've sold you as Riel. You can't change boats in midstream.

Matt: That's horses, Burns. *To Shane.* Riel has more scenes.

Burns: Horses?

Shane: Oh, in that case...

Burns: *To Yvonne.* Advise us.

Yvonne: Horses.

Burns: No, no. About Shane playing Dumont.

Yvonne: No, I don't think he should.

Shane: It's all ...

Burns: There, see!

Shane: ... all right. I changed my mind anyway. For the good of the series.

Yvonne: Who's going to play Riel?

Shane: I am.

Burns: Shane is.

Yvonne sees that she is going to have to work hard to be at her diplomatic best.

Yvonne: I'm sure you'd be wonderful.

Shane: Thanks.

Yvonne: But ... *They are afraid they already know what her next* *question will be* . . . couldn't you have found a Métis actor to play the part?

Burns: Oh, he'll look more like Riel once we give him a beard and . . . a bit of padding . . .

Matt: I don't think that's what she meant. . . .

Burns: Oh.

Matt: Is it?

Yvonne: Did you look for native actors?

Burns: Well, not yet. . . .

Yvonne: Because there are performers out there who would give their eye teeth to play Riel . . .

Burns: Well . . . not Riel. . . .

Shane: I'm written into the agreement.

Burns: It's the way we sold the series.

Matt: We needed his name. He's a rising star.

Yvonne: Is he?

Burns: Didn't you see "Black Lace at Midnight"?

Yvonne: No.

Burns: *Solemnly.* Very well done. Very fine acting.

Shane: Thanks.

Burns: He works all over the country.

Matt: It wasn't much of a script. . . .

Shane: Actually it was turkey time. . . .

Matt: But he was good. The other thing is he's got a financial stake in the Riel show. We've all put money into it. And a lot of emotional investment, too.

Yvonne: Why Riel?

"Ahs" and "ahas" from the men.

Shane: He's a revolutionary hero.

Burns: He's commercial. Riel's commercial.

Matt: It's the religion.

Shane: It's different with each of us.

Matt: *Enthusiastic.* I don't think anybody has ever gotten to the bottom of Riel's religion. He was a mystic and a prophet and a visionary, and what does it say about Canadians that our one outstanding frontier hero is this really eccentric, volatile religious revolutionary? What does that say about us? I don't know . . . but I figure it says something about us.

Yvonne: So it's going to be historical.

Matt: Yeah. I guess so. Is there something wrong with that?

Yvonne: Haven't you done it already?

Burns: Us? We've never done it.

Yvonne: Why don't you look at the present for a change?

Shane: *Joking.* Does it have a good part for me?

Joke falls flat.

Kelly: Shane.

Shane: I was just kidding.

Yvonne: *After a moment.* Maybe you don't want to change your project . . .

Matt: Everything's negotiable.

Burns: Within limits.

Yvonne: Could you go to some of the people?

Kelly: Tell them, Yvonne.

Yvonne: Why don't you go to skid row and talk to some of the people on the street. Find out how they got there. Maybe talk to the kids in foster homes, see what the system does for a people?

Burns: Well, maybe we could do that in the next project . . .

Matt: Wait, hear her out.

Yvonne: Go down to the States . . . talk to the descendants of people who fled from Canada after Red River and after Batoche. . . . See how they live in shack villages on the margin of American society — not white, not Indian, not black — show the suffering . . .

Matt: That could be very exciting.

Yvonne: What?

Matt: That really could be exciting. No, Burns, listen. We turn the series around. We turn it around. We make it a values-oriented thing. See what I'm saying?

Burns: Not exactly.

Matt: We do that. We set up a series of modern scenes that show the things that Yvonne is saying here and we ask the questions, you know, the important questions. Is this how we should treat our racial minorities . . . things like that.

Burns: But I sold them history.

Shane: What about Riel?

Matt: Oh, they'll get history, they'll get Riel, but it will be all juxtaposed with modern drama, you see what I mean?

Burns: Doesn't sound like VistaComNet material.

Shane: *Slowly.* I think I see what your getting at. Let me think here.

Burns: People are going to be looking at this on Superchannel.

Shane: I like it. It gives us a chance to make a real political statement.

Burns: People are going to be seeing this on Home Box Office.

Shane: Spice it up enough. They'll go for it.

Yvonne: *Sarcastic.* You could have a Mountie raping an Indian girl.

Burns: You've sold me. *Sudden thought.* Actually, that might do it.

Matt: Burns.

Burns: What? *Long pause.* Am I missing something here?

Yvonne: I don't know if I can handle this. *She gets up to go.*

Kelly: Wait, Yvonne!

Matt: I think we need you.

Yvonne: So do I, but I don't know whether I can handle it.

Shane: Wait. Don't decide right now.

Matt: Think about it. Take as long as you need.

Shane: I'd really like you in on this. We all would, right, Burns?

Burns: Sure.

Yvonne: Okay. Let me sleep on it.

She's off. Kelly turns to Matt as she exits.

Shane: Burns, I don't know how you do it!

Burns: What?

Matt: You've got the sensitivity of a wart hog.

Kelly: Matt . . .

Matt: What?

Kelly: You're an idiot. *Exit.*

Matt: *Stunned.* Me? *Pause.* Why am I an idiot?

Shane: *To Burns.* Is this a practice run or what?

Burns: Practice.

Lights come up on the witness stand of the 1885 court room.

Matt: *To Burns.* You're the guy who blew that. *Exits.*

Shane: Do I need the coat?

Burns: Do you want the coat?

Shane: Yeah. I'd like to try it.

Burns: *Calling off.* Kelly, we'll do it with Riel's coat. . . .

Kelly brings the coat to the witness stand.

Shane: Is that it?

Kelly: That's it.

She helps him into it as the lights go down on the library. Shane enters the prisoner's dock. Burns and Kelly withdraw.

Burns: *Over a studio intercom.* Ready?

Shane: Would you give me the lines of the judge and the lawyer?

Burns: *Sound of paper.* Okay. Judge: Prisoner, have you any remarks to make to the jury? If so, now is your time to speak. Lawyer: May it please your Honors. The prisoner at this time is entitled to make any statement he likes to the jury but I must declare before the court that as his counsel we must not be considered responsible for any declaration he may make. Judge: Certainly, but he is entitled and I am bound to tell him so.

Shane (as Riel): *Acknowledges the Judge and begins.* Your Honors, gentlemen of the jury: It would be easy for me today to play insanity, because the circumstances are such as to excite any man, and under the natural excitement of what is taking place today — I cannot speak English very well, but am trying to do so, because most of those here speak English — under the excitement which my trial causes me would justify me not to appear as usual, but with my mind out of its ordinary condition. I hope with the help of God I will maintain calmness and decorum as suits this honorable court, this honorable jury. You have seen that I am naturally inclined to think of God at the beginning of my actions. I wish if you — I — do it, you won't take it as part of a play of insanity. *Praying.* Oh, my God, help me through thy grace and the divine influence of Jesus Christ. Oh, my God, bless me, bless this honorable court, bless all those who are around me and change the curiosity of those who are paying attention to me, change that curiosity into sympathy with me.

To the court. The day of my birth I was helpless and my mother took care of me although she was not able to do it alone, there was someone to help her take care of me and I lived. Today, although a man, I am as helpless before this court, in the Dominion of Canada and in this world, as I was helpless on the knees of my mother the day of my birth.

The Northwest is also my mother, it is my mother country and although my mother country is sick and confined in a certain way, I am sure that my mother country will not kill me more than my mother did forty years ago when I came into the world.

When I came into the Northwest, the first of July 1884, I found the Indians suffering. I found the half-breeds eating the rotten pork of the Hudson Bay Company and getting sick and weak every day. Although a half-breed, and having no pretension to help the whites, I also paid attention to them. I saw they were deprived of responsible government, I saw that they were deprived of their public liberties. I remembered that half-breed meant white and Indian, and I have directed my attention to the suffering Indians and the half-breeds and to help the whites to the best of my ability. We have made petitions, I have made petitions with others to the Canadian government asking to relieve the condition of this country. We have taken time; we have tried to unite all classes, even, if I may speak, all parties. Those who have been in close communication with me know I have suffered, that I have waited for months to bring some of the people of the Saskatchewan to an understanding of certain important points in our petition to the Canadian government and I have done my duty. I believe I have a mission. With the help of God, who is in this box with me, and He is on the side of the lawyers, even with the honorable court, the Crown and the jury, I have a mission to prove that there is a Providence today in my trial, as there was a Providence in the battles of Saskatchewan.

Lights creep up in the library. It is morning. The library is empty.

Kelly: *Off.* I thought you'd be mad because I suggested you see the guys. . . . Come in. . . . I mean I brought you together so I feel kinda responsible. . . . Am I relieved to see you . . . I didn't even think . . . *Yvonne and Kelly enter.* . . . you'd show up today . . . but I didn't think it would turn out to be such a disaster — including my husband. *Offers a seat.* Be comfortable . . . and I have never been so mad at him in my life and I've been mad at him one or two . . . do you want some coffee . . . but there I am thinking what must she be thinking . . . meaning you, of course . . .

Yvonne: Woah.

Kelly: What?

Yvonne: Lighten up.

Kelly: It was a disaster, wasn't it? I was hoping we could keep in touch . . . but you'll probably never want to set eyes on us again. . . .

Yvonne: Kelly.

Kelly: Yeah?

Yvonne: I want to go in on this project .

Kelly: You do?

Yvonne: But I'm a little scared.

Kelly: Of them?

Yvonne: I don't know. . . .

Kelly: I wouldn't blame you. It's like they see you as a bunch of issues or something. There you are sitting in front of them and they just keep on spouting theories.

Yvonne: That's not exactly the problem. If I were spending my time speculating about Martians and one actually turned up, I don't know what I'd do. I might just keep on spouting theories.

Kelly: And you don't care that Shane gets to play Riel.

Yvonne: Yeah, I care about that. But if some Brit can play Othello . . . and I don't have much leverage in this situation. Maybe they'll let a native actor play General Middleton.

Kelly: *Laughing.* That would be good.

Yvonne: *After a moment.* I don't know. Maybe I've been working with my own people too long. See, when I started this, whatever it is . . . search, I guess . . . the thing I wanted was to work in the native community if I could. And it turned out there was this native-run school I could teach at. It's been good, Kelly. It felt like I was coming home. The people I work with have had a lot of the same experiences I have. We hurt in the same places. We want the same things. So this is different. I don't know whether it's a step forward or a step backward.

Kelly: It's better than three white guys trying to cook up a story all by themselves. I mean . . . you've got the answers, right?

Yvonne: But I don't. I'm still searching. I've got a different perspective, sure. But who knows if I'm right. I mean I know what's right for me . . . but I don't know if that's what they ought to be saying in the series. Or if it is — if what I have to say is exactly what Joe Public needs to hear about Métis — am I going to get it all into the show? Or is it only going to be part of the picture, or distorted or whatever?

Kelly: Sometimes I feel like I have to pry those three apart just to make a suggestion.

Yvonne: I could be a match for them, you know?

Kelly: Yeah . . .

Yvonne: But I'm not sure.

Kelly: You've got a problem.

Yvonne: Yeah.

Kelly: There are no guarantees.

Yvonne: It's a gamble.

Kelly: Is there also pressure not to work with white people?

Yvonne: I don't care about that. Why play it safe? I'm Métisse, eh? I own myself. That's what the Cree used to call us, *O-tee-paym-soo-wuk.*

Kelly: What does that mean?

Yvonne: We own ourselves.

Kelly: Oh.

Yvonne: It's not the pressure.

Kelly: What, then?

Yvonne: Trust.

Kelly: It's Matt, isn't it?

Yvonne: *Surprised.* How did you know? Yeah, he's the one that worries me.

Kelly: Matt thinks he's enlightened.

Yvonne: Enlightened. I know. I'd feel more comfortable with good old fashion self-interest.

Kelly: He's civilized. He's an artist. He's naive. He's naive about himself. I love him very much, Yvonne. But he takes so much for granted and he's got so much to lose.

Yvonne: You know something?

Kelly: What?

Yvonne: The first time I laid eyes on you, I said, "There is my least favourite kind of person." I have a natural prejudice against suburban blondes wearing . . . what kind of perfume are you wearing?

Kelly: Obsession . . .

Yvonne: I was sure it'd be Chanel No.5.

Kelly: See, I'm full of surprises.

Yvonne: I like you, Kelly. I do. How come you know so much?

Kelly: I don't know anything.

Yvonne: Is that the secret?

Kelly: *Laughing suddenly.* You've got me. *After a moment.* Yvonne, I think this is so important. Will you join the project? In spite of everything. In spite of Matt?

Burns: *Off.* So I says, "Who do you think you're dealing with. I'm walking out the door. You're not going to see me again. I'm walking." *Enter Matt and Burns.* So he says, "I didn't know you felt that way. I'll buy. . . . "

Kelly: Guess who's here?

Matt: *Going to her.* Yvonne!

Yvonne: Do you still need me?

Matt: Do we ever.

Yvonne: I'm in.

General jubilation.

Matt: *Going to her.* Terrific.

Burns: Welcome aboard.

Yvonne: Thanks.

Burns: I'll draw up a contract. Come on. We've got deadlines.

Kelly: *As Yvonne and Kelly follow him out.* This means you're a professional Métis.

Yvonne: I've never done it for money.

Burns: That's what we want . . . somebody fresh.

After they leave, Matt goes to his desk and then exits through his study door as lights down on library, up on the witness stand. Riel waits as the sentence is pronounced.

Judge's voice: *On tape or microphone.* Louis Riel, you have been found guilty of a crime the most pernicious and greatest that man can commit. You have been found guilty of high treason. You have been proved to have let loose the floodgates of rapine and bloodshed. You have managed to arouse the Indians and have brought ruin and misery to many families whom if you had simply left alone were in comfort, and many of them were on the road to affluence. It is now my painful duty to pass the sentence of the court upon you and that is that you be taken now from here to the police guardroom at Regina which is the gaol and that on the 18th of September next you be taken to the place appointed for your execution, and there be hanged by the neck until you are dead, and may God have mercy on your soul.

Sound of a gavel. Shane starts, breaks his stance, takes the coat off and wanders into the library area. He picks up a piece of music, "Riel's Letter," and starts to work on it. After a while Yvonne enters with a guitar.

Yvonne: You wanted this?

Shane: *Taking the guitar, somewhat absently.* Thanks, Yvonne. *She flops in a chair. He continues to work on the song with the aid of the guitar.*

Quand je partis, ma chère Henriette
Tu n'avais pas encore quinze ans

Do you know this?

Yvonne: No, what is it?

Shane: The song Riel made up for his little sister.

Yvonne: Riel wrote it? Sing it for me.

Shane: I'm still just learning it.

Yvonne: Go on.

Shane: And my French is probably all wrong . . .

Yvonne: Sing.

Shane: You asked for it. *Sings.*

Quand je partis ma chère Henriette,
Tu n'avais pas encore quinze ans.
Ma soeur, tu n'étais que fillette
Aux premiers jours du doux printemps.
Après mes travaux politiques
Vu le malheurs du Canada,
Je suis venu vous voir en groupe
Chez mon ami Normand Gingras . . .

And it goes on like that.

Yvonne: It's beautiful.

Shane: Yeah, it's nice isn't it.

Yvonne: What does it mean?

Shane: Can't you speak French?

Yvonne: Don't you start on me. . . . I've just been through all this with Matt. There are more different kinds of Métis than there are people and I'm one of the kind that can't speak French.

Shane: All right, all right.

Yvonne: So what's he saying?

Shane: Something like, "When I left you, you weren't fifteen years old. My sister, you were just a little girl in the first days of the sweet springtime. After my political labour for the sake of the troubles of Canada, I came to see all of you together at my friend Normand Gingras's house. Now you are visiting me in August and my heart is beating fast. Accept my welcome. I take you to my heart, I love you so much. The eyes that look upon you are the eyes of a happy man." *Sings.*

Reçois de moi la bienvenue
Mon coeur t'embrasse en soupirant
Lorsque mes yeux t'ont reconnue
C'était les yeux d'un homme content.

Yvonne: He was so tender . . .

Shane: For someone who "opened the floodgates of rapine and bloodshed."

Yvonne: Yes.

Shane: Tired?

Yvonne: *Nodding.* Being Métis is such hard work.

Shane: Why don't you quit for the night?

Yvonne: What's he trying to do? I feel like he's trying to pick me apart, every moment of my life, every last detail, every time I've been in love, every time I've cried. Is he going to use all this stuff?

Shane:ꞏ Not likely. He's very thorough. He likes to get as much of the picture as he can . . . and then dismiss it and kind of work out from it.

Yvonne: It's not fair. I lay out my little Métis heart and he just dismisses it? *Pause.* Your identity isn't just being white is it?

Shane: If you made me a consultant on white people . . .

Yvonne: Why would we need a consultant on white people?

Shane: I don't know. Say you did.

Yvonne: We know how you act.

Shane: I can't be an expert?

Yvonne: Not on white people.

Shane: Yvonne. . . .

Yvonne: Hmm?

Shane: Don't you feel like . . . sometimes just tearing the whole thing down? Like all the crap, the whole thing that we're locked into. You know, blow up the world and start all over again?

Yvonne: Me?

Shane: Yeah.

Yvonne: I wish it were that easy. What's wrong with you. . . . I thought you had it good . . . rising young star. . . .

Shane: Sure, I'm the greatest thing since sliced bread. Except that it's all hype. . . . I get turned into a product that sells, just like we're trying to turn Louis Riel into a product . . . and everything gets decided by some weird vague law of saleability and how much is at stake and I don't have the guts to say no.

Yvonne: Do you want to say no?

Shane: I'm an actor. I want to work.

Yvonne: It's a trap.

Shane: For sure.

Yvonne: Yeah, I've wanted to tear everything down. I even tried sometimes. Every time there was a problem they shifted me to another foster home. I had to learn to love people all over again every time. Finally I gave up trying. I was separated from my brothers and sisters. Two of them killed themselves . . . it wasn't just loneliness or depression or whatever with them . . . I know. They were furious. . . . They were raging inside. . . .they were mad at life. Me . . . I was mad too, but I kind of forced my way through the system. After that I started to look for what it meant to be an Indian . . . deep down. And that made me feel better . . .

Matt strides in with his script.

Matt: I think I've got the scene. . . . Will you try it out for me?

Yvonne: Matthew, it's getting late.

Shane: C'mon. We're just finishing up here.

They try to leave.

Matt: No, no. It's just a short scene. But I want to hear how it sounds.

Shane: Matt.

Matt: A guy slaves and labours in the silent lonely agony of his garret . . .

Shane: All right, all right. . . .

Matt: Okay, it's like this. It's a hundred years after he was hanged and Louis Riel comes back to talk to his people, all right. And he's asked whether he really was insane or not and he says he was obsessed. . . .

Shane (as Riel): Yes, obsessed. I was, too. One has to be obsessed when things must be changed. So obsessed and angry that the dead can be wakened. I had to be obsessed enough to rally the fear and the despair and the hunger of others and turn it into action. Obsessed enough to conceive of taking government into our own hands. And perhaps one has to be obsessed to obey God.

Yvonne: Were you obeying God?

Shane (as Riel): Yes.

Yvonne: You still believe that?

Shane (as Riel): Yes.

Yvonne: How do you explain that it all turned against you?

Shane (as Riel): God's ways are not our ways.

Yvonne: Our ways have been ways of poverty and oppression for one hundred years. For one hundred years we have been a people, without rights, without land, without identity. . . . For every one of us who declare we are half-breed and hold our heads high, there are a hundred who live in shame.

Shane (as Riel):   And am I to blame for that?

Yvonne: Some say yes. Some say Gabriel Dumont, for instance . . .

Shane (as Riel):   Ah, Gabriel. . . .

Yvonne: . . . could have defeated the Canadians if you had listened to him and let him fight the battle his own way.

Shane (as Riel):   When I got to Heaven, I went right up to the heavenly throne, you know. And I said, "Bon Dieu" (because French is the only language allowed in heaven), "Bon Dieu," I said, "I was waiting for you to send a miracle, what happened?" Well, the Good Lord shook his head, and he said — "What do you mean what happened? I sent you Gabriel Dumont." And then He said, "And if that wasn't enough I gave General Middleton to the *Anglais*! And you were standing around yelling please send a miracle. What do you want from me?" And He began to laugh and I had to laugh too, and then a good part of heaven was laughing. I wish I had understood in the first place.

Yvonne: I didn't know Heaven was such a humorous place.

Shane (as Riel):   It's been that way ever since the Métis started to arrive.

Yvonne can't believe Matt wrote that line but he gestures for her to continue.

Yvonne: What would you say to your people today? Would you tell us the same things you said a hundred years ago?

Shane (as Riel):   Yes. I would say take your lives into your own hands. What you do will be different than what we did . . .but whatever it is you must do it for yourselves. If you don't, you will gain nothing. Remember the strength that is among you. And one more thing: *laugh*! It is our tradition.

Matt: What do you think?

Yvonne: You think that's what Riel would tell us?

Matt: Yes.

Yvonne: Laugh?

Matt: Yes.

Yvonne: Laugh?

Matt: Well, Riel had a sense of humor. He was always making puns and things and Métis people have an inbred sense of humor. . . .

Yvonne: Let's hear it for the happy go lucky Métis.

Shane: Matt, we're talking about people dying here.

Yvonne: Look, this whole thing. . . .

Matt: I didn't mean it as a joke. . . .

Yvonne: This whole thing. I probably didn't have my head on straight with this. I think the best thing to do is just leave, all right? I'm not doing you any good . . . and I don't think you're doing me any either.

Matt: But why? I thought we were getting along so well. . . .

Yvonne: So did I.

Matt: I don't think we should do the film without you.

Yvonne: No, don't let me stop you. Do the film. I'm sure the public will eat it up.

Matt: You think so?

Yvonne: Why not. And the native people will get screwed again. *Exit.*

Shane: Matt, leave it alone.

Matt: I can't leave it alone. We've been working too long. . . .

Shane: Your thinking is all wrong on this.

Matt: No, no . . . if you can't change what fate hands out you have to laugh.

Shane: Or fight.

Matt: You don't know what you're talking about. It's a good scene!

Shane: Yeah, it's a good scene . . . for the wrong movie.

Matt: Like hell. What do you know anyway . . . you're just an actor.

Shane: Thanks.

Matt: All you've been interested in from the beginning is whether you have a big enough part. . . .

Shane: Yeah, maybe. But this part is never going to be big enough. I'm leaving the project.

Matt: Don't hand me that. Not with your investment. . . .You've got too much going for you. . . . You can't leave.

Shane: Watch me. *He gathers his things and walks out.*

Matt: It's late in the project. Everybody's tired, acting crazy. *At door.* Hey, come back! *Pause.* I don't get it. What's going wrong?

Exit Matt. Lights change. Burns on telephone.

Burns: Okay so what's going on? I thought everybody was happier than oysters. The place is a mausoleum. Matt hasn't been able to write a word in two days. . . . Shane hasn't shown his face. I don't know where he is. I can't locate him. Kelly is giving Matt the silent treatment. Everybody's been crying on my shoulder. Certain parties down east are asking me where is the script . . . they gotta have script approval they tell me, they gotta read the script. What do I tell them? Do I tell them there's a little hitch in our plans — a little friction — a few wrinkles in the old plot line? Not on your life. You gotta know how to handle Easterners. . . . I know how to handle Easterners. I say, "What the hell are you talking about? What do you think this is, some kind of hinterland out here where we don't know what we're doing out here? You'll get the script when we're bloody satisfied." That's what I tell them. But you guys — if you don't get it together and get it together soon, we're up the creek without a sail. *Pause.* Paddle. All right. So what happened? . . . That bad, eh? . . . Velveeta? What's white about Velveeta cheese? What do you mean, you can't work with him, Yvonne? Matt is the nicest, gentlest guy. I mean me, I could understand if you didn't want to work with me. I'm a mean son of a bitch. . . . What? . . . I regard that as an insult, Yvonne. I am not cuddly. Listen. . . . Listen to me. What is it? Aren't we paying you enough? Listen, I'll double it. . . . What's wrong with you? Don't you need the money? Name your terms. . . . No, name your terms. Anything. We're vulnerable here. We've got no room to manoeuver. Name your terms. . . . Yes, you are. Now, you are. You've got . . . what . . . information, experience that none of the rest of us has. You've made yourself indispensable. So talk. . . . Try me. . . . *Burns goes pale.* Do you mean that? God, what has he done to you? How can I tell him that? There's gotta be another way. . . . No, wait. I'll think about it.

Burns hangs up the phone slowly. The lights shift and the phone rings.
Yvonne picks up the receiver. This is the flip side of the conversation
we just heard.

Yvonne: ˉHello. . . . Who is thi . . . Burns? . . . I . . . Burns, I can't help
you. . . . Shane? Where is he? . . . Burns. . . . Burns. . . . Yeah. . . .
Yeah. Mhmm. Without a paddle. Up the creek without a paddle,
Burns. . . . Let's just say that tomorrow I'll be in Vancouver. . . . Yeah, that bad. . . . Oh, I don't know . . . it went all sour all
of a sudden. I didn't know it was going to be this way. I poured
everything out, Burns . . . I told him every story I had in me. And
it was like he processed it and it turned out all white . . . like Velveeta cheese or something. . . . Come on, Burns. I'm trying to say
I can't do it any more. I thought I was coming into this thing as a
kind of a partner . . . but . . . talk about exploitation. . . . I can't
work with him anymore . . . I can't. . . . At least I know where I
stand. Ah, no . . . with you it's blatant . . . out in the open . . . it's
unadulterated exploitation. It doesn't sneak up on
you. . . . Actually you're kind of cuddly. . . . sure. Yeah, you
are. . . . Okay. . . . No, . . . well how much is my soul worth anyway? You'll double it? Burns, it's not money . . . it's not
money! . . . There are no terms. . . . I'm not indispensable. . . . How did that happen? . . . There are no terms. . . . Okay,
but this you'll never go for. . . . The only way I could keep working on this is if you got Matt off of it. . . . You heard me. Look, I
don't expect you to do it. I'm just saying that's the only way I
could be involved. Look, Burns, I'm tired and I feel like a. . . . I
feel really rotten right now. I'm hanging up. . . . sure. *She puts
down the phone.* No. No. No!

Lights shift and come up on Riel's prison cell. A priest, Father André,
stands beside him.

Riel: But I have a mission. I was given a mission by God.
Look . . . still I carry the good Bishop Bourget's letter . . . see . . .

André: I have read it, my dear boy. . . .

Riel: *Reading.* But God will not abandon you in the dark hours of
your life . . .

André: Yes. . . .

Riel: . . . for He has given you a mission which you must in all
respects fulfill.

André: Renounce it.

Riel: But the Holy Church . . .

André: The Holy Church told you you had a mission and the Holy Church now tells you that the mission you followed was not one given by God.

Riel: But if it was . . .

André: It was not.

Riel: I would sin by renouncing it.

André: You sin by not obeying. *Riel has no answer.* It is the Church that possesses the keys of heaven and hell.

Riel: Yes.

André: Do you wish to share ever again in the Blessed Sacrament?

Riel: With all my heart, Father.

André: Do you wish to make of your life a sacrifice . . . will you give up that which is most precious to you as an act of obedience?

Riel: Yes.

André: Then swear.

Riel: Yes.

André: I submit to the Catholic, Apostolic and Roman Church.

Riel: I submit to the Catholic, Apostolic and Roman Church.

André: I renounce all the personal interpretations I have assigned to my mission and which are not approved by my confessor and director of my conscience.

Riel: *With difficulty.* I renounce all the personal interpretations I have assigned to my mission and which are not approved by my confessor and director of my conscience.

André embraces him and blesses him with the sign of the cross.

André: You have taken a good path today, my son, it is a path that will lead you back to eternal life.

Riel: Obedience.

André: Obedience.

André bustles off. Lights down on gaol. Kelly and Matt in library. Matt is drinking and becomes progressively higher as the scene progresses.

Matt: Nobody can tell me to get off a project that I started. Not Burns, not Yvonne, nobody. We've got contracts. I'm not backing down.

Kelly: I suppose it was my fault.

Matt: Hardly. How could it be your fault?

Kelly: It's obvious. I insisted on your having a consultant. I brought Yvonne in.

Matt: It was a good idea. It was the right idea, Kelly. I wouldn't have gone along with you if it hadn't been. We all said yes, finally, and it *was* the right thing to do. I still believe that. I can't imagine what we were thinking about. We were really arrogant S.O.B.s thinking we could do a program about Riel without working hand in hand with the Métis people.

Kelly: Yeah, you were.

Matt: It just didn't work out this time. I feel like somebody has just taken a baseball bat or something and slammed me in the gut. My whole . . . my whole sense of myself . . . sense of reality, is all junked up. You know, I felt like if people try hard enough . . . they can communicate because basically, at heart, everybody is the same, right? It's my business . . . and I'm good at it, right . . . creating real characters on the page. . . . And you know how I do it?

Kelly: *Patiently. She has heard him speak of the source of his genius on other occasions.* How?

Matt: By looking at myself. Because what is in other human beings is also in myself.

Kelly: By virtue of your shared humanity.

Matt: By virtue of our shared humanity. What?

Kelly: It's what you say when you give public readings at libraries.

Matt: That doesn't mean it isn't true.

Kelly: I didn't say that.

Matt: It is true. It is, isn't it?

Kelly: Oh, Matt.

Matt: Because if we don't have some kind of common . . . I don't know . . . essential humanity, why write anything, why paint anything, sculpt anything.... We're just crying out into the void. I can't understand what went wrong, Kelly. Do you know what went wrong? I can't understand how the communication broke down. I thought we knew each other. I thought we were close. It was like a ... like a sign of hope that people could get beyond racial barriers.... I thought we were really doing it right.

Kelly: Where I went wrong is thinking I could solve anything for anybody by bringing Yvonne in.

Matt: It was working.

Kelly: I just messed her up and you up and the project....

Matt: *Surprisingly caustic.* She did it of her own free will. She made the choice to come in on it. She just didn't have the guts to stick it through.

Kelly: She was hurting, Matthew!

Matt: Why did she have to inflict it on us? *Pouring himself anther drink.* Want another? *Kelly shakes her head.* It's only a TV program for crying out loud. Nobody needs to get so melodramatic about it. It's just a job.

Kelly: You don't believe that.

Matt: Why not?

Kelly: You were using that woman's life, her identity, the struggles of her people ...

Matt: Now you're talking like her.

Kelly: No, I'm talking like me! You're using all that as raw material for what is just a job? Just a job? Where's your common humanity?

Matt: Yeah. *Long pause.* Of course it's not just a job. I wouldn't be doing it if I didn't feel it was important. That's how I started this whole project. Riel is a prime example of the injustice this country has perpetrated on the Indians and the Métis. I wanted to expose that. I've always felt the arts have to be the social conscience of the country. I've always felt that. So how could Yvonne give up on us?

Kelly: When you're so high minded.

Matt: When I'm working with principles.

Kelly: *Cheeky.* It's hard to imagine. Do you think she should have been grateful?

Matt: Yeah, she should have been a little grateful. I'm not the enemy. . . . I'm not some redneck out there. . . . I take my share of white man's guilt. . . .

Kelly: You're mad, aren't you.

Matt: No I'm not. What right have I to be mad?

Kelly: You're furious, Matt.

Matt: Ease up, Kelly.

Kelly: Have it your way.

Matt: *Exploding.* What the hell do they think they're doing? I started this project, damn it! What makes them think they can take it away from me just like that. I had the original idea. Me. I am this series. I'm not going to quit. . . . I don't quit. I've got to see this through. They can't do it without me.

Kelly: Why not?

Matt: They'll fail. They don't have the talent. They don't have a writer. They don't have the time. It's a very complex series. . . . They don't have the know-how.

Kelly: If they succeed . . .

Matt: They can't.

Kelly: . . . you won't get any of the glory.

Matt: That's not what I'm interested in.

Kelly: That's what I like about you.

Matt: What?

Kelly: You're so honest.

Matt: I try to be. *Double take.* You didn't mean that, right? What did you mean?

Kelly: *Sudden realization.* I can't help you through this, can I?

Matt: Through what?

Kelly: You've had it so good for so long, and now you're in real trouble . . .

Matt: No I'm not . . .

Kelly: . . . for the first time in your life . . .

Matt: What kind of trouble am I in?

Kelly: . . . and you don't know how to handle it.

Matt: I started this project with the best possible intentions. . . .

Kelly: Like always.

Matt: And that's enough. Intentions are enough.

Kelly: Since when?

Matt: I mean that's where you have to start.

Kelly: Except for this time.

Matt: Kelly, you are really getting on my wick. It's all very well for you to make these gratuitous insults. . . .

Kelly: I'm not insulting you. . . .

Matt: All right . . . judgements about me . . . but it's all academic for you. You never had anything at stake, here. You've just watched the whole thing from the outside. You don't care if the whole thing collapses. It's not going to affect you. You're just going to go get your hair done, and maybe get a facial . . .

Kelly: Matt.

Matt: What?

Kelly: Don't do this.

Matt: Why?

Kelly: I care about this project. I care about you and you're making it hard for me. I care about all of you.

Matt: Let's not get sentimental.

Kelly: Work it out by yourself, then.

Matt: Work it out? It? What?

Kelly: And were you falling for her, too?

Matt: Yes. Who, Yvonne? No. . . . I don't know. I liked her that's all. It's intimate work, this. No . . . I probably wasn't falling for her. Doesn't make any difference now, does it? Where are you going?

Kelly: *As she exits.* To get my hair done. Maybe I'll get a facial.

Matt gets a copy of the screenplay and leafs through it sadly. He pours yet another drink.

Matt: You see, Louis? You see what happens when you start having visions? You lose. That's what happens. You'd know that, wouldn't you?

Lights up on the gaol.

Shane (as Riel): Death keeps guard at the door of my cell. Death peers at me behind my prison bars. Death watches at my door like a Labrador retriever keeping watch in front of the house. Death hovers over me like a great bird of prey. The gallows have been built against the wall of the gaol. There is a window with bars at the end of the hall and the night before my death they shall make of it a doorway to go out onto the platform. I am told that every appeal has failed. Every day I wait for word from John Macdonald authorizing my execution or granting another reprieve.

Matt: Reprieve? *Assuming his John A. Macdonald act.* I don't deny the many failings of my life. I don't deny my sins of omission and commission; but I trust that it may be said of me in the ultimate issue, "much is forgiven because he loved much," for I have loved my country with a passionate love. I have fought the battle of Confederation, the battle of Union, the battle of the Dominion of Canada. I throw myself on this house! . . . *Breaks the act.* What would he say? I don't have the documents. What would he say? *Improvising now.* I had a single overriding vision. To turn this collection of colonies and divided peoples, and wilderness and tundra and great jagged mountain ranges sawing at the sky . . . to turn all of the separate pieces of glory into one vast domain, a power in the world, a state like no other in the history of mankind. I saw — before it ever came to pass — a band of steel gleaming in the prairie sun, a great belt joining one ocean to another. And I saw locomotives drawing car after car of settlers chasing their own visions and I saw a new people flooding into the future working together to make an altogether new creation. I saw it. And it came to be . . . but not by itself. *Viciously.* I dragged it . . . I dragged it . . . I tore it . . . away from mere potential . . . mere possibility . . . mere wishful thinking . . . and made it a reality. I did what I had to do. And not all of it was good, or upright, or straightforward. And people died in the building of it. And people died in the finishing of it. But I did it! And no one will separate us

again. No one will drive a wedge between us. Certainly no
ignorant, savage, half-breed from the Northwest. Riel shall hang.
Riel shall hang though every dog in Quebec bark in his favor!

*Matt has worked himself up into a surprisingly emotional drunken
pitch with this speech. The effect should be that he is left staring
into his own soul and what he sees there is racism.*

Oh my God, I'm sorry, Louis. . . .

The lights shift to Riel in his cell. He is writing.

Shane (as Riel):   I have no gold or silver to leave to my children. I
pardon with all my heart those who have persecuted me; who
have, without any reason, made war on me for five years; who
have given me the semblance of a trial; who have condemned me
to death. I thank my wife for having been so good and charitable
to me, for the part she has so frequently taken in my painful works
and difficult enterprises . . . pardon me the sadness I have volun-
tarily and involuntarily caused her. I recommend to her the care of
her little children; to bring them up in a Christian manner. Yesterday and today I have prayed God to strengthen you and grant you
his gentle comfort so that your heart may not be troubled by pain
and anxiety. I embrace you all with the greatest affection. Please
be joyful.

The priest appears awkwardly at the door.

Shane (as Riel):   I am happy, father. My heart brims over with joy.

André: God is very present with us this day.

Riel: Will they let me speak, on the scaffold?

André: They will . . .

Riel: Ah. . . .

André: . . . but you should be like our Lord who spoke only seven
words on the cross. Your mission now is to show, not how you are
a prophet, but how a Christian knows how to die.

Riel: Then I sacrifice my last speech to God. *To someone off.* Mr.
Gibson, you want me? I am ready.

André: Bon. Allez au Ciel. *André stumbles as he goes.*

Riel: Courage, mon Père.

André: Courage, courage . . .

They begin to walk to the gallows. Yvonne walks into the scene watching after them.

Yvonne: Pray for us, Louis. Pray for us who come after. Pray for us in your distant future. We are proud to be called your children. Pray for all of us. Pray for those who have forgotten we are Métis. Pray for those of us who have grown up speaking our own language and those of us who know what it is to be Métis and are joyful. Pray for us who are still searching, still struggling to find out. Pray for us in our politics, in our struggles with the children of John A. Macdonald. Pray for us in our struggles with one another. Help us to be strong and may we be one.

Burns: *Over P.A.* Great! That's a wrap. That's a wrap. We've got it! *Calling to crew offstage.* Anybody have any problems with that? No? Fantastic. Fantastic.

Kelly: *Entering.* Beautiful.

Yvonne: It was? I didn't know I could do it.

Burns: Pack up the equipment. *To Kelly.* Was it okay with you?

Kelly: It was fine.

Burns: We'll look at the tape after supper.

Shane: *Joining them on stage.* Well, what do you say, Burns? Will it sell?

Burns: Will it sell? Who cares? It's what it should be.

Yvonne: Burns, what did you say?

Burns: *Suddenly awkward.* I don't know. Maybe it'll . . .

Kelly: Yeah?

Burns: . . . maybe it'll change people's minds . . . a little. I mean what can you expect . . . it's just a . . . but it's that good, I think.

Yvonne: Amazing.

Burns: Ah, shut up.

The four of them hug one another.

Burns: *Pause.* I wish . . .

Shane: So do I. *To Kelly.* How's he . . . ? I mean . . .

Kelly: I asked him to come. . . . But he's started writing again. . . .

Yvonne: Kelly, why did he back down, finally? Do you know?

Kelly: I think what got to Matt was that he always saw himself as Louis Riel, but when the chips were down he found out he was John A. Macdonald.

Yvonne: Hm.

Shane: What does that make you, Burns?

Burns: Don't look at me. Drinks, anybody? *Pause.* I'll buy.

The four of them leave the set. Back to the library. Matt is writing up a storm. He finally puts down his pencil and begins to read.

Matt: Welcome to Batoche National Historic Site. My name is Bertram and it will my privilege to be your tour guide while you're here on site. What I would like to do first of all is explain the main theme of the museum. The main theme of the museum is the tragedy of Batoche being a conflict of cultures. The conflict being between the white culture and the Métis culture and to a lesser extent the Indian culture. . . .

He looks up. I'd like to think we could work it out, Louis.

Writing. Hi.

Hello.

It's interesting, this.

Yes.

I love history, don't you?

Some of it.

Lights blackout.

THE END

Quartet for Three Actors

§

First Performance

Quartet for Three Actors was first performed January 9, 1987 at the Globe Theatre in Regina, with the following cast:

Mickey — William Vickers

Krull — Kenneth Kramer

Fran — Wendy Van Riesen

The production was directed by Pamela Hawthorne, designed by Ruth Howard and staged managed by Rachel Van Fossen.

Characters

Mickey: a comic actor, in his thirties

Krull: a classical actor, in his fifties, or older

Fran: a character actress, thirty or slightly older

Photo Credit: Tuan Nguyen

Wendy van Riesen as Fran, William Vickers as Mickey
Globe Theatre, Regina, 1987.

Act One

Work lights rise on a stage littered with props and costumes seemingly left over from old productions. Perhaps there is a metal step ladder, a lamp tree, risers in various shapes and sizes.

Mickey is the first to arrive. He is wearing a big coat with a rolled up script sticking out of the pockets. What is it about Mickey that makes us want to laugh? Is it a kind of foolishness waiting to burst out — or is it the depth of his despair? Checking to make sure he is alone, he tries out some props, swells to performance size, does a clown routine and sings.

Mickey: Those were the days, my friend, I thought they'd never end . . . la da da da da da da da da da da. . . . Forever and a day. . . . Life is a cabaret my friends, life is a . . . *Stops short. Shrinks visibly, sighs, puts the props aside and sits down.*

Enter Krull vigorously. He is removing a rather svelte overcoat and tweed cap. He also carries a leather script folder. He stops centre stage, examining the theatre evaluatively, tries out the acoustics. Krull projects the image of a serious artist. Perhaps this is what prevents him from noticing a now diminutive Mickey.

Mickey: *After a time.* Hello.

Krull: *Startled.* What?

Mickey: Hello, Krull.

Krull: Ah. It's so good to see you again.

Mickey: Nice to see you . . .

Krull: Don't tell me. It will come. It will come. Don't tell me.

Mickey: . . . Mick.

Krull: *Puzzled.* Mick. No.

Mickey: Yes.

Krull: No. *Triumphantly.* Mickey!

Mickey: *Sigh.* Yes. It's been a long time, hasn't it?

Krull: Mickey. *(Pause.) Death of a Salesman,* right?

Mickey: *The Lower Depths.*

Krull: Oh my God, *The Lower Depths.* Of course. Gorki. That was a while back.

Mickey: Yes.

Krull: You played? . . .

Mickey: The Goiter.

Krull: *He doesn't remember.* The Goiter. Ah yes, The Goiter.

Mickey: The comic bit at the end of the second act?

Krull: And you did very well too . . .

Mickey: With the dead body?

Krull: . . . I'm sure.

Mickey: And I run off with the police whistle in the third act, remember? *No answer.* I was just starting out then. . . .

Krull: Strange. I remember you, of course . . . but I thought it was *Salesman. (Pause.)* Aren't there supposed to be three of us?

Mickey: I think so.

Krull: No sign?

Mickey: Not yet. *Pause.* It's a fine theatre.

Krull: It's an interesting space.

Mickey: You can almost feel the audience, can't you?

Krull: Almost.

Mickey: Ghosts of old productions. . . .

Krull: It's a very distinguished theatre. Very fine reputation.

Mickey: Yes. You must have done the odd show here?

Krull: No. It's strange isn't it? But no. This is the first time.

Mickey: Me, too.

Krull: Well, it'll be good to get working again.

Krull sits on a box, and arranges himself, somewhat majestically. He takes out a silver cigarette case, offers it to Mickey, who shakes his head.

Krull: No stage manger?

Mickey: Not yet. It's quiet, eh? I thought I'd see someone out in the lobby. There wasn't anyone in the box office.

Krull begins to smoke. They wait. Mickey begins to rap on the stage floor.

Krull: *Annoyed.* Uh, Mickey . . .

Mickey: Solid.

Krull stomps delicately with his heel.

Krull: Quite.

Mickey: Considering.

Krull: Considering what? The ephemeral nature of theatre?

Mickey: Well, not . . . no . . . yeah, I guess. The whatever. Yeah.

Krull: It's a living.

Mickey: Sometimes. *Long pause.* I don't know why they're keeping us. . . .

Krull: There's not much we can do until. . . .

Mickey: Whoever.

Krull: Exactly.

Mickey: Have you read the script yet?

Krull: Skimmed through it. The salient bits, you know. How about you?

Mickey: More or less. Listen . . . maybe I could run across the street . . . someone could come and get me. . . .

Krull: If you like.

Mickey: *Starts to leave.* You want to come?

Krull: One of us should stay . . . in case . . .

Mickey: In case whoever . . .

Krull: Whoever . . . exactly.

Mickey: Of course. You don't mind, do you?

Krull: No, go right ahead.

Mickey: It's just that . . . well. . . .

Krull: You're thirsty.

Mickey: For a coffee . . . or something.

Krull: Go right ahead.

Mickey: Thanks.

Exit. Long pause. Mickey returns. Krull looks up.

Krull: Back already?

Mickey: It's not really fair to you, is it? It could be a long wait, all by yourself . . . nobody to talk to.

Krull: No problem.

Mickey: I changed my mind.

Krull: Go on. Have a . . . coffee if you want.

Mickey: No.

Krull: I'm telling you I don't mind. Have whatever you want. Whatever it takes.

Mickey: I'm not desperate.

Krull: I insist.

Mickey: I said I'd stay.

Krull: Go.

Mickey: I can't find my way out.

Krull: Why didn't you say so in the first place? Go through the lobby, down the stairs . . .

Mickey: But . . .

Krull: *Leading him off.* Look, I'll show you.

   They both leave. After a short while they re-enter from another direction.

Krull: No, this is not it.

   They turn around and leave. In a moment they are crossing the stage from yet another direction.

Krull: We'll just cut through here. . . .

Mickey: We've already been here.

Krull: No, we haven't.

Mickey: But this is the stage. . . .

Krull: No, it isn't.

Mickey: Yes, it is.

Krull: Not the same stage!

Mickey: Well, what stage is it then?

Krull: They must have more than one stage.

Mickey: But this is the one we were on before.

But they are off again. After a second, Fran enters. She is a peculiar looking person. She has thrown together her costume with eclectic panache. Her demeanor is extravagant, scattered, inspired. This is not a woman with both feet or even one foot on the ground. She looks around the theatre and takes a deep breath.

Fran: Okay, here we go again. *Checks to make sure she is alone.*

O Lord, *Pause*, won't you buy me a Mercedes Benz. *Recovers.* No, no. Seriously though, please help me through this. You know how I get scared at the beginning of things. Be with me and the other actors. Let the rehearsals not be too unpleasant. Don't let me make a fool of myself, again. Amen. I am not superstitious. I just believe in insurance. I know you've got the universe to run and all . . . but at the very least would you not stand back and laugh. Well, I get that feeling sometimes — that my trials and tribulations amuse you a little overly much. I listen for your guidance and all I get is a kind of giggle. *Pause.* I could have stayed at home, you know, and turned into a parsnip or something. Just once I'd like you to say something *unequivocal?* Don't tell me *Deep voice*, "I have set you free to work out your own destiny." *Own voice.* No sir, or ma'am . . .whichever. Because whenever I work it out? *Deep voice.* "Wrong!" *Own voice.* And when I say, "What's right, then?" you say *Deep voice*, "Sorry, I have set you free to work out your own destiny. Think of life as a great adlib." Jeez. I hate improvization. So much for morning devotions. *Pause.* Where is everybody?

Calling into the wings. Halloooo. Halloooo. *Receiving no answer she looks about, tries a prop or two.*

Singing. Tip toe through the tulips, through the garden. Oh won't you come along and tip toe through the tulips with me. *Relishing.* Stomp, stomp, through the tulips, through the garden. . . . Ooh won't . . .

She is just enjoying being on stage and letting herself go. She laughs and then reins herself in.

Yes. Well. *Goes out an exit and calls.* Yooohooo.

Krull: *Offstage.* Peculiar.

Mickey: Really strange.

Krull: There's a logical explanation. *Enters down an aisle with Mickey behind him.*

Mickey: *Startled.* Here we are again.

Krull: Very peculiar; but there's always a logical explanation.

Mickey: There has to be. But where is it?

Krull: It'll turn up. Wait and see.

Mickey: Right. *Long pause . . . then suddenly.* Isn't it funny how you walk into a place you've never been before and you don't notice how you got in? I didn't look behind, not once. Well, I saw the gargoyle over the entrance . . . but that was outside looking in. . . .

Krull: Was there a gargoyle?

Mickey: Ugly. *Demonstrates.* Hanging right over the door.

Krull: Yes. I suppose I didn't glance up.

Mickey: But once I came in I just followed my nose. I can't even remember what color the carpet was. If I'd known it was like a labyrinth or . . . well . . . a labyrinth, maybe I could have let my sweater unravel. . . .

Krull: Your sweater unravel?

Mickey: A long string of wool.

Krull: Well, we can just wait. Somebody will be along . . . sooner or later.

Mickey: It is strange, though.

Krull: A lot of theatres are very complicated. Especially the ones with a number of auditoria. You know, main stage, second stage, studio stage, recital hall, etcetera . . . puppet theatre. Have you ever played the Rumpole Centre? When I was there a witch from a certain Shakespearian play . . . well, apparently she thought she was late for her cue and rushed into the middle of the wrong play . . . a Noel Coward, if you please. She was two or three lines into the double, double toil and trouble bit before she realized. She tried to recover . . . something about . . . *Acting*, "Eye of Newt and Toe of Frog . . . I'm terribly sorry. Would you care for some more tea, Madam?" Then she scuttled off. Created a terrible stink. The actress was fired. Personally, I thought it was a nice touch. The only original thing in the entire production.

Mickey: Poor girl. Who was it?

Krull: I've forgotten her name. I didn't know her.

Mickey: *After a moment.* I suppose we just have to sit here and wait.

Krull: Somebody will show up, sooner or later.

Mickey: I guess. *Pause.* It's almost like we're in a play.

Krull: What?

Mickey: Like we're in a play.

Krull: You think this is a dramatic situation?

Mickey: What's your definition of a dramatic situation?

Krull: *Haughty.* One that gives me a chance to act. What's yours.

Mickey: Atmosphere.

Krull: *After a moment.* You are overly romantic.

Mickey: No, really . . . it's just like one of those plays.

Krull: Which?

Mickey: You know, those plays like. . . . I've done these kind of plays before. This one would be like . . .

Krull: Somebody has been here.

Mickey: *Looking around.* Yes, I think so. *Back to the subject.* This one would be like that Sartre play . . .

Krull: *With annoyance.* Sartre.

Mickey: *Examining the props.* Things are different.

Krull: The one where the characters are all in hell and can't get out? "Hell is other people." Pretentious line. That one?

Mickey: *No Exit.*

Krull: *No Exit.*

Mickey: Yes.

Krull: That one. But Mickey, let me ask you something. Let me ask you this: where is Jean-Paul Sartre today? Tell me that.

Mickey: Dead?

Krull: Exactly. For all his posturing. I'm not fond of supernatural or the mystical settings, Mickey. I like real scenes about real life.

Mickey: All I said was I've been in these kind of plays. That's all I said.

In bursts Fran.

Fran: Mickey, Darling!

Mickey: *Lighting up.* No kidding! Tell me it isn't true.

Fran: I had no idea!

They throw themselves into each other's arms like long lost lovers. Krull stands awkwardly by.

Fran: It'll be so good to work with you again.

Mickey: This is terrific, isn't it. Terrific.

Krull: *Coughing.* I take it you know each other.

Fran looks dubiously at Krull.

Mickey: I'm sorry. Do you know Victor Krull?

Fran: *Dramatically awed.* You're Victor Krull! *Rushing to shake his hand.* I'm really glad to meet you. I'm Fran Johnson.

Krull: Pleased.

Fran: Wow. They didn't tell me who'd. . . . This is great! I really admire your work, Mr. Krull.

Krull: My friends call me Krull.

Fran: Oh, thank you. Oh, this is going to be wonderful. Mickey

and . . . oh I can't think of anybody I like to work with
more . . . and now you, Victor — I mean Krull — because I've
really enjoyed . . . I saw *A Man for All Seasons.*

Krull: *Pleased.* Did you?

Fran: It was just great.

Krull: Well, there were a few problems in rehearsal . . . you
know . . . the director thought she should direct and all that . . . but
it turned out in the end, don't you think?

Fran: I thought so.

Krull: And you've done things with Mickey, have you?

Fran: Yeah.

Mickey: All summer.

Fran: We did the Downsville Summer Festival. We just closed last
week.

Krull: Missed each other terribly, have you?

Fran: It was a good summer, right, Mickey?

Mickey: Right.

Krull: And this so soon. . . . You're lucky.

Fran: Mickey was brilliant.

Mickey: She was . . . not me.

Fran: C'mon Mickey, you were brilliant. *To Krull.* He was brilliant.
Have you ever worked with him?

Krull: Yes, indeed.

Mickey: Well, I wouldn't exactly call it . . .

Krull: Some time ago . . . but yes. . . .

Mickey: I was just starting out. . . .

Krull: Showed promise, even then. . . .

Mickey: Do you think so?

Krull: Vaguely.

Fran: He's wonderful. This is going to be great. Right?

They hesitate.

Mickey: Ah, there's something we have to tell you.

Fran: What's that?

Mickey: Something peculiar. We can't find our way out.

Fran: Out?

Mickey: Of the theatre.

Fran: I know! Isn't it awful?

Krull: You knew?

Fran: It's like a maze, isn't it?

Mickey: Kind of.

Fran: Sometimes I really want to get out. . . . No, really! But I always end up back where I started. It's weird. I'll be sitting in the dressing room putting on make up, wearing somebody else's clothes, getting ready to say somebody else's words and pretend to be somebody I'm not. . . . I mean, does this happen to you?

Krull: Come again?

Fran: You know, you have to say, "What exactly am I doing? Get real!" You know, so I get out there and I have a really off night because I'm shaking my head inside.

Mickey: Yeah, but Fran.

Fran: So I swear I'm going to go out and look for real life, someplace. And then somebody gives me some juicy part or I get to work someplace I always wanted to work — so here we go again — and for sure, somewhere in the run the same thing happens all over again. . . . I'm sitting in the dressing room putting on make up, wearing somebody else's clothes . . .

Mickey: *Overlapping.* . . . putting on make up, wearing somebody else's. . . . Fran.

Fran: What?

Krull: We're not speaking metaphorically here.

Mickey: We can't actually figure out how to get out of the damn theatre.

Krull: This damn theatre.

Fran: Really?

Mickey: Really.

Fran: That's weird. You can't get out?

Krull: Precisely.

Fran: Why?

Krull: I think it has something to do with the building. There's something very deceptive about this building.

Mickey: We always end up back here. Do you know the way?

Fran: I think so.

Mickey: You want to try it.

Fran: Oh, I can get out.

Krull: Try it.

Without another word she leaves and then returns.

Fran: Amazing.

Krull: You see?

Mickey: Funny, eh?

Krull: It's almost like one of those nightmares, isn't it? . . . Those ones where you try to set off somewhere and you never get there. Every attempt to make progress is thwarted, sabotaged. . . .

Mickey: Yeah, I had a dream like that once.

Krull: Of course this is real life.

Mickey: Of course.

Fran: No doubt about it.

Krull: Right.

Fran: Unless I'm . . .

Krull: *At the same time.* Unless I'm. . . . *To Fran.* Sorry.

Fran: No what were you going to say?

Krull: No, no. After you.

Mickey: Of course I could be dreaming the whole thing. *The others glare at him.* Hypothetically.

Fran: It wouldn't have to be you, dreaming, you know. Why should it be you? It could be me just as easily.

Mickey: This place is getting to us.

Krull: If we were dreaming, which we aren't, of course, then it would actually be my dream.

The others stare at him.

It would be. Because I'm conscious, you see? I mean I'm me. Aware. Conscious of me . . . I. I cannot say with absolute certainty that either one of you is aware or conscious. For all I know you could be mere figments of my nightmare. Monstrosities dredged up from my id. . . .

Fran: Hey, watch it. . . .

Mickey: *At the same time.* Who are you calling monst . . .

Krull: Theoretically. All I'm saying is that I'm the single certainty here because I know I am conscious. Understand? When I dream I am conscious of being the dreamer. Only I'm awake. But if I weren't — if this were simply a very realistic nightmare — then I would be the dreamer and you two would be the . . . er . . .

Fran: Dreamees?

Krull: The only practical thing as with all of life is to behave as if it were not a nightmare. *Pause.* Whether it is or not.

Mickey: Actually it's like a play.

Fran: It is, isn't it? Like that . . . whatsit . . . *Hell is other People. (To Mickey.)* Did you see Henry's production?

Mickey: Yeah.

Fran: How did you like it?

Mickey: *Brightly.* It was all right!

Fran: You didn't like it, did you?

Mickey: I hated it.

Fran: I liked it.

Mickey: I hated it.

They appeal to Krull.

Krull: I missed it.

Mickey: It wasn't one of his best.

Krull: To tell you the truth, I've never seen anything of his I liked. *Chuckling.* In fact did you see? . . .

Mickey: *Quickly.* Henry and Fran are quite close.

Pause.

Krull: Of course I haven't seen all that much, actually. . . . He may be a nice person. . . .

Fran: He is. . . .

Krull: At any rate how do you propose we get out?

Mickey: If this were a play . . .

Fran: He is a nice person.

Mickey: Fran.

Fran: All right.

Mickey: If this were a piece of theatre and we wanted to get out . . . what then?

Krull: I suppose this sort of thing amuses you.

Mickey: *To Krull.* Just supposing.

Fran: It's just that pursuing two careers puts incredible strains on a relationship.

Mickey: I'm sure. Focus, Fran.

Fran: I guess we'd have to act our way out.

Mickey: Act our way out.

Krull: Nice thought.

Mickey: So where is everybody?

Everybody looks at watches.

Mickey: They're late.

Krull: They're like that, aren't they? Mad as hell when an actor's late . . . but they don't mind keeping us hanging around, twiddling our thumbs. There's a director for you.

Fran: What director? *They stare at her.* Did I read it wrong? *She fishes around in a bag.*

Mickey: There's gotta be a director.

Krull: There's always a director.

Fran: *Producing a document.* It's right here. Didn't you read your contract?

Krull: My agent reads contracts. I just sign them.

Mickey: I must've read it. It was a while ago. . . .

Fran: *Reading.* "Enter. Perform *Quartet*. Exit."

Krull: That's it?

Fran: Essentially.

Mickey: *Whimpering.* What about rehearsals?

Fran: I don't know. I guess not.

Mickey: . . . usually like a few weeks rehearsal. . . .

Krull: Blocking?

She shrugs.

Krull: Goodness knows I don't ask much from a director but I think somebody should tell me where to go. . . . *The others resist the temptation to offer suggestions.*

Fran: Enter. Perform. Exit.

Mickey: So it's true in a way. We will have to act our way out.

Krull: This is ridiculous.

Fran: Well, you know . . . the scenes are playable. Each of us has a nice bit . . . sort of centred on us.

Krull: On each of us?

Fran: Yes, in turn. I don't see the problem.

Mickey: You don't see the problem? We're in a theatre we can't find our way out of. We're supposed to perform these — what are they — short plays that have never been performed before. We have no director. We have no rehearsal time. Is this an accurate summary of our predicament?

The others nod.

Mickey: And you don't see the problem.

Fran shakes her head.

Mickey: *Exasperated.* Okay. *He gets his script.* The first movement of this quartet . . .

Fran: *Changing costume pieces.* In which you are the featured performer . . .

Mickey: In which I am the featured performer . . . is about a comedian?

Fran: Right.

Krull: Yes.

Mickey: *Light dawning.* Oh, that's it then, since comedy is the root of all revelation. . . .

Krull: Comedy?

Mickey: Yes. It's my credo. Comedy tells all, reveals all, bares life to the bone. . . . In which case when we play my scene . . . if I do my usual superb job . . . *Mickey locates a jacket and begins to put it on.*

Fran: Which you will.

Mickey: Which I will. . . . Then we shall know what all this is about, we shall understand the purpose . . . hell, we probably won't have to do the rest of the play whatever it is! We can adjourn to the pub!

Krull: I smell something revolting. You know what I smell? I smell experimental drama. Conceptual stuff. Stuff about actors being symbols! I heard about these two actors who went around for a year tied together with a rope and they called it performance art. There was another guy who never put on a play . . . he just advertized titles in the newspaper and he called that drama, conceptual drama! I hate experimental drama. People come to the theatre to see real people in real situations, not a bunch of metaphysical puppets on strings being jerked around by some playwright trying to play God. The job of theatre is to examine life, not theatre. I'm an actor. Pure and simple. Give me a character and I'll play it. Give me a story and I'll bring it to life! And I'm not going to be in a play about actors. I hate plays about actors. If anybody thinks I'm going to stand around expostulating on reality and unreality all night, forget it. I'm leaving.

Exits and returns after a moment.

All right, I can't leave but I can sure as hell go and stand in a vomitory.

Which he does, if there is one. If he can't find one, he will mutter something about wings and go and stand there. There is a pause.

Fran: I think he's upset.

Mickey: "I'm an actor." Big deal. He'll be back. This is how we get out, Fran. Seriously, whoever has put this whole thing together expects us to do our schtick and then they'll come along and show us the way out. It *is* some kind of of conceptual piece.

Fran: You think so?

Mickey: Of course. It's gotta be. It's the only thing that makes sense.

Fran: Maybe. But I think there's something else. . . .

Mickey: What?

Fran: I don't know.

Mickey: Do you have special insight into this?

Fran: I might have.

Mickey: Do you know the producer?

Fran: No.

Mickey: Then where do you get your special insight?

Fran: I think I'm psychic. There's something going on with me, Mickey! I think I go into trances. I'm waiting for the day when I drop off in the middle of a performance, you know, and Sarah Bernhardt or some other dead actress starts to talk. Actually I think in another life I was one of those priestesses at the oracle in Delphi . . . you know Delphi . . . from the Greek plays.

Mickey: Yeah, the Greek plays.

Fran: I don't know why I feel that way . . . but sometimes I see myself in a long white gown . . . a kind of a see-through thing . . . and I'm standing between columns and this smoke or something coming out of a crack in the rocks and strange words coming out of my mouth like a golden mist. Funny eh?

Mickey: *Gently exasperated.* Wonderful.

Fran: Isn't it? And scary.

Mickey: Very. So what has all that got to do with all this?

Fran: All what?

Mickey: All this!

Fran: Something. *She concentrates.* Wait.

Mickey: The sooner we do the scene . . .

Fran: Wait.

Mickey: . . . the sooner we get to the pub.

Fran: *Pronouncing.* Let us make our own worlds here. Let us make worlds where we may come and go as much as we want. We just have to play it. Such is the source of truth. Such is revelation. So be it.

Mickey: That's it?

Fran: It isn't?

Mickey: Fran, I like you a lot and I think you're a good actress, okay? . . . And communicating with spirits is all right. . . . I prefer drinking them myself. . . .

Fran: We know.

Mickey: And creating our own world is okay, but face it, it's still only theatre.

Fran: Maybe I didn't get it right.

Mickey: *Sitting.* I need a drink.

Fran: *Sitting down grandly.* Of course, you little darling. Of course. *Calling.* Waiter! *Pause.* Waiter! That's your cue!

Krull rushes on as a waiter.

Fran: One more brandy and soda please.

Krull: A brandy and soda, Madam?

The lights alter. The actors are stunned for a moment.

Mickey: *Softly.* Someone's on lights.

String quartet music begins to play.

Krull: What the hell is that?

Fran: Production values. Somebody's in the booth.

Between them materializes a table covered with linen, crystal, candles, flowers.

Mickey: All right!

Krull: Let's . . . let's talk about it a little. . . .

Mickey: You can stand around and talk about a scene all you want . . . but finally you gotta just do it, right?

Krull: But this is ridiculous.

We become aware of the sound of others just out of sight — low conversation, tinkling of crystal, occasional laughter of people enjoying themselves.

Fran: A brandy and soda for me. And a Pink Lady for the gentleman.

Mickey: A Pink Lady?

Krull: A Pink Lady it is. *Rushes off.*

Mickey: A Pink Lady?

Fran: I think it's cream and gin and stuff.

Mickey: I drink beer. Why are you ordering my drinks for me?

Fran: Because I'm paying for them. Do you know much about art?

Mickey: Art who?

Fran: *Coquettish.* You don't, do you?

Mickey: I don't know, any more. I just don't know.

Fran: Oh, Harv. You're so amusing.

Mickey: It's just as well, isn't it . . . considering I'm a . . .

Fran: Comedian?

Mickey: *Glum.* Yes.

Fran: Don't worry. You'll hit it big again. I know you will. Anyway, getting back to art . . . there are three things I want to do.

Mickey: Three?

Fran: I want to go to France and see the Mona Lisa . . . you know something about the way that painting is painted it looks at you no matter where you are in the room.

Mickey: I guess it does.

Fran: Have you seen it?

Mickey: I've seen pictures of it.

Krull: *Returning.* A brandy and soda for the lady and a Pink Lady for the gentleman.

Fran: Thank you so much.

Mickey: *Brightening up.* Is this real?

Krull: Will that be all?

Mickey: Do you have any beer?

Krull: I beg your pardon?

Fran: *Fiercely to Mickey.* Shhht.

Mickey: Nothing.

Fran: Everything is lovely.

Krull: Thank you. *Hangs back.*

Fran: Then you know what?

Mickey: What?

Fran: I want to go to Italy and see Michelangelo's statue of David.

Mickey: The one with his penis chopped off?

Fran: No.

Mickey: It is so.

Fran: No it isn't.

Mickey: I've seen pictures.

Fran: That's someone else. And then I'd like to go to Egypt and study Egyptian art.

Mickey: I think there's real gin in this.

Fran: Because Egyptian art is amazing.

Mickey tries to turn himself into an Egyptian two-dimensional figure.

Fran: What are you doing?

Krull: *Stepping forward.* Would you like to order your dinner, now?

Mickey: Egyptian.

Fran: *Apologizing to the waiter.* Once a comedian, always a comedian. Just a load of laughs, isn't he. Honestly.

Krull: A comedian?

Mickey: *Modestly.* Well . . .

Krull: You're Harvey Ledbetter, aren't you?

Mickey: *Toying.* Not really. Yes, I am. Aw shucks.

Krull: *Confidentially.* I'm a fan of yours, Mr. Ledbetter.

Mickey: Well, thanks . . .

Krull: *Dropping his waiter's dignity to do an imitation.* "Bigelow, Bigelow, come aaawwwwn in!!! Where do you want it? . . . You're this far *(Half an inch),* from this *(Fist),* you big palooka!" Eh? Eh? Eh?

Mickey: Yeah. That's me all right.

Krull: *Abruptly resuming his waiter demeanor.* Dinner, Monsieur, Mademoiselle?

Fran: Would you like me to order for you, Harv?

Mickey: I can order.

Fran: I just . . .

Mickey: I can order!

Krull: Perhaps you need a little more time. . . .

Fran: Perhaps. . . .

Mickey: Do you know what you want?

Fran: *Affirmative.* Hmmhmm.

Mickey: Then we'll order.

Krull: Very good, Monsieur.

Mickey: What d'you want?

Fran: I'll have the Coquille Saint-Jacques as an appetizer . . .

Krull: Excellent, Mademoiselle . . .

Fran: The Truite Amandine . . .

Krull: Yes. Ensuite?

Fran: Et ensuite La Salade des Trois Petites Rigolettos Au Retour du Marché En Aimant avec l'amour du Chef.

Krull: *Dancing and kissing his lips in ecstasy.* Formidable, formidable. Excellent choice. Comme merveilleux. Bon, bon, bon, bon!

Mickey is flabbergasted. He is checking both menus to see what she said and how much it cost.

Krull: *After a pause.* And you, Monsieur?

Mickey: Wait a minute, wait a minute. *Consults menu.* What's this crud?

Fran: Delicately put.

Mickey: *To waiter.* Would you put this in plain English.

Krull: That is the Raw Ground Sirloin with Basil.

Mickey: Raw?

Krull: Very tasty, Sir.

Mickey: Where's the beef dip?

Krull: Heh, heh. We have had a run on beef dip this evening, Sir. I'm afraid we're out.

Mickey: Where's the Salisbury steak?

Krull: *Dry convulsions.* That's very amusing, Mr. Ledbetter.

Fran: You're doing this on purpose.

Mickey: Liver and onions.

Waiter so amused he is unable to speak.

Mickey: Leevair undt Ognions? No liver and onions.

Krull: *Gasping.* Would you care for a hot beef sandwich with gravy?

Mickey: Pork chops.

Krull: Yes indeed.

Mickey: *Laying down the menu triumphantly.* There.

Krull: That'll be one order of Le Cochon de la Maison.

Mickey: *As Mickey.* Will the food be real, too?

Fran: Better bring Mr. Ledbetter one more Pink Lady. *To Mickey.* Keep your concentration.

Mickey: Where do you get off telling me I don't know anything about art.

Fran: You don't.

Mickey: I'm an artist. How can you say that?

Fran: Harvey, you're a comedian.

Mickey: Are you trying to tell me. . . . Wait a minute! A comedian *is* an artist!

Fran: In that case who isn't an artist? Harvey, you don't understand the difference between art and entertainment.

Mickey: There is no difference.

Fran: Of course there is. Entertainment just keeps your attention. Art takes you out of this world.

Mickey: That's exactly what I can do. Well, maybe not any more . . . but I used to. . . .

Fran: You never did. You just kept them laughing. *Pause.* Of course you were very good at it. . . . *Pause.* And you'll make a comeback. . . . *Pause.* Maybe. Anyway I'll take care of you.

Mickey: Why?

Fran: You're fun to have around.

Mickey: I've been working up some new material. High art. I'll put it beside Michelangelo with his penis missing any day.

Fran: Have you ever thought of taking up painting?

Mickey: Do you want to see it?

Fran: I could buy some paints for you . . . and an easel . . . and one of those cute smocks with the beret. . . . Sit down. This is a restaurant.

Krull: *Rushing up.* May I get you something else?

Fran: He wants to do his act.

Krull: His act?

Mickey: New material. A new kind of routine. I want to try it out.

Krull: But this is not exactly the . . . we don't even have a . . .

Fran: See, they don't want you . . .

Krull: Of course it would be a first for us. . . .

Mickey: Of course it would be a first for you. Your restaurant will become world famous as the place where Harvey Ledbetter stopped in and did his thing. . . . The intro, Maestro! *Sings a funky fanfare.*

Krull: Wait, wait . . . let me explain to everybody. Introduce you.

Mickey: Terribly kind, terribly thoughtful.

Krull: Ladies and Gentlemen, if I may have your attention for a moment. You may not have noticed but Le Café Fille de Joie et Cuisses de Grenouille is very privileged to have among its dinner guests the famous comedian Harvey Ledbetter. *Pause for applause.* Harvey Ledbetter. Well, you may remember him as Joe in the short lived situation comedy, "Cacciatore and Collard Greens"? Or you may have seen his many stage shows and remembered his endearing characterization of Little Egg Head. Yes?

Scattered applause.

Le Café Fille de Joie et Cuisses de Grenouille does not normally present live entertainment, but this evening, Mr. Ledbetter has kindly offered to perform one of his unique — how do you say — numbers. So without further adieu, Mr. Harvey Ledbetter!

Applause. "Harvey" stands up on a serving cart which sort of rolls about on the stage.

Mickey: Thank you, thank you. Thought I'd try out some new material on you tonight. Kind of a test run if you know what I mean. . . . Hope it hits you right in the old funny bone. Hey, were you outside today? Windy day, eh? I was waiting for it to blow over and. . . . Ask me how windy was it. It was so windy it blew my mind. . . . Get it? It blew me over, it was so windy. It was so windy that this dame fell right into my arms. I said, this is some windy! Never been that windy before. It was so windy that my cat blew in. It was so windy that red turned the colour blew. It was so windy that the wicked witch of the west stayed home. It was so windy that I got lonely and cold. . . . Get it? You know, four strong winds. . . . Never mind. How about the answer? There were answers blowing all over the place. Who has seen the wind?

Would you tell me that? The wind in the willows was redundant. *Singing.* "Just a little breeze seemed to holler Louise!" And this dame who fell into my arms . . . said she'd been just swept off her feet. . . . *To Fran.* This isn't working.

Fran shakes her head.

Mickey: Have you ever watched the way people walk down the street in a wind storm? *Demonstrating.* Some people walk at a forty-five. Some people get propelled along. Some people try to duck under it. Some people offer the line of least resistance. Some people hold onto their hats. Some people hold onto their hair. "Hahaha . . . I know what you've got on. Look, Mommy he's got a furry on his head!" Some people carry umbrellas. . . .

Generally there is great chaos. The waiter tries to intervene.

Krull: Mr. Ledbetter. Just wonderful. Just wonderful!. Your dinner is ready, Sir. Let's give him a big hand!

Scattered applause.

Sadly. You used to be so good. "Bigelow, Bigelow, come aaawwwwn in!!!" Whenever I heard that I used to roll on the floor! Here. Another . . . *Another Pink Lady and brandy and soda.* With our compliments. *Exit.*

Mickey: There, see?

Fran: See what?

Mickey: Art. *Long pause.* Knock knock.

Fran: Who's there.

Mickey: Art.

Fran: Harv . . .

Mickey: Art Who.

Fran: Art Who?

Mickey: Art for Art's Sake. Get it?

Fran: Harv . . .

Mickey: I don't like it anymore. I don't get anything out of it. I can't even get a laugh out of the bastards. *Rising.* Can't a guy get a decent drink around this place . . . instead of this elephant piss. Pink elepha . . . *Sitting down.* Aw. . . .

Fran: That routine could be good. . . . I mean . . .

Mickey: Is it funny? Is it? *No answer.* Right.

Fran: Maybe you should take up poetry. I always wanted to have a relationship with a poet.

Mickey: I used to think I could save the world — laughing — making them laugh. Hey, if they were laughing they wouldn't have time to make bombs. . . . If they were laughing they wouldn't be able to blow people's brains out, rape the women, pillage the village, exploit the masses . . . whatever. It was the way for me to do my bit, see. I figured it was enough. To stand up. Hear the laugh sweep in. And, just as it crests, to top it and build it until they're helpless out there, eh? And I'm breaking up with them. . . . Now . . . what? It's an automatic thing. Like tickling. They laugh? So what. And sometimes they don't laugh.

Fran: So what?

Mickey: Then it's worse. There's something like a cold wind blowing through me . . . dead leaves blowing on a wire fence. Geez, they're taking a long time with the grub.

Fran: Take it easy.

Mickey: I am. I am. All right? I am taking it easy.

Fran: That's the difference between art and comedy. You don't have to worry about whether people laugh or not. Art is beyond laughter. Art is for the discriminating few. . . .

Mickey: For the truly superior?

Fran: Yes.

Mickey: For those who can afford it.

Fran: Everything has its price.

Mickey: *That does it.* I have to get out of here.

Krull appears with the food — steaming and sumptuous. Mickey almost upsets him in his flight.

Mickey: Let me through!

Fran: Harvey!

Krull: Sir?

Mickey: I'm out! I'm . . . *But the lights begin to black out.* No!

The stage reverts to its original setting. The characters remain frozen in their scene briefly — Mickey almost out the door. Then Krull dumps the food in a prop box.

Mickey: They pulled the lights on me! I was going to get out! They pulled the lights on me!

Fran: Don't look at me.

The control booth is accessible. Mickey runs up an aisle and pounds on the window.

Mickey: Hey, you in there. Who are you? I want to talk to you, Turkey! Get the hell out here and talk to me. Now! I wanna know what's going on! That was a good scene. . . . Why didn't you let me out? And another thing, where did you get that material, anyway? Where did you get it? I said get out here! *No response. Finally he comes back.*

Fran: Give up, Mick.

Mickey: What are they doing with us?

Fran: We'll find out.

Krull: What's your problem?

Fran: Too close to home?

Mickey: Yeah, I've been feeling like that . . . like dead leaves against a fence.

Fran: Blowing in the wind?

Mickey: Last winter I was doing a show. Every night when I came to the theatre I had to walk past people begging for money. Young people, old people, girls with pale faces . . . stretching out their hands. . . . I felt really guilty!

Fran: What were you doing at the theatre? Drawing room comedy?

Mickey: No. That's it. We were doing a docudrama about unemployment. Yeah. It was like wind, eh? No answers, no voices . . . just wind and special effects.

Fran: We had something real there for a minute, didn't we?

Mickey: The comic who can't hack it.

Krull: I could have had a somewhat larger role, don't you think?

Hastening to add. Not that you didn't do a perfectly adequate job, Mickey.

Mickey: Thank you.

Krull: Some of it was quite fascinating.

Mickey: Thank you.

Krull: Although I think you could have followed the script a little more faithfully.

Mickey: I followed it.

Krull: You did?

Mickey: To a tee.

Krull: Then the script must have kept changing. I hardly knew where I was. *He turns away.*

Fran: *To Mickey.* I thought it was working.

Mickey: We didn't get out.

Fran: You got a drink. More than one.

Mickey: It's not the same thing.

Fran: You were in a restaurant.

Mickey: But it wasn't out.

Fran: Then we'll have to try something else.

Krull: *Returning.* Of course, I thought I played the waiter rather well. *Imitates his performance and then returns to himself.* And I believe I have a more fulsome role in the next one.

Mickey: You're very co-operative all of a sudden.

Krull: Of course.

Mickey: *Imitating.* "But if anybody thinks for one minute that I'm going to stand around and expostulate all night about what's real and all that . . . "

Krull: "Give me a good story and I'll bring it to life." Let's get on with it.

Everyone rushes to prepare, consulting scripts to see what they need, picking props, costume bits. Finally everything is assembled and they assume a starting tableau. Nothing happens.

Fran: Set the scene.

Mickey: Make it outside somewheres.

Fran: Right.

Krull: Outside it is. Brand new situation. Brand new characters. Brand new setting.

As he speaks the stage seems to undergo an alteration.

A great, green, manicured lawn . . . dotted with ornamental shrubbery. Tall hedges over there . . . and there. Ah. . . . And my character is what? An actor, an old retired actor, drinking his coffee out of doors.

Fran hurries off.

Krull: *Picking up a newspaper.* Reading the morning paper . . . brooding over natural catastrophes and fresh disasters . . . all strangely distant from this idyllic paradise. Isn't acting wonderful!

Fran returns. Her costume is a rather plain summer dress. She places coffee on a little wrought iron table.

Mickey: *Putting a chair under him.* Until you're too old to remember your lines . . .

Krull collapses into a very ancient version of himself. Mickey puts a rug over his knees.

Mickey: . . . to remember your lines.

Krull: Eh?

Mickey: Too old to remember your lines.

Krull: I'm sorry.

Fran: *Prompting.* There seem to be a number of . . .

Krull: Oh, yes. . . . There seem to be a number . . . *quite* a number of fresh catastrophes . . . er . . . disasters in the paper this morning, don't you think?

Fran: Yes, Father.

Mickey: We always called him Father.

Krull: Coincidental, it seems?

Fran: He insisted on it.

Krull: Look, a volcano last week . . . an earthquake this week — in two widely separated countries in South America — and another one . . . another one in Italy and then a tremor in San Francisco. One wonders where next.

Mickey: Yes, Father.

Fran: When after long absences he appeared we assumed a kind of filial decorum.

Mickey: Can I get you anything else?

Krull: May.

Mickey: May I?

Krull: Jennifer?

Fran: It was our Mother's name.

Krull: *Rising.* This chair feels somewhat — I'd like another one — shaky.

Mickey: I'll help. . . .

Fran: It means going back to the house.

Krull walks a few tottering steps. Turns. Spots the chair he had just risen from.

Krull: Never mind. That one will do nicely. *He shakes the others off.* I'm quite able, thank you.

They watch him make his way back. Sitting. Much better. Jennifer?

Fran: Francine.

Krull: What?

Fran: I'm Francine, Father.

Krull: Of course you are. What did I say?

They are silent.

Earthquake. Do you remember the description of the earthquake in *The Foundations*, Francine? *Launching forth.* "How could we have noticed? The ice was tinkling in the cocktail glasses. . . . The champagne glasses were clinking in one toast after another . . . the orchestra played a waltz . . . the ladies' sweet laughter rose over the chattering of the chandeliers above our heads. It was only when the floor lurched that we fell silent. There were few screams, remarkably few. We lost little dignity even as the entire west wall crumbled. The night city lay ruined before us. A blood red glow spread long flickering shadows . . . fingers reaching towards us. An earthquake alters one's perspective, makes one think of things never before thought of, returns one to a land completely changed." . . . Is this your fiancé, Francine?

Mickey: Francine has had two husbands and she's looking for a third.

Fran: It's Michael.

Krull: Michael. Do you hear from him? I've heard he is doing well. He never comes anymore. Never writes. Ungrateful child.

Mickey: It's me, Father. I'm here now. . . .

Krull: He came once to see me do Oedipus. Remember Oedipus? My greatest triumph. Triumph. I used to shun that word. Just a journeyman actor I used to say. But now . . .

Fran: One has to have triumphs in one's life. . . .

Krull: One has to have had. He came backstage afterwards and said he couldn't take it any more. I've forgotten what he couldn't take anymore. Was it me?

Mickey: It was. He hasn't forgotten. . . .

Krull: He went to the other side of the world. Australia or someplace. Where was it?

Fran and Mick: New Zealand.

Mickey: But I'm back now. Can't you see me?

Krull: Of course I can see you. *To Fran.* What a peculiar young man. Are you sure you want to marry him?

Fran: I don't have a fiancé, Father. This is Michael. Of course you recognize him, don't you.

Krull stares at Mickey for a long time and then turns back to Fran.

Krull: I suppose they don't want to marry the daughter of an actor, even one as distinguished as I.

Fran: I'm sorry, Michael . . .

Krull: Was it the homosexual scene in the film? My first movie and I am typecast forever as a screaming queen. The tabloids! The muckrakers. Surely they had only to look at you and your brother Michael to see that I was no slouch on that front. Eh? They could have asked your mother . . . she could have given them an earful. You remind me of her, Francine. . . .

Fran: He says that often now. Not so much then.

Mickey: I didn't mind that he wasn't here. When he did come home, his fame came with him like sour rain clinging to his clothes.

Fran: I was thirsty for a taste of his glory. I would wait at the door with the newspapers . . . the interviews and the reviews. . . .

Mickey: I had to stifle my yawns and listen, eyes wide, mouth open, to his stupid stories about receptions with kings and presidents. . . .

Krull: I didn't do well by her, Francine.

Mickey: Of course you didn't, you old fart. Famous philanderer of three continents.

Krull: But I loved her. Who is this boy?

Mickey: Michael.

Krull: Whatever happened to Vincent?

Fran: Long over.

Krull: And Stanley.

Fran: Over.

Krull: Over . . . like that?

Fran: Like that.

Krull: Why, Francine? Do you know?

Fran: I guess none of them measured up to you.

Krull: Then I've done you a disservice. *But he is pleased neverthe-less.* Are you really Michael?

Mickey: Yes.

Krull: You have come back.

Mickey: Yes, Father.

Krull: In spite of everything?

Mickey: Because of everything.

Krull: What does that mean exactly? Because of everything.

Mickey: I don't know. I guess I wanted to say to you that . . . I don't know . . . things. . . . Find out. Do you know what I mean?

Krull: You never could express yourself concisely.

Mickey: And he always expressed himself too concisely.

Krull: Are you going to stay?

Mickey: Not for long.

Krull: Good. I suppose you're laughing, aren't you . . . to see me like this? How are the mighty fallen, is that it? God, how I despised you — you and your mean little spirit — always whining. . . . How can I be anybody? . . . Everybody always introduces me by my father's reputation. . . . Do you know what you did . . . you took the edge off my success! You were always there . . . reproaching me for my fame.

Fran: Father!

Krull: He did! He did! He all but took happiness away from me. . . .

Fran: *To Mickey.* He gets like this sometimes. More and more . . .

Mickey: Some happiness . . . if I could spoil it so easily. What good was it?

Krull: What good? What good? In my day I shook the world, Michael, I shook the world with my voice . . . with the very gesture of my hand . . . the earth would tremble. *He rises.* Thousands — millions — were silent when I spoke. I could bring them to tears with a whisper. I could bring terror to their souls in a storm of passion! I can still do it!

But he has to sit down again. Jennifer? Where's Jennifer?

Fran: She's not here, Father.

Mickey: She's dead, Father. While you were out making the earth tremble, she was here dying.

Krull: Was it worth it?

Fran: It had to be.

Mickey: Why?

Krull: I could have been out working in the fields with the farmers. Sun drenched. Winnowing the hay, or whatever it is they do . . . planting grain to feed the multitudes. I could have been here taking care of my family — growing into a gentle funny old man. You might never have had that trouble back then, Michael. We won't speak of that, but you might have become moderately successful. . . .

Mickey: I am moderately successful — where I am — at what I do. I run a store. I sell odds and sods of things. It's a living.

Krull: But is it art?

Fran: Never say your life wasn't significant. I've lived by your life. Your fame has been my bread and milk. . . .

Krull: Bread and butter. It's kept you in allowance. . . . Get out of my sight. Both of you. *He begins to weep in his senility.*

Mickey: I hate self-pity in myself and others. But there was only so much room and his presence could fill a whole theatre. It took me so long to feel like anybody at all.

Fran: If there's nothing in what he's done . . .

Krull: All shades and images . . . all phantasmagoria . . . signifying nothing. . . .

Fran: . . . then where can I stand? He was always bigger than life — a man of the theatre — connected in a long line to Olivier and John Barrymore and Henry Irving and Keane and Garrick and Burbage . . . and if he crumbles so does the whole history of English-speaking theatre. And so do I.

Krull: "How could we have noticed? . . . " I was very good in that part, wasn't I? "How could we have noticed? The ice was tinkling in the cocktail glasses. . . . The champagne glasses were clinking. . . . " I made the lines dance as delicately as fine crystal. "The orchestra. . . . The one two three played two three . . . do you hear? Orchestra played a waltz. The ladies' sweet laughter rose over the chandeliers chattering above our heads. It was only when the floor lurched that we fell silent. We lost little dignity even as the entire west wall crumbled. . . . Blood red glow spread long flickering shadows . . . fingers reaching towards us."

He has risen. He walks towards the image he has created in his words, but encounters the boundary of the physical state.

Fran: Father . . . you can't . . .

Mickey: Where does he think he is?

Fran: . . . you can't go there . . . not any more.

Frustrated, Krull kicks over some of the stage junk.

Krull: What is this? Who put that . . .

The lights fade out. The actors revert to normal, somewhat dazed.

Krull: Oh.

Mickey: I almost thought we'd done it. . . .

Fran: Me too.

Krull: My friends, that is acting.

Mickey: But it didn't get us out.

Krull: No.

Mickey: No new insight. No voice of God, no revelation of the secrets of existence. . . .

Krull: Well it must have meant something. You can't have all that *acting* and not have it mean something. *Appealing to Fran.* It meant something, didn't it?

Fran: Yes, Krull.

Mickey: What?

Fran: It was very impressive. It proved . . . well, it's all leading up to something I'm sure.

Mickey: It proved earthquakes don't mean anything. *Disgusted.* Earthquakes!

Krull: I suppose wind means something? *Imitating the Harvey Ledbetter routine.* "Boy was it windy today . . . some people walk sideways. . . . "

Mickey starts to pout.

Mickey: What I did in my scene wasn't so bad either. *Appeal to Fran.* Was it?

Fran: You were both very good.

Krull: Of course. . . . But you see . . . his was comedy. If we're going to find meaning we don't look to comedy because there's always a greater portion of unreality in comedy, don't you think?

Mickey: No. Besides mine wasn't just comedy . . . it was about comedy. It was just as serious as yours was. Heart-rending. It's the clown with the tear in his eye. It's basic to the human condition.

Krull: Not as basic as pure tragedy.

Mickey: It is so.

Krull: *King Lear*!

Mickey: Oh, *King Lear*. People think they can solve anything by saying *King Lear*. . . . *Pygmalion*!

Krull: *Pygmalion*?

Mickey: Shaw.

Krull: I know who wrote *Pygmalion*. . . . *Hamlet*!

Mickey: Overrated!

Krull: What!

Mickey: *Playboy of the Western World*!

Krull: Irish! *Death of a Salesman*!

Mickey: Let's talk about viability. *The Norman Conquests*!

Krull: *Disgusted.* Oh, Ayckbourn. *Long Days Journey into Night*!

Mickey: Long. *Billy Bishop Goes to War. (Pause.)* Canadian.

TOGETHER: *Waiting For Godot*!

Pause.

Krull: That's a tragedy.

Mickey: *At the same time.* It's a comedy.

Krull: Tragedy.

Mickey: Comedy.

Krull: It's a . . .

Mickey: It's a . . .

Fran: *No Exit.* It doesn't matter. Neither of you got us out of here, did you? What's with you guys? *They stop.* You're like a pair of rutting moose.

Krull: I beg your pardon?

Fran: I've had a thought that makes me very uncomfortable, very disconcerted. *Pause.* What if all this is totally fictitious?

Krull: How do you mean?

Mickey: You mean totally fictious?

Fran: Hmmhmm.

Krull: Perhaps you could elaborate?

Mickey: Krull . . . she means us too.

Fran: What if we are only characters? . . .

Krull: Of course we're characters . . . we're actors playing characters.

Mickey: She means what if we actors are also characters.

Krull: Is that what you mean?

She nods.

Krull: Us? The three of us, just characters?

She nods again.

Krull: You're saying we're some kind of literary device?

Fran: Maybe.

Krull: That's impossible. We have backgrounds. We have personal histories outside of this story. I've got two kids at home — and a wife.

Fran: That's true. I've got Henry. *Although she's not sure. . . .* I guess.

Mickey: Yeah. That all proves something. And I'm divorced. I've got no kids and I've got a dog, Pluto, and I've got a drinking problem. *Pause.* That doesn't prove anything.

Krull: Yes it does. Why not?

Mickey: All characters have histories. It doesn't mean a thing. Well developed characters have well developed histories.

Krull is stumped.

Fran: Yeah.

Krull: I am not fictitious.

Fran: But supposing we are, and supposing this is a play and supposing we do get out, what happens then?

Mickey: We could terrorize the audience.

Krull: Audience?

Fran: Seriously.

Krull: Yes . . . I suppose there must be an audience out there. It feels like an audience. It's giving me that old surge of adrenalin.

Fran: Seriously. What if this is the only . . . what if we *depend* somehow? . . .

Mickey: *Softly.* On being in this?

Fran: When I was a little girl my parents would come in to my bedroom to tuck me in and say prayers . . . and I had this funny feeling that when they left the room they would disappear . . .you know? They would just puff out and then when morning came they would kind of light up and get going again.

Krull: So what's that got to do with us?

Mickey: I think that's the point, Krull.

Krull: We're not being tucked in. Oh. You mean. . . . No. I'm much too substantial. I know I am.

Mickey: There is an element of uncertainty here . . .

Krull: Nonsense.

Fran: I don't want to believe it, either. It's just that I don't feel all that substantial right now.

Krull: That way madness lies. To say — to even contemplate that when this play is over so is our existence? We're actors. We'll live on beyond these characters to play others, a long unending succession of characters. Well, I suppose it will come to an end eventually. . . .

Mickey: *To Fran.* It doesn't matter. Let him think whatever he wants if it makes him happier.

Fran: *To Krull.* Right, forget I said it, Krull. I'm sorry.

Krull: I will. *Pause.* That scene left me unsettled though. It seemed a little . . . I don't know . . . relevant? I do depend on performing for my sense of — what? Worth? If that's all it comes to in the end — a doddering old man reciting the shards of forgotten plays — I didn't take it so personally when I read it the first time. Shades of . . . of . . .

Mickey: Mortality?

Krull: Impermanence.

Fran: *Consulting a script.* Well, this might shed some light.

Krull: Yes?

Fran: Intermission.

Mickey: An intermission.

Fran: That might tell us something about the state of our existence — whether or not — etcetera.

Krull: Etcetera. When?

Fran: Soon.

They sink into a long pause. Finally Krull does a Jimmy Durante imitation, singing and dancing "Inka Dinka Doo." The others are amazed.

Krull: It's something I always do when confronted with the spectre of my imminent demise. It helps somehow. *Finds a hat.* "Inka dinka dee, inka dinka doo, this is a song for croonin', inka dinka dee, inka dinka doo, I've got the whole world croonin' . . . "

Mickey gestures for the hat and tries a chorus with prompting from Krull.

Mickey: You're right. It helps a bit. *Tosses hat to Fran.*

Fran: *After a line or two.* Amazing. *Hat back to Krull.*

Krull: "Eskimo belles up in Iceland, they got their own pair o' diceland, Inka dink. *Etc., ending on a particularly off note.* "That note was given to me by Bing Crosby *(Beat.)* and boy, was he glad to get rid ot it."

And the lights fade to black. After a time the house lights rise. The actors have disappeared and it is the **END OF ACT I.**

Act Two

Scene: As before. The three actors are on stage.

Krull: "Inka dink, inka dinka doo." There. *Pokes himself.* Just as solid as before the break. Just as glorious. Just as brilliant.

Mickey: Could have been worse.

Krull: *To Fran.* See? We're still here.

Mickey: We'd have to be, wouldn't we? The show's not over.

Fran: Ask yourself what we did during intermission. *This gives Krull pause for thought.*

My scene's coming up. *Fran goes off and starts to do strange physical and vocal warm ups.*

Krull: *Reacting.* Now what?

Mickey: Her scene's coming up.

Fran: *Talking to someone inside.* Let's get a few things straight, all right? What if I goof up . . . will my ego self-destruct? What if Henry and I break up, can I stay in this forever? Don't let me vomit. Is there some other method of gaining eternal life? Please make me superb. Don't let me go into a trance in the middle of the scene . . . and if I do, can it be on somebody else's line? What place do my own inter-personal relationships have in a career dedicated to the pursuit of art? Will this be successful? Will it get good reviews? Will the audiences flock to see me perform in an otherwise mediocre piece of organic waste? If the answer to any of these is negative please don't let me know. Don't let my costume fall off on stage. Don't let my breasts pop out. Am I pregnant? Will Henry marry me? Do I want him to? Is he having an affair with his administrator? Don't let my voice go unnaturally high. Amen.

The others are staring.

Warm ups. *Further.* It's better than a cigarette and a belch.

Mickey: You're really nervous.

Fran: No I'm not.

Mickey: I've never seen you this nervous.

Fran: I'm cool.

Krull: *Gently.* We all get nerves. They're nothing to be ashamed of.

Fran: *Yelling.* I am not nervous! I am calm and collected. Get away from me! *Long pause.*

Look . . . a lot depends on this one, right? The way I see it . . . this is our last chance. I mean there are only three of us and you two bombed out. . . . Well, maybe you got us somewhere but not far enough. We don't know how to get out and we don't know why we're here. . . .

Mickey: And we don't know whether we're real.

Fran: Anyway, this is our last chance. It's all up to me. Tell me I'm wrong. Please?

Mickey: You're right.

Krull: Yep.

Fran: Yeah.

Krull: What are you going to do? We've been through laughter and tears. What's left?

Fran: We've gotta fly. Just take off and fly.

Krull: Good luck.

Mickey: Give her hell, Fran.

Fran: *But she breaks.* I'm sorry . . . I used to do a lot better. I never had nerves . . . jitters. I guess I got a little too cocky. . . . You know what happened? I was playing one of the large centres. . . . They had a whole bunch of plays on at the same time and I went into the wrong play. . . . I was playing one of the weird sisters . . . and I ended up in . . . what?

Krull: A Noel Coward?

Fran: Yes . . .

Krull: *Doubled up.* Was that you?

Fran: *Dismayed.* You saw it?

Mickey: He saw it.

Fran doesn't know where to hide.

Krull: That was funny. I've never seen anything that funny!

Mickey: *Trying to be helpful.* He told me you improved the production.

Krull: You're legendary! I always wanted to meet you.

Fran: *Trying to disappear.* Oh, no.

Krull: It was wonderful! What's wrong?

Fran: It was like falling off a horse. Ever since then I've had to force myself to get back up on stage. No matter what I do . . . I think I'm in the wrong play.

Krull: You were fantastic. Anybody who can recover that fast. . . .

Fran: *Small voice.* He saw it. . . .

Krull: Should be able to add inestimably to . . . this.

Fran: I could die.

Krull: Don't do that. Act.

Mickey: This might be the one.

Krull: We're counting on you.

Mickey: Don't blow it.

Fran: You're doing me a world of good.

Krull: Where are you?

Fran: All right. A hospital. Sunshine Heights — a hospital for the mentally disturbed. Filled with broken humanity . . . wandering around the wrong stage in the wrong costume.

Krull: An asylum . . . wonderful . . . you get to play a mad scene. Somebody should have thought of that for my bit.

Mickey: *Consulting his script.* Are they actors?

Fran: It doesn't say. They're just human beings.

Krull: But they're crazy . . . same field. I love these little plays.

The stage is gradually altering form and color, becoming disconcerting. The actors are assembling their costumes.

Mickey: There has to be a common theme.

Krull: Masters of delusion.

We are in a patients' lounge in the hospital. Krull assumes the manner of a severely disturbed patient and wanders out of the room. Mickey shifts upwards in age. Fran enters wearing a bathrobe, looking somewhat unkempt.

Mickey: *Overly avuncular.* Frances!

She tries to avoid him.

Mickey: Frances!

She continues to avoid him.

Mickey: Come on, you know me, don't you? Mike. Your Uncle Mike.

She stops and examines him.

Mickey: Now say Hello. Hello. That's it. Let's sit down and have a nice long chitchat shall we?

Fran: *Weakly.* Mikey?

Mickey: That's right, Mike, Uncle Mike. Have things been going better for you, Frances?

She stares at him.

Mickey: *As if to a deaf person.* Have you been feeling better, Frances?

Fran: I don't know who you are.

Mickey: Your uncle.

Fran: What uncle?

Mickey: Mike.

Fran: I don't have ...

Mickey: *Roaring.* Don't say that! *More quietly.* If you keep on denying reality, Frances, you'll never get better. You'll never get better. You want to get better don't you?

She nods helplessly.

Mickey: Of course you do. It was a nice day so I drove up. I haven't been up since last spring. Do you remember when I came up last spring?

She shakes her head.

Mickey: Well we can't remember everything. I'm getting forgetful myself. I've taken to writing lists of things. Do you believe that? And I used to remember everything. Fine head for details. I think it's the fluoride they put in the drinking water. Oh, they tell me they don't but who can you believe? Aunt Martha says hello.

Fran: I don't . . .

Mickey: Your parents were here last week. Yes, you remember your parents but you don't remember your aunts and uncles, is that it?

Fran: Some of them . . .

Mickey: But not your favorite Aunt Martha and Uncle Mike.

Fran: No.

Mickey: Don't say that. *Pause.* You know it's a long way for your parents to come. And they're not getting any younger, are they? You should get well soon and come back and live closer to them. They haven't got all that long, surely. Why don't you get well and make their last years happy?

Fran: It isn't up to me.

Mickey: Oh, yes it is.

Fran: I know who you are. You're . . .

Mickey: Uncle Mikey. Pretend.

Fran: Why?

Mickey: If we can't get well we can pretend to get well. It's almost the same thing, isn't it. *More of a statement than a question.* Pretend you know me. Say, Uncle Mike.

Fran: Uncle Mike.

Mickey: Progress.

Fran: I feel so bad about my parents. They had such hope for me. When I was a child they would tuck me into bed and say that I was a princess and that I was bound for wonderful things. And now . . .

Mickey: Look at you.

Fran: Look at me.

Mickey: You know what's wrong with you?

Fran: I wish I did.

Mickey: Lack of will power.

Fran: No.

Mickey: Yes. That's all that's wrong with you. You went out into the world and you had a few setbacks . . . a few defeats. And what did you do? You ran away.

Fran: I had to.

Mickey: That's nonsense and you know it, Frances. I went out there. Defeats? I was beset on every side. I was, Frances. I made enemies. There were people putting poison in my drinking water. They followed me. . . . They would phone me and hang up without saying anything. They even got the government after me . . . they reviewed my tax returns . . . they tapped my phone. . . . Do you know why? Because I knew too much. I knew what they were up to and I wasn't afraid to say so. Rat poison in the drinking water. I said it, right out. And the Queen — Queen Elizabeth the Second — why does she go on all of those royal tours? Drug dealing. They tried to get me, Bolshie Commie bastards. But I didn't run. I stayed. Guts. *Looking around.* Hey listen, tell me something.

Fran: Sure.

Mickey: What's it really like here, really? Is this really a cuckoo bin?

Fran: No.

Mickey: I knew it! What is it, really?

Fran: An interplanetary transport module.

Mickey: I knew it! How does it work?

Fran: I can't say.

Mickey: *Louder.* How does it work?

Fran: It's a secret.

Mickey: You're afraid to tell me, right?

Fran: Yes.

Mickey: Because you'll be punished, right?

Fran: Yes.

Mickey: Maybe even tortured. Just nod your head.

She does so.

Mickey: I knew it! Who's in charge?

Fran: Strange forces.

Mickey: Socialists.

Fran: I think they have origins outside the solar system.

Mickey: Socialists.

Fran: It's so wonderful.

Mickey: Brainwashed.

Fran: Every night I ascend on columns of fire faster and faster until I am hurled beyond the stars to new worlds I never dreamed of. I see strange and marvellous sights. The universe is saturated with color and sound. Did you know that? It's alive with fire. Every night I am ablaze with the flames of creation. Strange spirits speak to me and tell me wonders in tongues that I can't translate into human language. I'm like an eagle soaring among the galaxies . . . a great eagle spreading light as great as the nebula.

Mickey: So that's what they're up to.

Fran: Who?

Mickey: *Faltering.* Who knows?

Fran: Uncle Mike?

Mickey: Never mind. Frances you have to come down from all that stuff.

Fran: I do. They bring me down every so often. . . .

Mickey: Stay here and fight. Join the ordinary folk . . . like me and your Aunt Martha. Forget stars and extraterrestrial beings and all that stuff.

Fran: They exist. I hear them. I hear them even now.

Mickey: No doubt you do. But what about us?

Fran: Such is the power of their communication . . .

Mickey: Frances . . .

Fran: Shhh.

Mickey: Fran . . .

Fran: Shhh. *Suddenly bursts into alien language.*

Krull: *Rushing in as doctor.* Are you playing Doctor again, Mikey? Go back to your room.

Mickey: *Mickey retreats.* I was just trying to help.

Krull: *Turning back to Fran.* Young lady, can you hear me? Can you hear me?

Fran: *Reverting to English.* I hear you.

Krull: You're safe now.

Fran: I hear you. That is A-Okay. Thanks.

Krull: I want you to relax.

Fran: We have been assured that our orbit conforms to expectation. *Pause and then with urgency.* Central, we are showing a red light on the panel. Something is wrong. The alarms are going off. . . .

Mickey provides sound of alarms. He becomes more and more agitated as Fran does.

Krull: *To Mickey.* Take it easy.

Fran: Are you duplicating, Central?

Krull: *Trying to enter into her fantasy.* No, everything is normal here.

Fran: Oh my God, the cockpit is filling up with smoke. *She begins to panic and choke.*

Krull: We show no problems on our end.

Fran: The bulkhead is hot to the touch. The thrust engines are going to blow, aren't they, Central? Aren't they?

Krull: Don't panic. Things are fine, just fine.

Fran: The computers are going wild!

Krull: The computers are normal.

Fran: I've got to get out. The cabin is on fire.

Krull: It's all an illusion. Come back to us ... relax ... come back to us ... you're hallucinating. Ride it out.

Fran: I don't understand what you are saying.

Krull: I said it's all in your head!

Fran: Not receiving you, Central. ... There is fire in the cabin. ...

Krull: There is no fire. There is no smoke. You're safe. You are with us safe and sound, Frances. Listen to me.

Fran: I have to get out of here!

Mickey: Have to get out! Have to get out! Have to get out!

Screaming and choking Fran rushes to the entranceways and is thrown back every time. Mickey is imitating the alarms and hurling himself against the walls, the floor, in response to Fran.

Fran: Let me out! I can't get out!

Finally she collapses. The doctor rushes to her. The lights return to normal.

Mickey: So what does all this tell us?

Krull: Mickey?

Mickey: The first two scenes were about acting, this one was about ...

Krull: Mickey.

Mickey: ... about escaping from real life. There's a sort of connection. ...

Krull: Give me a hand, Mickey. *He is bending over Fran.*

Mickey: *Rushing over.* Sorry. *He shakes Fran gently.* Fran? Fran? C'mon, Honey ...

Krull: Must have gotten a little carried away.

Mickey: *To Krull.* Water or something?

Krull: Where?

Mickey: Try the washrooms or something. I don't know.

Krull: Are there washrooms?

Mickey: Even fictitious characters have to piss.

Krull: Don't be crude.

Mickey: Where'd you get the booze in the first act.

Krull: Off the props table. Where else?

Mickey: Look on the props table.

Krull: *Starting off.* All right. *Turning back.* No, forget it. We're not doing a scene right now. There won't be any props for this.

Mickey: You're scared, aren't you?

Krull: Me? No.

Mickey: You scared of going offstage.

Krull: No, of course not. . . .

Mickey: Afraid you'll puff out?

Krull: Lay off.

Mickey: It's all right.

Mickey puts Fran's head down and leaves. Krull waits for a moment watching the entrance. Mickey does not return. Krull moves towards Fran. He folds up one of the costumes and puts it under her head.

Krull: Mickey?

No answer. He folds Fran's hand. Still no Mickey. Fran begins to groan and move. Suddenly she comes to and sees Krull bending over her.

Fran: Hi.

Krull: Hello.

Fran: Did we get out? *She sits up and looks around.* I guess not, eh?

Krull: I guess not.

Fran: That's it, then, our last chance. I'm sorry.

Krull: No, no. It wasn't your fault. You have wonderful flair, wonderful spontaneity.

Fran: Thanks, Krull.

Krull: No substitute for control and technique of course.

Fran: Thanks.

Krull: But fascinating to watch . . . fascinating.

Fran: I thought it would work, I really did. You know, between the heat and the fire and the hallucinations . . .

Krull: Pride goeth before a fall.

Fran: What good were they . . . our stories?

Krull: Our attempts to escape?

Fran: Yeah. What good were they?

Krull: So here we are then. For the duration.

Fran: Until the end.

Krull: Well, this isn't a bad place to spend our time. We can do all kinds of little things. You know, vaudville sketches, one-acts, if we can find a few scripts around the place. Perhaps we could work up something fairly major . . . although the cast is somewhat small. . . .

Fran: *Suddenly.* Where's Mickey?

No response.

Fran: Where is he?

Krull: Oh, he . . . he went for some water.

Fran: Oh.

Krull: He's taking a long time to get back. *Pause.* I should have gone myself. I didn't want to. I'm feeling less and less comfortable going off.

She goes to an entrance and peers out.

Fran: I see what you mean. It's almost . . . it's like kind of closing in. Mickey's out there in all of that. Poor guy. He's a good person, Mickey. We've been in a lot of things together. People took to him . . . *take* to him right away, don't you think?

Krull shrugs.

Fran: I remember the first time I met him. Do you remember the first time you met him?

Krull: No.

Fran: I said to myself, "Here's something new in my life. Here's a new person." I thought he'd be an adventure. . . . He had a special kind of humor. People were starting to imitate his style.

Krull: Were they?

Fran: Sure, all the time. Didn't you notice?

Krull: I guess I wasn't following closely enough.

Fran: I don't think he was having as much fun in the last couple of years. A lot of the joy had gone out of it. Do you think he'll make it back?

Krull: I'm sorry . . . I can't say. . . .

She begins to sob.

Krull: Perhaps you would like . . .

Fran: *Taking his handkerchief.* Thanks.

Mickey: *Becoming visible in the aisle of the theatre.* Are you okay, Fran?

Fran: I'll be all right in a minute. *Take.* Hi Mickey!

Krull: Thank God.

Mickey: Why?

Krull: We thought we might have lost. . . . Never mind. Where's the water?

Mickey: *Coming to the stage.* I couldn't find it.

Fran: Where were you?

Mickey: Trying to find some water. So. How are things going?

Fran: Oh, great, great.

Krull: Fine, fine.

Mickey: What happened to you? You were out cold.

Fran: I don't remember. Sarah Bernhardt, I guess.

Mickey: Oh.

Everybody appreciates the little joke. They fall silent.

Krull: *Finally.* What's it like?

Mickey: What?

Fran: Out there.

Mickey: Oh, that. Well, it's not much. *He doesn't want to say more but finally.* It's dark.

Krull: Dark.

Mickey: I got lost. There are a lot of passageways. They're pitch black. I couldn't help it. In some of the passages I felt cold breath blowing on the back of my neck.

Krull sings "Inkadink" to himself softly.

Mickey: I thought I'd never find my way. Then I was back here. Sorry about the water.

Fran: Don't worry about it.

Mickey: I was wishing I had a light. I hated being that scared. I was wishing you were there . . . you aren't afraid of these things . . . are you?

She doesn't answer.

Mickey: These mysteries. You're not afraid, are you?

No response.

Mickey: So what do we do now?

They all sit down in separated parts of the stage. After a time Mickey begins to laugh. The others look at him.

Mickey: Did I ever tell you about my friend Harry? I used to play golf with Harry. What a son of a bitch. Handicap of God knows what — something astronomical — and still he always whips the pants off me. And it's not just a matter of: "Harry . . . congratulations." "Thanks, Mickey . . . better luck next time." He humiliates me! "I don't know why I play golf with you, Mickey. It's boring. You're pitiful. Get lost." Anyway one day down at the club house we spot Jesus Christ in the locker room. We are both very surprised. Harry says, "I didn't know you liked golf." He says, "Thought I'd give it a try. I wanted to see where everybody spends Sunday." Harry says, "You wanna make it a threesome?" "Why not," says the Lord. We toss. I tee off. I do my usual lousy shot into a sandtrap. Harry is the same patronizing son of bitch. Then he drives a spectacular one — pin high, drops within two feet of the cup — good even for Harry. So listen what he says to the Lord. "Don't let that throw you," he says. "Just do your best." So, Jesus gives the golf ball a kind of awkward slam — you could tell it was the first time — and the thing flies off in the opposite direction to the green. It goes flying out over the clubhouse roof towards the highway. Harry is rolling on the ground . . . doubled up with laughter. You could tell the whole history of Christianity had been discredited in one stroke. Anyway just as the ball gets out there a semi-trailer comes roaring down the road and the ball lands on roof of the semi, bounces off into a lake and sinks. A minute or two and a fish comes up and spews the ball onto shore! A squirrel grabs it and takes it up a tree! A bolt of lightning comes out of a cloud and splits the tree! The ball bounces up into the air. An eagle swoops down and catches it and soars into the sky, drops the ball onto the wing of a passing Air Canada DC9. It falls off. A twister blows in out of nowhere and deposits the ball onto the green for a perfect hole in one. I'm watching Harry and Harry is watching the ball with his mouth open. Finally he turns to Jesus and he says, "Are you going to fool around or are you going to play golf?"

The others laugh.

Mickey: Yeah. *He is happier.* You still want a drink of water? *He heads off.*

Fran: No . . . it's okay.

He returns.

Fran: If I get thirsty we can do a play about a woman at a drinking fountain. *Laughs again.* Golf. What made you think of that?

Mickey: I don't know. I identify with it.

Krull: He thinks he's Jesus Christ.

Mickey: I think I'm the golf ball.

Krull: *After a moment.* Let's do a play about a classical actor . . . at the peak of his career . . . a man who wants to get off the stage occasionally and sit back and just enjoy his international reputation.

Mickey: Let's do a play about getting sloshed.

Krull: I may have passed it, though. My peak.

Fran: Surely not.

Krull: People don't think of me much when they're casting anymore.

Fran: I can't believe that.

Krull: I belong to the old school. Nobody needs the old school anymore.... No one wants to hear beautiful language spoken beautifully.

Fran: People probably think you're out of their price range....

Krull: I work cheap. If I told you what I'm doing this for you'd be embarrassed. This is my first stage play this year. I'm not getting offers anymore, Fran. If things keep up like this I shall have to begin accepting commercials.

Fran: I didn't know.

Krull: Few do. I have my pride.

Mickey: I'm always getting offers. The sound of the phone used to set the heart a-thumping. Now, I don't want to go anymore, I don't want to do anymore. Why, eh? Why?

Krull: Mickey, you have a career stretching out before you, a shining highway of opportunity. I wish I were in your place.

Fran: Come on, Mickey . . . you still like it, don't you — the Biz?

Mickey: There's no business like show business....

Krull: You can take the boy out of the theatre — under normal circumstances — but you can't take the theatre out of the boy....

Fran: *To Krull.* Maybe he's just tired of playing games.

Mickey: Maybe.

Fran: I'm getting that way. I'd like to do something real, something *for* somebody.

Mickey: Yeah. But who?

Fran: Anybody.

Mickey: You know those beggars I told you about . . . the ones that used to stop me on the way to the theatre? I never gave them any money . . .

Krull: Once you start you never . . .

Mickey: . . . except once. It was this old guy, see. And he's sitting in a corner out of the wind and he's got his hat in front of him, a cane across his knees, like this, and he's strumming the cane and he's singing, *(in a hoarse monotone,)* "You are my sunshine, my only sunshine. . . . You make me happy . . . " I walked past him and then I cracked up and I went back and threw some money in his hat. I couldn't believe it.

Krull: That's pitiful.

Fran: You gotta admire the guy. Street theatre, right?

Krull: But what did it get him?

Fran: A couple of bucks.

Mickey: Fifty cents, actually.

Krull: Surely you're not saying our lives are like that of a beggar in the streets, are you?

Mickey: Just better paid.

Fran: Only slightly.

Krull: Acting is a noble profession.

Fran: How?

Pause.

Mickey: Tell us.

Krull: Just a second. Just a second. *Pause.*

Well . . . we elevate people's minds, sometimes. We . . . er . . . raise the spirits of the odd . . . perhaps we have on occasion brought a smile to the lips of a depressed or even suicidal personality. And once in a while — of course you wouldn't want a steady diet of this sort of thing — but once in a while we challenge our audiences. *Taken with the idea.* Yes . . . we challenge our audiences to make the world a better place . . . you see? Challenge. Surely we don't have to justify our lives beyond that . . . do we? Well?

Mickey: It doesn't do it for me, Krull. I want more.

Krull: But what more is there?

Pause, and then Fran and Mickey begin to search through the script again.

Krull: What are you doing?

Mickey: There's gotta be something.

Fran: There is, there's one more.

Krull: Is there really?

Pause.

Mickey: One more?

Fran: The last movement.

Krull: There is indeed. So we perform once more and then we're finished.

Mickey: *Alarmed.* Finished?

Krull: Who gets the lead part?

Mickey: Maybe we should put it off as long as we can.

Fran: We've all been assigned supporting roles.

Mickey: Don't you think we should put it off?

Krull: Supporting who?

Mickey: Let's do something else.

Fran: *Strangely.* We can't. We're in the middle of it. Look.

Krull: *Reading over her shoulder.* "Let's do something else."

Mickey: "We can't. We're in the middle of it. Look."

Krull: What's that line?

Fran: "It's cold, isn't it, all of a sudden . . . "

And all of a sudden it is.

Krull: It *is* cold.

They look about for coats, put them on like cloaks and huddle together.

Mickey: Better?

Krull: Not much.

Fran: *Softly.* Now.

The lights begin to change. There is the sound of a storm and the actors huddle closer against the cold.

Fran: There's an owl watching me.

Krull: An owl?

Mickey: Where?

Fran: It has one eye shut and light gleams in the other.

Krull: I see nothing. There's nothing to be seen in here.

Mickey: Do owls live in caves?

Fran: This one does.

Mickey: Maybe it's a bat.

Krull: Bats don't watch.

Fran: I'm caught in its one long shaft of cold light.

Krull: It does feel uncomfortable in here . . . like someone watching. Could it be that one of their? . . .

Mickey: Don't even think it.

Fran: Nobody knows about this place, I promise.

Mickey: I'm cold.

Fran: This is a place where they would never dare to come. It's also a place where weird things happen. Nobody ever feels comfortable here.

Mickey: We should have stayed down there . . . where it's green and there are trees. . . .

Fran: Down there we'd be dead.

Mickey: *Reflecting.* That's true, too.

Krull: Better dead down there instead of starving to death up here.

Mickey: Yeah!

Krull: *Second thought.* No.

Fran: We are not here forever.

Krull: *Gloomily.* I know.

Fran: I mean . . .

Mickey: You've told us a hundred times. *Mimicking.* "I'm taking you to a hiding place — a sanctuary from our enemies. . . . "

Krull: "A holy mountain where we can fast for a while and seek guidance." We know, we know.

Mickey: I wish I'd never gotten mixed up with you in the first place.

Krull: Same goes for me.

Fran: I thought you were committed.

Krull: We should have been.

Fran: To the cause. To the cause. I never promised things would always go well. A few days ago we were riding the crest of the wave. Now we're in a trough. But it was worth it wasn't it? You have to admit things were pretty spectacular for a while.

Mickey: Sure, sure. But you antagonized people.

Krull: The wrong kind of people.

Fran: I spoke only the truth.

Mickey: There's a time and a place for everything.

Krull: Might have been better if you'd let me deliver the messages.

Fran: Why?

Krull: Well I'm closer to their sort of people. . . . I've got background. Besides, the great prophets have all been men. It's because of our voices. We can make the words ring out. Women tend to get shrill.

Mickey: *To Fran.* You should have sent me with the message, really.

Krull: You . . . that's a laugh.

Mickey: That's the point. Laughing is the point. I could have put things in a more humorous sort of way. Kind of gotten in below their belt so to speak. Gradually, bit by bit, I think we could have effected real change: gotten rid of the leaders one by one . . . returned power to the people . . . stopped the exploitation of the masses . . . all that sort of thing. *To Fran.* But no; you had to have a showdown.

Krull: If you hadn't pulled off the miracle, we'd be sleeping in our own bed tonight. Nobody likes miracles. They're too ostentatious.

Fran: You think it was too much?

Mickey: It was kind of. I mean it's one thing for a prophet to claim to be telling the truth . . . it's another to prove it. A lot of the politicians took offense.

Krull: Not to mention their religious advisors.

Mickey: Just to call down fire from heaven like that and burn up the monument to Mammon like that . . . lacked . . . I don't know . . . taste.

Fran: I found the golden calf offensive.

Krull: But a lot of up-to-date thinkers are saying we've been too quick about that. Material wealth ought to be thought of as a sort of spiritual concept.

Fran: Greed is greed. I know idolatry when I see it. Spiritual concept. Hah. It was time for confrontation.

Krull: It's no use telling you anything, is it? You're so damn sure of yourself. . . .

Mickey: If you had to destroy anything, why didn't you pick something cheaper? Do you know the price of gold these days?

Fran: But I didn't actually do the destroying myself.

Krull: Oh, that again.

Fran: I didn't.

Krull: Well, just who got mad then? And who called down the fire?

Mickey: *Looking out the entrance way.* It's sure they won't track us down for a while — there's a regular blizzard blowing up out here. *To Fran.* So you'd better get at it, eh?

Fran: At what?

Mickey: The mumbo jumbo. You know the spiritual guidance stuff.

Krull: Yeah. Get at it. That's what we need . . . confer with the powers that be, why don't you.

Mickey: And while you're at it tell them some fire would be nice right about now . . . just a little bonfire maybe.

Fran: I resent this skepticism. After everything I've done for you. After the faithfulness you have always shown me. This sounds very much like apostasy.

Mickey: Look, it was all right down there. . . . I mean we didn't have a lot to do anyway. I didn't have job. *Points to Krull.* He didn't need a job, being a genteman of leisure. Along you come prophesying judgement in the land and challenge for change and all that. So we signed up. Sure it was kind of exciting, pretending there were greater things than we dreamed of . . . that there were expectations from up there . . . that we could talk to the powers above and all that. It was even a lot of fun shocking people and spouting off about how the society was going to the devil . . . but I thought we were just providing entertainment.

Krull: I certainly didn't think we'd get people mad at us.

Mickey: I wasn't counting on this. Look at us. Fugitives. Holed up in a cave in a mountain.

Krull: *Mumbling.* With a crazy lady who thinks an owl is shafting her with his eyeball.

Fran: Pardon?

Krull: So if this is a place where you can get the word, you'd better get it quick.

Mickey: Yeah, show us. And no hokey pokey this time.

Fran: All right, all right. *Praying like she did at the beginning.* Oh Lord, we've provoked the fury of the unrighteous, we've afflicted the well-heeled and not healed the afflicted. They're hunting us down like wild game. And the bottom line is we're scared. . . .

Mickey: Not me. . . .

Krull: Speak for yourself. . . .

Fran: *To them.* You're not scared?

Mumbles.

Fran: We're scared. We were just trying to make improvements and we've been cited as subversives. There's a price on our heads. We've been chased away from our homes. We're holed up here and we aren't sure what we're doing any more, and frankly, we wouldn't mind if you told us.

The wind increases.

Fran: Well, I'd rather stay in here. All right. All right.

Mickey: What?

Fran: We're supposed to go and stand on the top of the mountain.

Mickey: Oh no.

Krull: Forget it.

Mickey: Right, forget it. Tell whoever that we're not moving. Talk to us in here.

Fran: On the mountain top. There or nowhere.

Krull: That's the word?

Fran: Those are the terms.

Mickey: You don't know how cold it is out there.

Fran: *Starting out.* It's up to you.

Krull: Well, we've come this far. . . . *He starts to follow.*

Mickey: All right, all right. This had better be worth it.

They struggle out against the blizzard and climb. A stepladder perhaps becomes the mountain.

Mickey: Maybe we could just stand on the side of the mountain.

Fran: Up.

Krull: You should have told us about this in the beginning.

Fran: I didn't know in the beginning.

Krull: Some prophet.

Mickey: The wind is blowing the mountain apart! God!

Fran: No, it's not God. It's wind!

Mickey: I can't hear you!

Fran: I said it's wind!

The Others: We know that!

The wind dies down. The sun comes out.

Krull: Thank heaven that's over. *Suddenly.* This isn't a mountain. This is a goddamned volcano.

Mickey: *Looking down.* You're right.

Krull: You led us up a goddamned volcano!

There is a great rumble and the earth shakes.

Mickey: This volcano is a live volcano.

Krull: This volcano is about to blow up. *To Fran.* See what you've done. We should have stayed down and taken our chances.

Mickey: Help!

They all save each other from falling down the mountainside. Finally the shaking stops and there is another roar as the stage becomes ruddy with flame.

Fran: This is where we burn to death.

Krull: I knew it. I knew it.

Mickey: I wish I'd never laid eyes on you.

Fran: The feeling is mutual.

Krull: Is this your supreme being?

Fran: Of course not. This is nothing compared to God.

They are at the top of the mountain.

Fran: Prepare to die and meet thy maker.

Mickey: I don't want to!

Krull: Me neither!

Fran: Prepare to die and meet thy maker.

Krull: Put it off!

Mickey: We can always come back later!

The fire and the roar of it reach a crescendo and then cease abruptly.

Mickey: What's happening?

Fran: Listen.

Krull: I hear nothing.

Mickey: Just silence.

They are awe-struck.

Fran: A silence like the ringing of bells.

Mickey: A silence that whispers.

Fran: You can hear?

Krull: A silence full of voices.

Fran: An awful silence.

Pause. Do we ourselves perceive something in the silence, something almost at the threshold of hearing?

Fran: There's hope here.

Mickey: If I could believe that . . .

Fran: Listen.

Krull: I can almost hear what it is. . . .

Mickey: What's it saying? What?

Fran: To make kings and prophets.

Krull: Prophets?

Mickey: Kings?

Fran: Kings who will comfort the prophets and prophets who will judge the kings and people who will rise up in ecstasy and dance a wild dance of freedom and kindness. . . .

Mickey: All that?

Krull: Are you sure?

Fran: Listen.

Mickey: Listen.

Krull: Yes.

And the sound of music rises and the lights change. The actors stand, stunned for a while before they begin to take off their cloaks.

Mickey: That changed things somehow.

Fran: I can feel a difference.

Fran: The air feels fresh again . . . like after a warm summer shower. . . .

Mickey: Have we gotten out, somehow? No . . . we're still here. . . . This is still the stage. . . .

Fran: It's the still edge of a volcano . . . isn't it? No. . . .

Krull: But whose scene was it? *The music disappears — and then. . . .* My goodness! I can see the audience. . . .

So do the others.

Mickey: Funny thing about listening to silence. It clears the mind somehow.

Fran: I knew we would be able to see them, finally. And there they are.

Krull: Just the audience I would have wanted. Wonderful looking bunch . . . most of them.

Mickey: Let me try to analyse this. . . . I can't.

Fran: In that scene . . . it's like when we really faced the idea that there might be nothing there. . . . Then somehow . . . we found there was — at least there could be — something.

Mickey: First nothing and then *voilà* . . . like the moment the lights go down at the beginning of a play: first nothing and then . . . everything.

Fran: Yeah . . .

Light begins to pour through an entrance way.

Krull: The doors are opening.

Fran: They are!

They watch the light rise.

Fran: Amazing.

Krull: So we can go out now.

Mickey: Uhuh.

Krull: But what will happen to us?

Fran: Don't be afraid. When we walk out there we'll find people — millions of them — all the people in the world . . . and somewhere there'll be an old man . . . sitting on a lawn chair, an old actor, muttering away to himself, worried about his performance. . . .

Mickey: And the comedian?

Krull: Of course. We'll see him trying to work out a new routine . . . *To Fran.* . . . Right?

Fran: Right.

Mickey: And a woman somewhere who can't take life on earth and tries to fly among the planets.

Fran: Yes, she'll be there.

Krull: But we did well by them, I think.

Mickey: Of course.

Krull: We caught their essence and now it's over.

Fran: Except for the exit.

Mickey: I don't really want to go yet.

Krull: Actually I don't either.

Fran: Think of all these people. Some of them are going out for after-the-theatre supper and some of them want to see the news . . . and there are baby sitters to think of . . .

Mickey: We've got us to think of.

Fran: . . . and more.

Krull: What more?

Fran: You know, being kings and prophets — powerful like kings, inspired like prophets, and all that.

Mickey: Oh great. They get to be inspired and we get to be what? Memories.

Krull: That's our job, isn't it! Making kings and prophets. Do you think we did?

Fran: *Sizing them up.* Little kings and minor prophets. At least they know what they can try for.

Mickey: We never know what effect we've had . . .

Krull: It's the price we pay, Mickey, for our brief moment of glory. Once I worked in a small theatre in a small town that only ran plays for two weeks. On opening night they would put up the closing notice in the Green Room. It was like a sentence of death the day you're born. It's the price we pay. We act. We walk off the stage and there's nothing left. Inkadinkadink. . . .Well . . . except them. . . . *Indicating the audience.* They're left.

Mickey: Right.

Fran: Come on . . . give them back to themselves. Let's take our exits.

Mickey: How did you get so courageous all of a sudden? All right, *Looking fearfully towards the entrances . . .* who goes first?

But Fran is already on her way out one entrance.

Mickey: Fran!

She is gone.

Krull: So be it. *Krull goes next — another way.*

Mickey: Krull! *Krull begins to go . . . hesitates, spots a prop cane, strums it like a guitar while singing in an old beggar's voice.*

You are my sunshine, my only sunshine . . .

A wave of happiness sweeps over him. He makes a little gesture that says to the audience, "Your turn," and he leaves.

THE END

Afternoon of the Big Game

§

First Performance

Afternoon of the Big Game was first performed January 16, 1988 at The Globe Theatre, Regina with the following cast:

Ogie — *James Timmins*

Diane — *Diana Belshaw*

Kevin — *Kevin Bundy*

Bill — *Richard Thornton*

Floyd — *Thomas Hauff*

Sharyl — *Donna White*

Sports Announcer — *David McKnight*

The production was directed by Kenneth Kramer and designed by Jo Dibb. Lighting was designed by John Gilmore. The stage manager was Deborah Adelstein.

With many thanks to the Blythe Festival, where this play was first workshopped August 21, 1987, under the direction of Diana Belshaw.

Characters:

Ogie: Old

Diane: Ogie's daughter. Middle aged

Kevin: Diane's son. Teen-ager

Bill: Diane's second husband. Middle aged

Floyd Stark: Bill's supervisor. Middle aged

Sharyl Stark: Floyd's wife. Middle aged

The Sports Announcer

Scene

The basement rec room of a suburban split level house in Regina. It is 1987, early autumn. There is the suggestion of a very modern, very large television set — but the device is somewhat metaphorical. Entrance is down a stairway.

Photo Credit: Patrick Pettit
Thomas Hauff as Floyd, Kevin Bundy as Kevin, Donna White as Sharyl, Diana
Belshaw as Diane
Globe Theatre, Regina, 1987.

Act One

Ogie (O.G.) walks on stage alone. He is in his seventies — not ancient, but old enough. His face is weathered, intelligent, informed. He is a man of strong character and only gradually do we detect that the strength of his intellect and body has been undermined. There is a slight difficulty in forming words, in keeping thoughts together.

Ogie: *To the audience.* I do not think this is where I live. I should not be welcoming you as though. . . . Were you met at the door? Sent down here? They told me, the people who live here, that you were coming. I think they told me. It's very important, this game, eh? I understand it is . . . a . . . very . . . game. Well, since you are here, would you be interested in a few you might call them *pre-game activities.* Who are the players? *Quick grin.* I'll introduce you to the players. First there is my daughter, Diane. *Calling.* Diane? *As he waits.* They call this the rec room. We used to call them basements. . . . Diane? Diane's my daughter, the pride of the litter. She's twenty years old. She's in her third year at the university. She won't take guff from anybody. She has principles and she stands by them. She's going down to Selma, Alabama and march with those freedom marchers next week. What do you think of that? Yes, she gets called a radical and what not . . . but nobody has ever explained to me adequately why that's not a compliment.

Diane has entered. She is middle aged, dressed for company, not at all what we have been led to expect. She is far from being tough. There is a look of vulnerability about her. She is bringing down a tray with party snacks.

Diane: Ogie?

Ogie: Yes?

Diane: Who are you talking to?

Ogie: Your guests.

Diane: They aren't here yet.

Ogie: Who are these people then?

Diane: They aren't here yet.

Ogie: Where's Diane? I thought Diane was coming.

Diane: Look at me, Dad.

Ogie: *To the audience.* "Dad" she calls me. But I've never seen her before.

Diane: I'm Diane. *As she busies herself about the room.* Try and stay with us today, Ogie. I want it to be nice. Do you remember who's coming? Bill's supervisor and his wife are coming. Bill's supervisor.

But this is too much for him and he wanders off.

Diane: Why don't you warm up the TV.

Ogie: The teevee.

Diane: Don't touch anything. Don't eat the dip.

Ogie: What kind of dip?

Diane: Crab. Don't eat it.

Ogie: I like crab.

Diane: Yet. Don't eat it yet. I want it nice when they come.

Ogie: Virginal.

Diane: Yes.

Ogie: Virgin crab.

She exits.

Ogie: *To audience.* I don't know her. The next player is . . .

Kevin enters. He is a teen-ager at an awkward stage. He turns on the television set.

Kevin: Hi, Gramps.

Ogie: My son, Kevin . . . no . . . my *grandson* Kevin. He looks like . . . *Pause.*

Kevin: You know something?

Ogie: He reminds me of . . .

Kevin: This room should be for serious football fans only. If they want to frig around they should go upstairs.

Ogie: What was that?

Kevin: Every time there is a really important game we get guests, right? We hafta get guests. Big football fans — they know everything about football — they're really *enthusiastic*. So they get down here and five minutes . . . two minutes . . . they're friggin' around yackin' about barbecue sauce or some stupid thing . . . what kinda firewood you should use. . . . *Imitating.* "Oh, I like birch — it smells so nice. . . . " *Another voice.* "Well, personally I like spruce — a little cheaper . . . easier to keep going . . . and boy it makes for a dandy fire. . . . " I don't know, all's I know you can't hear the play-by-play.

Ogie: Life is full of injustice, Kevin.

Kevin: It is. And there's nothing I can do about it. I can't shift them upstairs. It's not my house. What can I do about it?

Ogie: I don't know.

Kevin: I'll get my Walkman and plug it in my ears and maybe then I'll be able to listen to the friggin' football game — even though I bet they all said that they were coming over to watch the big game . . . the game that will decide whether or not we even have a chance at the playoffs — or whether we're going to lose again the way we've been losing all my life.

Ogie: Who's playing?

Kevin: *Gives him a look that reads "Et tu, Brute" and supreme pity.* You used to be such a great fan. *Exits.*

Ogie: *To the audience.* Ah, the scorn of the young. It was a joke. I know who's playing. Let's bring Diane's husband down here. *Pause.* Allen. Don't let him fool you . . . he may seem like a shy, artistic sensitive type . . . but he's sharp as a tack. Just the kind of young fellah I thought she'd go for. Interested in politics, too. I like him a lot.

Bill descends the stairs. He is sleek, middle-aged, successful, supremely self-confident . . . for the time being.

Bill: Everything okay down here? Got the telly going, Ogie?

Ogie: I guess you're supposed to be Allen.

Bill: Oh, geeze. No, I'm not Allen. I am *Bill*. I've only been married to your daughter for eight years. She left Allen. Got that straight?

Ogie: More or less.

Bill: And please don't go on about Allen when the Starks get here.

Ogie: Who?

Diane: *From the head of the stairs.* Bill?

Bill: The Starks. *Up the stairway.* Yeah?

Diane: I don't think we have enough ice.

Bill: I bought a bag of party ice. I filled up the ice bucket.

Diane: You think of everything!

Ogie still looks blank.

Bill: That's who's coming, Ogie. Sharyl and Floyd. Floyd works on the floor above me . . . when he's working.

A doorbell chimes.

There they are. *Quickly.* Don't tell Floyd I said that, Ogie. I was kidding . . . he's my boss . . . okay? A very fine man, Floyd. And Sharyl, that's his wife.

Doorbell again.

Calling. Nobody getting that? *Exit.*

Ogie: *Confused.* Did I mention Diane's husband? *Frown.* I don't believe that is the man. *He dismisses that.* It must be clear by now that you are seeing things through my eyes. . . . And you might find a problem with this. I get things a litte mixed up sometimes. Either that or things *are* a little mixed up. They say my short-term memory cuts in and out on me . . . there's a kind of a short in the wiring somewhere. That's what they say, although I don't discount the possibility that . . . it's actually the world that's changed. I find things don't hold together. It's getting harder to proceed from A to B without something getting in the way. 'Course it's always been a struggle, human beings being what they are. Some people get from A to B and want to stay at B, and other people hanker to get back to A again and let's not even talk about reaching for point C. *Pause.* I'm not sure whether you're following me. *Sighs.*

There are noises down the stairs.

So much for the pre-game activities. Get yourself set for the kick-off.

Diane: No, no, you're not late . . .

Floyd: She had to wear green and white tights, for crying out loud.

Sharyl: Oh, stop it, Floyd . . .

Floyd: And she couldn't find them. "Sharyl, wear anything, we're already late." "Oh no," she says. "I gotta have my green and white . . . it's a Rider game."

They descend into view. Sharyl is wearing something expensive and impressive. Not green and white tights.

Floyd: I says, "You want to be a cheerleader at your age? Come on!" If she'd had her way we'd still be looking for them.

Sharyl: Honestly, you just go on and on.

Floyd: Sometimes, Sharyl, I like to catch the beginning of things.

Bill: Aw, the game hasn't even started yet.

Floyd: Just sometimes.

Bill: What are you worried about? You don't have to worry. Sharyl, you look good in anything.

Floyd: I told her that. . . .

Sharyl: You did not. Thank you, Bill.

Floyd: Well, I meant it.

Bill: You're welcome.

Diane: Same thing happens to us. Doesn't it, Bill?

Sharyl: What an interesting rec room.

Diane: Do you think?

Sharyl: Hm-hm.

Diane: Bill decorated it.

Floyd: *To Bill.* 'Dja do the fireplace yourself?

Bill: Yep. And I'm putting in a wet bar over there.

Floyd: Handy.

Diane: Make yourselves comfortable. Have some dip. It's crab. Just make yourselves acquainted. Bill?

Bill: They already know each other.

They have a coded signal which means, "get their drink orders, stupid."

Bill: Right. What's your poison?

Sharyl: Poison?

Ogie: I haven't heard anybody say that for a while.

Bill: You name it, we got it.

Floyd: Beer?

Bill: You got it.

Sharyl: Anything?

Bill: Anything.

Sharyl: A spritzer please.

Bill: You got it.

Floyd: Light?

Bill: *On his way.* Right.

Floyd: Thanks.

Bill: *Stopping on the stairs.* Ogie?

Ogie: Er . . . *Long pause.*

Bill: *Giving up.* Forget it. *Leaving.* I'll bring you something.

There is an awkward moment between Oggie and the others.

Diane: This is my father. He's living with us. Sharyl and Floyd.

Sharyl: *Stretching out her hand.* Mr . . .

Diane: He likes to be called Ogie.

Floyd: *Shaking hands.* Ogie, pleased to meet you.

Ogie: Pleased . . . I . . .

Diane: Well grab a good seat. . . . Any bets?

Ogie: *Wandering to the audience.* I thought I was being introduced to somebody.

There is a large sports press booth hanging over the stage. It has been scarcely noticeable but now suddenly it dominates the stage. Lights rise up on a CBC Television "sports announcer."

Announcer: The CFL on the CBC!

Music.

Kevin: *Running down the stairs.* It's on, it's on. *He carries a Walkman radio which he will plug into his ears whenever the conversation gets too loud.*

Announcer: I'm Clark Morgan here in Exhibition Park on the beautiful shore of Lake Ontario. I'll be bringing you the exciting play-by-play of today's contest between the Saskatchewan Roughriders and the Toronto Argonauts. The Saskatchewan team is presently residing in the basement of the Canadian Football League. Toronto is on a winning streak having won three out of its last three games. Nevertheless, we could still be in for a very interesting afternoon. In an interview taped earlier today, Toronto head coach, Bob O'Billovich told CBC reporters, *Puts on an O'Billovich cap,* "You can say what you like about the Saskatchewan team . . . but you can't ever take 'em for granted." *Takes off the cap.* The teams are lining up. David Ridgway will be kicking off for the Riders . . .

Everybody lines up in front of the television set. Bill comes down the stairs with a tray of drinks.

Bill: Here we are, everybody. *And serves them by standing in front of the screen. The spot goes out on the announcer.*

Announcer: The ball is on the tee . . .

Floyd: You know, I could never build a fireplace. That's an accomplishment.

Diane: Bill's got a knack.

Floyd: Got your wood for the winter?

Bill: Yep.

Announcer: There's the kickoff.

Bill: Birch.

Sharyl: *Taking her drink.* Oh, you're a sweetie, Bill.

Floyd: Birch.

Bill: Cut it myself. Did you meet Ogie?

Floyd: *Taking his drink.* Thanks, Guy. Yes.

Bill: He's kind of our mascot for the game . . . right, Ogie?

Announcer: Toronto Argonaut Darrell Smith receiving . . .

Bill: I brought some ginger ale, Kevin.

Announcer: Smith puts on the speed . . .

Bill: Here.

Roar of crowd swells.

Announcer: Look at him go.

Kevin is disgusted but can't say anything.

Diane: This is mine?

Announcer: The fifty.

Bill: That's yours, Sweetie.

Announcer: The forty.

Diane: Cheers.

Announcer: The thirty.

Bill: Wait a minute, wait a minute. *He gets rid of the tray and sets his drink.* Cheers.

As Bill moves out from in front of the TV set we hear the announcer and the sound of a crowd going wild. The spot comes back on the sportscast desk.

Announcer: And he's brought down on the twenty-eight. An incredible return on that kickoff by Darrell Smith of the Toronto Argonauts . . .

Kevin: What happened? What happened?

Floyd: Great start.

Sharyl: What a nice drink. What kind of wine are you using, Bill?

Bill: Just something we had kicking around in the fridge. What is that stuff, honey?

Kevin: The twenty-eight yard line. Geeze.

Diane: You bought it. Chateau something.

Announcer: The Boatmen are lined up at the Riders' thirty yard line. . . . We're waiting for the snap . . .

Floyd: Bill, how are you getting along with . . . you know . . . your assignment?

Bill: At work?

Announcer: There it is . . .

Floyd: Yeah.

Sharyl: Here we go, shop talk.

Diane: Men.

Sharyl: Men.

Announcer: And it's a handoff to . . .

Bill: Oh, it's tough.

Announcer: No it isn't! That was a fake. . . . It's a pass to Fenerty and . . . *Crowd roar* . . . it is incomplete.

Kevin: Good.

Bill: Not that I can't handle it. But you wouldn't be human if it didn't get to you some times. Actually, it's easier than I thought it'd be. I just take the attitude: "Well hell, it's gotta be done. Somebody has to do it."

Perhaps the announcer is mouthing the play-by-play at this point. We and Ogie are tuned out.

Floyd: Should have been done a long time ago.

Bill: Overdue . . . right. *Frankly.* And now that I'm at it, I find it interesting. Every case has a different twist, you know? There's a different challenge every time. Actually it can be even . . . well . . . kind of fun.

Sharyl: What do you do, Bill?

Bill: I fire people.

Announcer: Renfroe lobs the ball just over the heads of the linemen and . . .

Ogie: Why do you do that?

Kevin: *Screaming.* Oh no!

Announcer: . . . the pass is complete.

Ogie: Eh?

Announcer: And the Argos have a first down on the Rider ten.

Ogie: Why?

Diane: *Involved in the game.* We're in trouble now.

Kevin: You said it.

Ogie: You.

Bill: *Surprised that Ogie is addressing him directly.* Huh?

Ogie: Why do you fire people?

Bill: Because it's my job, Ogie.

Ogie: Who do you work for?

Bill: I work for the Province. Why won't that stick with you? *To the others.* He asks me that two or three times a day. *Apologizing for the interruption.* Sorry.

Ogie: *To everybody.* I never could understand why Diane left her first husband for him.

Bill: Ogie.

Ogie: He is a perfectly nice fellow, of course . . . but he and she seemed opposite. *Searching for the word.* Diametrically.

Announcer: It is a long pass to Dwight Edwards . . .

Ogie: It shook me when she broke up with the first one — young Kevin's father. Bill here and I get along all right.

Announcer: . . . complete!

Ogie: But I liked the other one.

Bill: Diane, maybe your Dad could watch upstairs.

Diane: Why, what's the troub . . . ?

The crowd roars.

Announcer: And it's a touchdown! Toronto makes that important first touchdown against Saskatchewan only three minutes into the first quarter!

Diane: *Disgusted.* Oh, come on.

Kevin: Where's the defense?!

Ogie: What happened? *Everybody ignores him.* Did they score?

Diane: Yeah.

Sharyl: Who?

Floyd: Who do you think?

Kevin: Toronto.

Sharyl: Oh.

Announcer: And the kick is good. The Toronto Argonauts, seven. The Saskatchewan Roughriders, nothing. You are watching this game on the Canadian Broadcasting Corporation: The CFL on the CBC. *Fanfare.*

Vague sounds of a commercial.

Bill: Well, they'd better get their hind ends in gear, that's all I have to say.

Floyd: *To Ogie.* I hear you used to be in farming, er . . . Ogie.

Ogie: Farming? Yes, I used to be a farmer.

Floyd: A good sort of life, I suppose?

Ogie: Yes, it was a good life, you could say. Sometimes.

Floyd: And I suppose a struggle at other times?

Ogie: Yes, a struggle.

At this point a past memory cuts in. Since we are seeing things through Ogie's eyes, this should not be senile meandering but rather acute and real.

Ogie: It's going to be a struggle, boys, but I say we're going to have to go through with it.

Crowd roars.

Kevin: Oh, yeah! That's more like it.

Floyd: *To Ogie.* Pardon?

Ogie: I said we're going to have to go through with it.

Announcer: And so the Riders are in a pretty good field position to start their first drive of the game.

Ogie: The banks are robbing us. The big vested interests back East are robbing us. Seems like even the weather is robbing us . . . the wind is stealing the earth away. . . .

Announcer: The weatherman has given the fans here a fine afternoon to watch football.

Ogie: The rain? I guess the rain has just given up on us. So I say it's going to be a struggle.

Announcer: Saskatchewan Quarterback Jeff Bentrim back to throw . . .

Ogie: We all know how desperate things are.

Floyd: As a farmer . . .

Announcer: No, it is a handoff to Bender. . . .

Floyd: . . . how do you feel about free trade?

Ogie: Some of you can't hardly feed your young ones. . . . I hear tell of people starving to death. . . .

Announcer: It is Bender up the centre . . .

Ogie: The banks are foreclosing . . .

Announcer: . . . and Saskatchewan will not gain more than a yard or two on the play.

Ogie: We can't seem to win for trying.

Floyd: What is he talking about?

Ogie: We have to pull together or we'll go under.

Bill: Some ancient agitation.

Ogie: It's plain the system is against us. Well then, we have to change the system. It stands to reason.

Floyd: What was he, a CCFer?

Ogie: The CCF, yes. Why not?

Announcer: It is a Saskatchewan second down on the forty-eight yard line.

Ogie: Sure the government's to blame. But who put in the government? Oh, not you, eh? It's real hard to find anybody who actually voted for the government. The first time in the history of the province that a party has been elected with no votes.

Announcer: Bentrim back to pass . . .

Ogie: No, we did it to ourselves. We put them in there knowing full well how they operate. And surely to Moses, if the way the government operates is wrong, don't we have to start over again and rig up something else — something that'll operate right. And don't tell me about the other party. They had their chance and look what happened. Same damn thing.

Announcer: It's a long one. . . .

Ogie: Anyway, that's all I have to say. I'll sit down and listen to the rest o' ya.

Crowd roars.

Announcer: And Armstrong hauls it in and steps out of bounds. So it's Saskatchewan on the Toronto thirty-five, first and ten to go.

Floyd: Is he all right?

Bill: Ignore him.

Floyd: You have a lefty in the house.

Bill: Slightly demented died-in-the-wool socialist.

Floyd: Hard to find these days.

Bill: Thank the Lord, eh?

Floyd: That's how they used to think. Let the government do it all. Any problems with the economy of the country . . . then it's up to the government to solve it for us.

Ogie: What's the government for?

Bill: Blame everything on the government, eh Ogie? Too much rain? Blame it on the government. Too little rain? Blame it on the government. Can't sell your wheat? Blame it on the government.

Ogie: That's why we want to set up this new Co-operative Commonwealth Federation, you see . . . the CCF, a whole new system . . .

Bill: Ogie? This is Earth calling Ogie.

Diane: Don't, Bill.

Floyd: This is the 1980s, Ogie.

Bill: All that stuff's over with.

Ogie: *Dismayed.* It can't be . . .

Bill: You're living in the past.

Sudden roar from the crowd.

Announcer: Bentrim throws a beautiful pass. . . . Armstrong backing up and. . . . Oh! Interception!

Bill: Where are Lancaster and Reed when we need them?

Announcer: Rodney Harding of the Toronto Argonauts just rolling over the Riders.

Kevin: You think Lancaster never threw an interception?

Announcer: Look at him go.

Floyd: Not so as you'd remember.

Announcer: Nobody can even lay a hand on him. He's still moving. And it's a touchdown. The score is now thirteen for Toronto and zilch for the Saskatchewan team.

Kevin: Anyway there's no Lancaster anymore. There's no Reed. And things are rotten. The Riders are looking like my gym class at school. And it's not like they're playing the best team in the CFL.

Ogie: That's debatable. *He has their attention.* Toronto's looking better every game. They might go all the way this year.

Bill: Welcome back.

Announcer: The point after is good and Toronto leads by fourteen. Saskatchewan has yet to score.

Diane: *To the announcer.* We know, already. Don't rub it in.

Pause.

Bill: Do you remember the last year we went to the the Grey Cup? Almost won it, too.

Sharyl: What year was that?

Floyd: 1974.

Kevin: Against Ottawa?

Floyd: Right.

Kevin: '76.

Floyd: No it wasn't. It was 1974.

Kevin: The last time we went to the Grey Cup?

Floyd: Yeah.

Kevin: In Toronto.

Floyd: Yeah.

Kevin: Against Ottawa.

Floyd: That's what I said.

Kevin: 1976.

Bill: Kevin.

Kevin: But it was. And Ottawa won it in the last twenty seconds with a pass to Tony Gabriel.

Bill: Mr. Stark knows a lot about football, Son. Don't contradict him.

Floyd: *Moving to higher ground.* Of course 1966 was the game.

Kevin: You got that one right.

Floyd: I was there.

This garners respect from everybody.

Kevin: Really?

Floyd: Yeah, really. I was at that game.

Kevin whistles on the intake.

Sharyl: I didn't know that.

Floyd: You don't need to know everything.

Sharyl: No I don't, do I?

Floyd: No.

Sharyl: *To the others.* Of course we hadn't met then.

Floyd: I was on a special course ... leadership and business management ... you know the kind of thing. There was a big test coming up on the Monday, but chains couldn't have kept me at the books ... not that day. ...

Bill: I guess not!

Floyd: No sir. I bought a ticket off a scalper ... an arm and a leg! I ate peanut butter sandwiches for a month after that and let me tell you I *relished* every bite. That day was the best day of my life.

Diane: Oh, come on. Not the best.

Sharyl: Believe him. He means it.

Floyd: Oh, I can still see that final quarter. There's a touchdown on the very first play of the quarter. . . . Lancaster fires a shot straight through the line to George Reed . . .

Kevin: Campbell, wasn't it? *Catching himself.* Sorry.

Floyd: I meant Campbell — Hugh Campbell. But when George Reed ran thirty yards for that last touchdown, just high stepping it like some Lippizan stallion . . . I almost . . . excuse me, ladies, . . . well, let's say I almost had a bowel movement. The crowd went crazy. I mean, we went in there that season . . . we were the underdogs . . . maybe   twenty   to   one   against   our   winning. . . . There was a big headline in the *Vancouver Sun:* "Surprise! It's Saskatchewan." I never felt so proud of this place . . . never before, never since. Now, no matter how often we lose, I still see that Vancouver Grey Cup . . . kind of superimposed over the game like maybe a movie. . . . We've got a lot to be proud of. Don't let anybody tell you any different.

Ogie: Yep, we have a lot to be proud of. . . .

Floyd: Yeah.

Ogie: Wheat Pool, Co-ops, CCF . . .

Bill: We're talking football here, Ogie. Isn't it time for your nap?

Ogie: Nap?

Bill: Yeah.

Ogie: *Puzzled.* No. *Pause.* "No CCF Government will rest content until it has eradicated capitalism and put into operation the full programme of socialized planning which will lead to the establishment in Canada of the Co-operative Commonwealth." *Proudly.* You know where that came from? The Regina Manifesto, signed in 1933. I was there. I was at the signing! Of course, they changed it later on, cut out the bit about eradicating capitalism, about the same time that radical got to be a swear word. But that was it: 1933. Nothing wrong with my memory, eh?

Floyd: *Indicating the television.* Now, watch this.

Bill: *To Diana.* I told you this was a bad idea, didn't I?

Diane: What?

Kevin: Yeah!

Floyd: See.

Announcer: And a nice pass to Tron Armstrong / *Throughout this text, the SLASH(/) within one character's speech represents the cue for the "following" character's speech to overlap.* . . . I think that'll be good for a first down. No, they've called for a measurement . . .

Bill: *Over the announcer from "/".* Putting your father and Floyd in the same room.

Diane: *Annoyed.* What?

Bill: Aren't you listening? He's ranting again . . . all this left wing stuff. . . . He was just spouting the Regina bloody Manifesto for crying out loud!

Diane: *Laughing.* Was he?

Bill: The Regina Manifesto.

Diane: That's Ogie.

Bill: Not funny, Diane.

Diane: What do you want me to do?

Bill: Why didn't he go to the Senior Centre this afternoon? Why didn't he go to the Senior Centre?

Diane: He didn't want to go to the Senior Centre. He wanted to stay here and watch the game.

Announcer: So it is second and a foot to go.

Bill: You should have made him go.

Diane: Not if he didn't want to.

Kevin: Block, block, block you idiots!

Floyd: *To Bill.* Look at this.

Bill: Yeah? Oh, no.

Announcer: And Bentrim is carried back for a net loss on the play of maybe five yards. Saskatchewan will be forced to punt.

Sharyl: Sometimes I think I don't quite understand this game.

Kevin: I don't think I want to watch anymore.

Ogie: What did you say?

Kevin: They're doing us in, Grandpa. It's sickening. It's like slow death, execution by inches. . . .

Ogie: *Nazi accent.* First ve vill pull aut der finkernails undt zen der finkerss. . . .

Kevin: It's not funny.

Ogie: Come on. Undt zen der armsuss. . . .

Kevin: Ja, first ve vill pull aut der finkernails.

Diane: Undt zen, zen ve vill cut off der finkers.

Ogie: *British accent.* Oh, I say, not my fingers. . . .

Diane: Ja, der finkers.

Kevin: Undt zen ve vill pull aut der armsuss.

Diane: Undt zo on. Until der is nuzzink left.

Kevin: Nuzzink! You underschtandt?

Ogie: *Exaggerated Oxford accent.* I'm afraid so. Very well, I am resigned to my fate. But would you be so kind as to respect my last request and dispose of my bodily parts in the following manner. . . . Each time you lop one off, take the severed extremity on one of your air raids and drop it over Old Blighty with a note saying this was sacrificed for love of my country.

Kevin: Of course, Mein Herr. Iss leasht ve can do.

Diane and Kevin: Vait a minute.

Kevin: Vhat do you sink?

Diane: Do you sink ve are schtupit?

Kevin: Ve know vhat you are tryink to do!

Diane: Finker py finker . . .

Kevin: Arrum py arrum . . .

Diane: Legk py legk . . .

Diane and Kevin: *Punchline.* You are tryink to escape!

Diane, Kevin and Ogie laugh. The others are puzzled.

Diane: *Explaining.* Family joke.

Floyd: Oh.

Bill: Their humor runs to the gruesome.

Ogie: *Losing it again.* Humor?

Announcer: There was a flag on that play. Holding against Toronto. / That will be a penalty.

Ogie: *To Floyd, over Announcer at "/".* Humor is an important element.

Announcer: / First down Saskatchewan

Floyd: It sure is.

Announcer: Saskatchewan retains possession. . . .

Ogie: Well, that's good, anyway.

Announcer: And it is the end of the first quarter.

Kevin: But now the wind's against them.

Ogie: *Comforting.* Don't worry, *Hesitant.* Ke . . . Kevin. There's a lot more game left, eh? Anything could happen.

Kevin: *Somewhat mollified.* I guess so.

Sharyl: Your son really gets involved, doesn't he?

Diane: Too much.

Sharyl: I think it's sweet. Does he play?

Diane: He just watches. You don't have kids?

Sharyl: No, we just have each other . . . and a dog. I think I missed out.

Diane: A dog would be less of a worry.

Ogie: *To Kevin.* How about a small wager.

Kevin: How much?

Ogie: Two bits we win.

Kevin: I'd be robbing you.

Diane: It's like he doesn't have any other interests. . . .

Kevin: *To his mother.* What?

Diane: Nothing.

Ogie: I'll lay you odds.

Kevin: What odds?

Sharyl: *Indicating Ogie and Kevin.* The two of them get along so well.

Diane: They used to. Dad's condition is getting worse. It doesn't help.

Ogie: I know they're talking about me.

Diane: When I left Kevin's father he didn't have anybody except Ogie. . . .

Sharyl: And you.

Diane: Not even me. . . . I kind of lost myself for a while. Quite a while, I guess.

Sharyl: Oh . . .

Diane: At any rate . . . I think Ogie's going down like this . . . hurts him the most.

Ogie: Down? Well, I suppose. We aren't getting any younger, are we? Any of us. *To Kevin.* Ten to one.

Floyd: I'd take it.

Announcer: Complete to No. 32, Walter Bender . . .

Kevin: Go, go!

A moment of suspense and then all the men groan.

Announcer: . . . and he is brought down at the Argo forty-five. A solid hit by linebacker Don Moen and Bender is taking a while getting to his feet. It will be first and ten for Saskatchewan when we return with the play-by-play on this key Argo-Rider game.

Commercial.

Bill: *Jumping up brightly.* Well, let me freshen up the drinks. Sharyl?

Sharyl: Exactly the same, thanks, Bill.

Bill: Floyd?

Floyd: Sure, I can handle another one.

Bill: Anybody else?

Diane hands him her glass.

Bill: *On his way up the stairs.* Tell me if anything good happens.

Floyd: We'll keep you filled in, won't we, Ogie?

Ogie: Certainly, we'll keep you ... er ...

Floyd: Filled in on the game.

Ogie: On the game.

Floyd: Well now, Ogie.

Ogie: Yes?

Floyd: You like being called "Ogie," right?

Ogie: Not much I can do about it.

Floyd: *This is his version of redbaiting.* You can't tell me you believe in all that old CCF bullroar, not in this day and age, eh?

Ogie: Yes. I believe in the Co-operative Commonwealth, yes.

Floyd: The NDP don't even believe it any more ... and they're communists.

Sharyl: Ogie. Isn't that an unusual name! What's the background to that name. Is it Icelandic?

Ogie: Communists? I don't think so.

Floyd: Next thing to.

Ogie: We called it the Co-operative Commonwealth Federation back then in the thirties — closer to what we were intending, you see. And that was the start of the New Democratic Party.

Floyd: *Mocking.* No!

Ogie: It's true. People forget. I take it you don't vote NDP?

Floyd almost chokes and the women laugh.

Ogie: Was that funny?

Sharyl: If you knew.

Ogie: What are you, then?

Floyd: Let's just say I'm a committed Progressive Conservative. Of course some people will say I ought to be committed, right? ...

Ogie: Progressive Conservative. There's a contradiction in terms.

Floyd: We're not the ones trying to turn the clock back to nineteen thirty.

Ogie: That's true.

Floyd: Darn right.

Ogie: You're trying to turn it back to the year zero.

Floyd: *To Sharyl.* What are you laughing at?

Ogie: You probably won't be happy till you get things back before the creation of the universe — back to the original chaos.

Floyd is flummoxed for a second and then he laughs drily.

Floyd: You're quite a character, aren't you?

Ogie: *To Sharyl.* Not Icelandic. Old Guy.

Sharyl: Pardon?

Ogie: Old Guy. Where Ogie comes from.

Diane: O.G. for short. All us kids used to call him the Old Guy.

Ogie: What a bunch.

Diane: Even Mom.

Ogie: I don't know why I took it from them. No respect.

Diane: *Affectionately.* No, you old guy . . . why should we give you any respect?

Ogie: *Suddenly weeping.* Your mother.

Diane: No, Dad. . . .

Ogie: Why did she leave me, Diane?

Diane: She didn't leave you, Ogie. She died.

Ogie: You all left me.

Announcer: A long bomb . . . this time to . . .

Diane: I suppose we did . . .

Announcer: . . . Tron Armstrong. . . .

Diane: . . . leave you, always. . . .

Announcer: It is going to be an intercept by McCrary . . .

Kevin: No!

All eyes on the game. The crowd is going wild.

Announcer: No . . . Armstrong has it! Seemed like Armstrong just reached right through McCrary.

Floyd: Go!

Kevin: Move!

Announcer: Armstrong: forced out at the Toronto thirty yard line.

Kevin: *Satisfied with the yardage.* Ah!

Announcer: And Saskatchewan is back in this game.

Floyd: *Calling up the stairs.* Hey, Bill, you missed something good!

Muffled response.

Floyd: Can't hear you. *Chuckling.* He is going to be madder than hell. *To Diane.* Bill never told me he married a Red.

Diane: He didn't. I married a Blue. I wasn't anything.

Ogie: Why?

Diane: *Turning to her father with pain.* I couldn't be what you wanted me to be. I can't stay here . . . Ogie . . .

This is double playing somehow both for Ogie and Diane. She a younger version of herself. Flashing, creative.

Ogie: Don't leave me, Diane . . .

Diane: Don't lay this on me, Ogie. You know I can't stay. Would she have wanted me to?

Ogie: I don't know how I'm going to get along without her.

Diane: You're strong.

Ogie: I never told your mother how much I depended on her.

Diane: She knew. Come on, Old Guy. I'll come and see you every so often. But the fact is . . .

Ogie: You are off to change the world.

Diane: Yeah. It needs it.

Ogie: Where did you get that notion?

Diane: You know damn well where I got that notion.

Ogie: When you come back from Selma.... Sure you have to go ... I know. I'm proud of you. But when you come back, eh? Just for a while, Diane ... until I get myself organized.

Diane: I can't take her place, Dad.

Ogie: Can you see yourself living here ... ever?

Diane: It would choke the life out of me.

Ogie: Just like your brothers....

Diane: I'm sorry, Ogie.

Ogie: I'll never get them back here ... big city big shots.... Now you.... I didn't expect you to give up....

Diane: Give up? Look I'm on my way to Selma ... you call that giving up? I'm a fighter, Ogie. You made me this way....

Ogie: You'll go risk your life for colored people in Alabama, but you won't fight along side of the farmer in this province. I've fought for this farm....

Diane: I know.

Ogie: Tooth and nail. And your grandparents before me. And you just spit on it, you and your brothers. I can't work it myself. What am I going to do with it?

Diane: Sell it to a co-operative ... give it to a commune or something. You always said that was a great thing.

Ogie: Not when it's your land.

Diane: Some socialist.

Ogie: If you give up the land you give up the story of it.... How my mother and my father came here in an ox cart.... How ...

Diane: We've heard that story, Ogie. How they lived in a sod house ...

Ogie: ... with a piano and a sofa ...

Diane: ... carted all the way from Ontario.

Ogie: Two school teachers from Clinton, Ontario determined to be farming ...

Diane: ... sucked in by the fancy promises of the land speculators.

Ogie: And they made it. Almost killed them ... but they made it!

They passed all that on to me. This is land sown with the sweat of my parents — and mine. . . . Darn near killed me too, but things'll be better next year. . . .

Diane: I've got to go. The bus will be coming down the road any minute. Give up, Ogie. The family farm is obsolete.

Ogie: I beg your pardon?

Diane: Private ownership is on its way out. It's either the people or the big capitalists . . . and you can't fight them from Maidstone. I want to be where the action is.

Ogie: But this is it. This is what it's all about. The family farm is the best way to do it — the most efficient, the most natural . . .

Diane: Face it, you've got the worst land in the worst part of the worst province of the country. . . .

Ogie: The bread basket of the world.

Diane: Was it ever?

Ogie: *Pause.* Of course.

Diane: There's got to be a change, Dad.

Ogie: Don't leave me, Diane.

Diane: Radical change.

Ogie: There's got to be a radical change. She could have been me, thirty years before. You won't stay down there.

Diane: Can't fight Ross Thatcher from Alabama.

Floyd: So she said "Margaret Thatcher! Now that she's for another term, she'll turn our poor old country around . . . wait and see." I'm telling you, that's what we need here. Another Margaret Thatcher.

Ogie: The bus will be out at the gate.

Floyd: Pardon?

Ogie: Keep yourself safe, Diane. Well, don't back down either. Look those state troopers right in the eye, damn rednecks. But come back safe.

Announcer: And the Saskatchewan Roughriders gain another first down at the Toronto twenty. For the first time in the game

Saskatchewan has a march going. . . . They have gained forty yards in just five downs.

Bill brings the drinks down.

Bill: Here we are, everybody. *As he serves.* What's happening?

Floyd: We just got three touchdowns.

Bill: We did? Hah, hah, very funny.

Kevin: We're on their twenty.

Bill: Hah, hah, very funny.

Kevin: We are.

Announcer: There's the snap. Bentrim fakes a handoff to Armstrong.

Bill: *Doubletake.* Hey, we are.

Kevin: See, I told you.

Announcer: He's stepping back, looking for a receiver. . . .

Sharyl: Floyd . . . will you get my sweater out of the car?

Announcer: It's going to be a sack. . . .

Sharyl: Floyd. . . .

Announcer: No . . . he got it off. . . .

Diane: Are you cold? I can turn the air conditioner down.

Exclamation from the watchers.

Announcer: And it is incomplete, deflected by defensive back Jake Vaughn.

Sharyl: No, then everybody else would be uncomfortable. I just have cold blood. Floyd.

Floyd: Just a minute.

Diane: I'll get you something.

Sharyl: No, it's all right.

Announcer: When we return it will be second down and ten for the Riders.

Sound of commercial.

Floyd: *To Sharyl.* What do you want?

Sharyl: My sweater. I'm cold.

Floyd: Why didn't you get it yourself?

Sharyl: The car is locked.

Floyd: Why didn't you say so?

Sharyl: You didn't ask.

Floyd: How was I supposed to know?

Sharyl: Would you get it for me?

Floyd: *Getting up.* Which one?

Sharyl: There is only one.

Announcer: Bentrim is stepping back. Heavy pressure from Toronto. Down the centre to Ray Elgaard. . . .

Sharyl: Floyd.

Floyd: *Throwing her the car keys.* Here.

And he sits down again. Sharyl exchanges a look with Diane and goes upstairs.

Announcer: It is complete for a first down at the Argo ten.

Bill: Now, you bastards, move it in there. *To Diane.* See where the ball is?

Diane: Yeah.

Announcer: There's the snap. Bentrim steps back . . . now he steps forward into the pocket . . . Armstrong going deep into the end zone . . . Bentrim is fumbling the. . . . He loses the ball! There's a pileup. . . . Who is going to come up with the . . . ? It is Toronto!

Great groans all around.

Announcer: The Toronto Argonauts have recovered the ball on their own five yard line. . . . And there is a shot of Rider Head Coach, John Gregory, looking absolutely devastated, absolutely devastated! So close, and yet so far.

Bill: Looks like Melnyk, Friday morning.

Diane: Melnyk?

Bill: He didn't have a clue. I knock at the door and he says come in. I open the door and just stand there with the box so I can see his reaction. "Is that for me?" "'Fraid so, Melnyk," and I pull out the white envelope.

Floyd: He had it coming.

Bill: God's gift to the Department of Justice.

Floyd: So he thought.

Bill: Anyway I walk in and plunk the box down on his desk. "Your personal effects in here. Leave everything else just the way it is. We'll send the box on in a couple of days . . . and we've got a nice employment counselor for you to talk to." He says, "I can't leave now. I've got too many projects on the go. Nobody else knows how to handle them." "Sorry," I say. "Your position has been abolished." He has little drops of sweat on his forehead, "Listen, Bill — I know I've been involved in the Saskatchewan Government Employees Union, I know I've signed the odd petition here and there, I know I went to the NDP old fashion picnic . . . but it was just for the potato salad. I'm really a Conservative. I've been on your side the whole time!" So I say, "Then you should understand what we're trying to do here."

Floyd: What did he say to that?

Bill: What could he say?

Floyd: You have real style, Bill.

Bill: I've worked it down to a fine art.

Floyd: These people should be able to figure out what's coming. They bury their heads in the sand.

Bill: They think what they're doing is so all-out important nobody will ever want to get rid of them. None of them expect it. Not a one.

Floyd: Of course nobody is secure.

Bill: Right.

Floyd: Everybody should be checking the exits.

Bill: Try and tell them that.

Floyd: Even us.

Bill: Right. Even us.

Sharyl enters with her sweater, an extraordinarily stylish creation. Simultaneously there is a roar of enthusiasm from the television and this attracts the attention of the men.

Floyd: Look at that.

Diane: It's gorgeous.

Sharyl: Thank you all.

Floyd: I meant the game.

Announcer: And Renfroe makes a thirty-five yard pass to Gil Fenerty. Spectacular, simply spectacular. And Toronto has a first down at its own forty yard line.

Diane: Look at this, Bill.

Bill: Beautiful.

Floyd: It should be. It cost enough.

Bill: What? The wife or the sweater?

Floyd: Both.

Hah, hah. Sharyl burst into tears. Diane takes her over to a corner and tries to comfort her.

Diane: All right?

Sharyl: Yeah.

Diane: Sure?

Sharyl: Okay. I bought this in Montreal last month.

Diane: It's really nice.

Sharyl: It's me, isn't it?

Diane: Definitely.

Sharyl: This is the first chance I've had to wear it. *Pause.* Tell me something. Is he a scumbag or is it my imagination?

Diane: You know him better than I do.

Sharyl: Just your first impression.

Diane: Well, possibly.

Sharyl: He's proud of it. He doesn't care what people think of him. He doesn't care how he makes me feel and I'm supposed to love him for it. *She tries to get herself together.* I'm sorry. Is yours like that?

Diane: Sometimes.

Sharyl: Not enough to make you get out, I guess.

Diane: No. What about you? *Embarrassed.* I'm sorry. That's none of my business.

Bill: Keep the camera on the ball, eh . . . come on.

Diane: Bill makes me feel safe. That makes up for a lot. He makes me feel safe. That's why I married him. Okay, I was out on the end of a very shaky branch. I decided to crawl back before somebody sawed it off.

Floyd: Hit him! Hit him!

Sharyl: It's funny why people get married, eh?

Diane: Sort of.

Sharyl: Seemed to me like the only thing to do. My father approved of him . . . of his . . . what did they use to say? His prospects. My mother was charmed, tickled pink. He was a "good catch." I was a "good catch." We got married.

Ogie: All they need is a little inspiration.

Kevin: A little blocking might help.

Diane: I was trying to out-radical my parents. *At Sharyl's raised eyebrows.* Not with Bill . . . with the other one . . . my first husband. And out radicalling my parents took some doing.

Sharyl: I bet.

Diane: You've seen Ogie. My mother was worse. She came on gentle, but she was like steel . . . her outrage at social injustice . . . you know the type. United Church Women. So I was pushing and trying to outdo them and . . . or maybe it was what I thought they wanted of me — that they wouldn't be satisfied with anything less. . . .

Sharyl: And?

Diane: And finally I got scared and I beat a retreat.

Sharyl: What was your first husband like?

Diane: This is my retreat.

Bill: Oh no. I'm going to cry.

Diane: He was a hippie. An artist, sort of . . . a sculptor. He worked with garbage . . . building queer shapes that nobody liked. We never had any money . . . lived in a mess. We went after causes like bull terriers, every possible cause. If there weren't any current ones we made them up. Anti-nuke, native rights . . . waffle. . . . You name it we were out there carrying our little placards around.

Kevin: Pass. Complete. Pass. Complete. Pass. Complete. What's going on!

Diane: Then I had Kevin and somehow. . . . I was scared and I tried to bring it up . . . but Allen told me it was the petit bourgeois coming out in me.

Laughter from men.

Floyd: *Laughing.* We're ridiculous!

Bill: Understatement.

Diane: So I shut up and then I met Bill . . . and he looked at me as if I was the most amazing thing that ever happened to him. You know where we met?

Bill: Watch it.

Diane: In a bank. I should have listened to my parents and stuck to the Credit Union. We had an *affair* . . . you know, like you see in movies. He even rented an apartment we went to on his lunch hours. He took care of everything. He took care of me. He's that kind of person, see.

Bill: *Mock fright.* Oh, scary!

Diane: And by then. . . . Allen and I were kind of destroying each other so I said, "All right let's shift ground here." And I took Kevin and left. Bill and I got married. We bought this house and I've been happy ever since.

Sharyl: Really?

Diane: More or less.

Sharyl: I didn't mean to get so upset. I don't know what came over me.

Diane: It's all right. Happens to all of us.

Sharyl: Thanks.

Diane: It is a nice sweater.

Sharyl: I know. *Moving over to the gathering huddled around the television set.* What's happening, boys?

Diane is left standing by herself. Ogie moves up and comments to the audience as if she were an exhibit.

Ogie: I think now that this is my daughter, Diane. I haven't seen her for a long time . . . but I would say it is the same person only different. How did she get like this — so dependent . . . so afraid? What happened to the feisty girl she used to be? I don't like to think that changes for the worse are permanent. When is Diane coming back? I wonder when she'll come back?

Diane: *Annoyed.* What are you talking about, Ogie?

Without waiting for an answer she walks back to the group.

Bill: So Toronto has managed to get all the way to the ten yard line and it is second down for the Toronto Argonauts.

Floyd: It took them four plays to get down there. Do you believe it? Four plays.

Sharyl: That's a lot, eh?

Everybody turns to look at her. Then they are drawn back to the set.

Announcer: Renfroe is ready to throw. He's looking for a receiver in the end zone. Saskatchewan is putting on the pressure. And James Curry . . .

Yea, go, etc.

Announcer: . . . James Curry climbs right over the Toronto offensive guards and slams Renfroe into the turf! Oh, that hurt. So it is third down for Toronto and eighteen yards to go.

Sharyl: Who is that mean man?

Floyd: He's paid to be mean.

Bill: Perfectly legal.

Announcer: And Argo placekicker Lance Chomyc is coming on to attempt a field goal. Renfroe . . . being helped off the field, looking a little dazed. . . .

Ogie: There should be a rule about that kind of thing.

Floyd: Just like a socialist.

Kevin: Hey, Gramps . . . that was for our side.

Ogie: Our side?

Floyd: Regulate everything, right. Solve everything with rules.

Ogie: You mean I've been rooting for wrong team?

Floyd: Already too damn many rules.

Kevin: I suppose there's no chance of his missing this one.

Bill: And he's kicking with the wind . . .

Floyd: *To Ogie.* Of course, you'd disagree with that, wouldn't you?

Ogie: Nope. Looks to me like the wind's with him. You can tell by the way those cheerleaders' skirts are whipping up. . . .

Sharyl: Ogie!

Ogie: What there is of them.

Bill: You're not supposed to be looking at that!

Ogie: I'm old enough.

Announcer: And it's good.

There is a visible and sudden deflation.

Announcer: Which brings the score to Toronto seventeen, Saskatchewan nothing.

Kevin: *Bitter.* Great. How long have we got?

Announcer: And there is a minute and a half left until half time here at Exhibition Park in Toronto.

Sound of a commercial.

Kevin: Great.

Diane: Don't take it so seriously, Kevin.

Sharyl: It's just a game.

Kevin, Floyd and Bill turn to her in disbelief.

Sharyl: Well, it is.

Kevin: Just a game.

Diane: There are more important things in life.

Kevin: Like what?

Diane: Like school for one.

Kevin: Sure.

Diane: Did you do your homework?

Kevin: I've got the rest of the weekend.

Bill: As long as you keep your priorities straight.

Kevin: Why? So I can live like you?

Diane: Kevin.

Kevin: Well, just what is so important? To have a split-level in Lakeview? To have a swimming pool? . . .

Bill: Now don't say you don't appreciate the pool.

Kevin: To have a job with the government so you can go around firing people?

Bill: There's more to it than that, Son.

Kevin: I'm not your son.

Bill: True enough.

Diane: What's eating you?

Kevin: Nothing.

Diane: What is that supposed to mean?

Announcer: Chomyc kicks a good one. It is hanging in the air. Tron Armstrong is under it. / He's got it at the twelve yard line. He puts on the moves. . . . There's a lateral to Walter Bender. Bender manages to run it up to the thirty . . . the thirty-five yard line . . . and he is brought down.

Diane: *Over the announcer at "/".* Well? Talk to me, Kevin.

Kevin: Quiet, I'm trying to listen to the game.

Diane: That's not the way to talk to me.

Kevin: You don't care. Just let me listen.

There is a sudden silence.

Diane: When I was your age. . . .

Pause.

Ogie: What?

Diane: When I was his age I had something to live for.

There is the sound of the crowd again.

Announcer: First and ten for Saskatchewan. Bentrim back to throw. He has time. Now he's in trouble. He's gonna be sacked. No, he shovels it off to Bender. He gets away . . . but no . . . they're going to call him down. The officials are calling it dead. The loss will be three. It will be second and thirteen.

Bill: Kevin, you're wrong. I'm not just firing people for the fun of it. It's not really fun throwing men and women out of work . . . destroying careers, giving them a life of uncertainty and hopelessness . . . making them wonder how they are going to feed their families. Do you think I'm doing that for the fun of it? It's just as hard on me as it is on them. But there are principles at stake, aren't there, Floyd?

Floyd: Of course.

Bill: You don't quite understand politics, not at your age, but you'll get to understand them, won't he? There are principles at stake.

Ogie: What sort of principles?

Bill: Here we go again. We've been through this, Ogie. You're too stubborn to understand.

Ogie: Have another crack at it.

Bill: All your politics come out of the Depression.

Floyd: Let's give it a try, Bill. For the boy's sake, here, eh?

Bill: He's not interested.

Kevin: Yeah, I'm interested.

Bill: He won't listen.

Kevin: Sure I will.

Everybody stops to watch the next play.

Announcer: Bentrim rolling to his right. Screens it off this time . . . to Conrad. And Conrad gets close to a first down. It'll be third and less than a yard to go.

Floyd: Go on.

Bill has to think hard. Principles haven't been occupying the front of his mind recently.

Bill: Well, for a long time the ordinary people have been shut out of things. The government was trying to take over everything. Especially here in Saskatchewan. Now that the Conservatives are in, we know we've got to give the ordinary people a chance to make it on their own.... All big government does is ... well ... it shoves itself in and spoils their chances, doesn't it? Right, and that's where I come in, see? I'm helping to reduce the size of the government so that the little guy will have a chance to make it on his own.

Ogie: He's not really firing anybody. He's creating opportunities.

Floyd: That's right.

Bill: Don't agree with him, Floyd.

Announcer: Well, they are about a foot and a half short of a first down and Saskatchewan is going to gamble.

Floyd: It's really about freedom, Kevin — freedom to take the initiative ... freedom to exercise your imagination, freedom to make a ...

Ogie: Killing.

Announcer: Bentrim is in and under.

Bill: See what I mean.

Announcer: He keeps the ball. Yes. He'll have the first down.

Floyd: Freedom to make a mark in this world.

Ogie: What about freedom from being exploited by the rich people? Freedom to have a say in what the government does for the people? ...

Floyd: As long as it's socialist.

Ogie: Freedom from the people who just want power. ...

Bill: Give up, Ogie. *To Kevin.* You understand what we're talking about?

Kevin: No.

Announcer: It is now first down and ten for the Roughriders. Tod Brown is wide to the right, Tron Armstrong to the left. And in the first six months of our second term we have dismantled or semi-privatized or curtailed the activities of the Saskatchewan Dental Plan . . . Bentrim hands it off on the inside to Bender . . . the Saskatchewan Drug Plan, the Native Courtworker Services, Community Colleges and Adult Education. . . . He gets a couple of yards . . . the Legal Aid Society, and the Human Rights Commission. We have cut off funding to The John Howard Society, Planned Parenthood and the Association of Métis and Non-Status Indians. And he is belted by Marcellus Greene of the Toronto Argonauts. Oh what a slam! We are going to put this province back on it's feet!

Ogie: But it wasn't off its feet.

Bill: He is now.

Announcer: Bentrim is trying to get up . . . he looks shaken.

Floyd: There ought to be a law against that.

Ogie: You have to make good laws to do good things. Of course the Grits and the Tories are going to call us communist and dictatorship and all that . . . and they know we're not. That is a smear campaign. We have a more democratic idea of government than they have. Sure. All government is is the combined co-operative power of the people, see? Government is us!

Bill: Ignore him . . . he's off and running.

Ogie: What was that? What was that?

Floyd: Who does he think he's talking to?

Ogie: Let me give a warning here.

Bill: I don't know. Some election campaign . . . maybe a CCF convention. I don't know.

Ogie: If the CCF gets in and starts going 'round acting like a big free enterprise corporation . . . we're done for. The way I see it if we lose sight that we're the common people acting in common for the common good . . .

Kevin: Grandpa, don't go all crazy on us.

Diane: Ogie, that's all over . . . that's long gone.

Ogie: These people say, "Society operates by greed — the profit motive." Oh, they don't call it that. They call it market forces. They think that if the forces of the market place can have free reign, everything will all be perfect. Perfect for who? And they call *us* naive! *Suddenly.* Diane! It's all coming apart on me. Diane!

Diane: Take it easy, Dad.

Ogie: Where's your mother, Diane?

Diane: She's not here. Not any more. But I am.

Bill: She's been having nothing but trouble with him. It's wearing her out.

Floyd: I can see where it would.

Bill: I'm thinking about finding a nursing home for him and taking Diane on a long cruise or something.

Sharyl: That's sweet of you.

Bill: Oh, I'm not all bad. Pretty bad but not all bad. I was going to ask you, Floyd, you know about these things. What are the chances of my taking a little extra time off?

Floyd is thinking.

Bill: Pretty limited, eh?

Floyd: Not necessarily . . . but . . .

Bill: I was thinking about putting down a down payment . . . you know. . . . It's for the cruise of your life . . . that kind of thing. . . .

Floyd: I wouldn't make any long-range plans if I were you . . . not for a while . . . not that involve big expenditures. . . .

Bill: Why not?

Floyd: Well like I said, nobody should feel too secure.

Bill: Oh yeah. . . . But I . . . I'm good. I'm really competent. . . .

Floyd: These are hard times. It's not a question of competence. It's a question of percentage cuts. . . . Maybe that would count for something. . . . Listen, I don't want to spoil your party here. . . . Can't this wait until Monday?

Bill: I'm one of the cuts? *Pause.* Well, I'll be damned.

The sound of the gun going off. Some of these effects, although emanating from the television, sound like real life.

Announcer: And there is the end of the first half. The Toronto

Argonauts are seventeen and the Saskatchewan Roughriders are yet to score. Stay tuned for our half time features.

Bill: Couldn't you put in a good word for me?

Floyd: I have already.

Bill: And?

Floyd shrugs . . . and it is the **END OF ACT I.**

Act Two

Ogie is talking to the audience. The rest of the characters are seated around the television in a kind of portrait grouping. Everyone now knows about the firing and everyone except, perhaps, Ogie looks very grim. Drinks have been replenished. In fact a case of beer and a couple of bottles of liquor have been brought down and are on the coffee table for people to take at will. Bill is violently chomping his way through a bowl of taco chips.

Ogie: Well, *Referring to the others,* not exactly a happy family portrait. Of course losing one's job can't be a joyful affair, precisely. Something like losing one's farm. But I thought what's-his-name, there ... Bill ... would be able to take this sort of thing more in his stride. Isn't he supposed to be some kind of expert on firing? Of course that's probably a little different then *getting* fired. Still one would think he'd welcome a move into the private sector career market ... especially since he's so competent.

He contemplates Bill for a moment. A very disgusted individual. Maybe he's mourning the loss of that big tropical seas cruise he and Diane were counting on. They didn't tell me about it but I had my suspicions aroused by the two brochures they left on the coffee table — one from the travel agent and the other from "Sunset of Life" Nursing Home. *Disgust.* Sunset of Life.

Sharyl whispers something to Floyd and he turns to Bill.

Floyd: Maybe Sharyl and I should go home, people.

Bill: No, no. Stay.

Diane: Maybe ...

Bill: No.

Floyd: You probably don't feel like partying. . . .

Bill: *Viciously.* I said stay!

Floyd: All right. *To Sharyl.* See?

Pause. Everybody starts to talk at the same time and then they abruptly stop, waiting for someone to begin. No one does so they start to talk again. They stop.

Floyd: Go ahead.

Diane: No, you go ahead.

Floyd: No, after you.

Bill: No, go ahead.

Sound of marching band, crowd. Lights up on the announcer.

Announcer: Welcome back to the second half of this Saskatchewan-Toronto game at Toronto's Exhibition Stadium. There are about thirty-five thousand fans here on this pleasant autumn day . . . and most of them are very happy indeed that the home team is leading the Western Riders by a score of seventeen to nothing. Although they say a game isn't over until it's over, Saskatchewan turned in such a disappointing lacklustre effort in the first half one has to wonder if they shouldn't just pack up and go back to Regina. They have been completely outclassed by the Toronto club.

Bill: Well?

Floyd: Well, I was just going to say that maybe it's just as well that I told you. Better to know in advance, eh? Soften the blow? I mean that's the least I could do for you.

Bill: Thanks.

Floyd: It's completely against policy. . . .

Bill: I know.

Floyd: I was supposed to tell you in the morning. We were supposed to clear your floor of the other employees.

Bill: In case I run amok. I know the routine.

Floyd: Of course you would.

Bill: Yep.

Floyd: The employment consultant'll be in to see you first thing.

Bill: With a box of tissues.

Floyd: You'll get the executive-class treatment. A wonderful severance package. Try to act surprised, okay?

Announcer: Chomyc is teeing up. Tod Brown and Armstrong back to receive the kick.

Pause. Sound of the crowd.

Announcer: Tod Brown has it at the twenty, makes it to the twenty-five, the thirty, the thirty-five and he is tripped up by Glen Kulka as he crosses the forty yard line.

Diane: What are we going to do?

Bill: Your guess is as good as mine.

Floyd: I suppose this wouldn't be a good time to ask you for a donation to the Party. . . . Just a joke.

Bill gets up and turns off the television set. The light goes out on the announcer.

Sharyl: Floyd.

Kevin: *Yelling.* Hey!

Floyd: It was just a joke.

Bill: Sorry.

He turns it back on again. The announcer lights up again.

Announcer: A fifty yard kickoff, a twenty yard return.

Ogie: There's something I want to say about all of this but I don't really know what it is. Not yet. Who are these people? Of course I know who they are, off and on: my daughter and her son, her second husband, her son's stepfather. Their friends, such as they are. You see, I do know their . . . designations. But I have such a hard time recognizing them as people. What are they about? What is it they want out of life? Something. I know that. And they want it with a certain desperation . . . whatever it is. Are they getting it?

Kevin: *To Diane.* When I get out of school there won't be any jobs anyway . . . leastways that's what everybody says.

Diane: Is that your problem?

Kevin: Well, I mean it's not like it's the major existential preoccupation of me as a representative of today's youth or anything. But it seems to be in the air around here this afternoon.

Diane: So watch football for the rest of your life.

Kevin: Might as well. Saves me from being a geek.

Diane: Kevin, this isn't a good time. *Pause.* You're not a geek.

Kevin: Close to it. But I've got this area of expertise, see. I can't exactly play football . . . but I can stand next to a cheerleader on the sidelines and explain what it means. That's my strategy. So far it isn't working.

Ogie: The boy is growing up in a vacuum. There is in this household a complete absence of ideals. And/or ideas. There aren't many of those either.

Announcer: It is a handoff to Conrad. Conrad drops the ball!

Kevin: Of course I'm not the only one.

Announcer: The Boatmen recover at the Rider thirty-two.

Ogie: What is it you want — as human beings in life?

Bill: Not now Ogie.

Ogie: What?

Bill: Please, not now.

Ogie: Was I talking out loud?

Bill: I want my job back. It doesn't make sense, Floyd. If you want to reduce the size of the civil service, don't fire the people who fire people.

Announcer: There's the snap.

Floyd: Whose down is it?

Kevin: Toronto.

Announcer: Renfroe steps back. . . . Where did he come from? Mike McGruder appears out of nowhere and flattens Renfroe. . . . Wait a minute . . . the ball is loose. Saskatchewan has it. Saskatchewan recovers on the. . . . There are flags down on the play. Holding. . . . Against Toronto! For once Saskatchewan gets a break.

Floyd: Well, Bill . . . we didn't make the decision lightly, you know. Somebody put you on the list. . . .

Bill: Who?

Floyd: I don't know. Somebody. I've forgotten.

Bill: Bastard.

Floyd: And then I took you off, and then . . .

Bill: Floyd, I've always been politically correct.

Floyd: Well maybe a little too much so. . . .

Bill: What?

Floyd: We've moved into a different stage here. We're trying to be a fully professional civil service. It's an image problem. Some people felt you were getting a little too cheerful about firing your colleagues.

Ogie: Now I know it's the world that has gone crazy. Now, if the NDP had gotten in . . .

Diane: You want to know what I want, Ogie? I just want to be an ordinary wife married to an ordinary guy with a job that puts bread on the table. I want to sit around in my ordinary rec room watching an ordinary football game. . . . But oh no . . . one guy's just been fired, one guy lives in 1933, and somehow, before the afternoon is out, we're probably going to have to prove the superiority: Captialism or Socialism.

Kevin: And my reason for living is going down the tube with the Riders.

Diane: And my son will commit suicide if we lose the game.

Kevin: If? Fat chance. *When!*

Sharyl: All I want to be is extraordinary.

Floyd: Can it, Sharyl.

Ogie: Oh, we are all extraordinary. Look at us. Diane, when you were born I looked at you and I said, this is the most wonderful amazing little person in the whole world.

Diane: But I wasn't.

Ogie: But you were . . . until what happened?

Diane: I got middle-aged. I got tired.

Announcer: Armstrong is in the clear.

Ogie: Is that all?

Kevin: Hey!

Announcer: It goes to Brown at the fifty and it is complete. Brown stopped at the fifty-five. A first down for Saskatchewan at the fifty-five.

Ogie: I got middle-aged ... and I got *old.*

Announcer: When we return it will be first and ten for the Riders at centre field.

Ogie: That's no excuse for turning into an archconservative.

Diane: I'm not archconservative. ... I'm apolitical.

Ogie: *Shocked.* Diane, that is worse.

Floyd: He's right. You might as well be a Liberal.

Announcer: Bentrim back, looking for a receiver. And it is another long pass ... complete! To Ray Elgaard and he is squeezed out of bounds on the Argo thirty-two yard line.

Diane: Can't a person be a human being? That's the trouble with this province. By the time you define yourself as to what party you belong to, and what wing of what party — and whether you're pro business or anti business — or pro American or anti American or pro free trade or anti free trade or pro labour or anti labour ... pro abortion or anti abortion ... you've got no room to move — no space to just sort of stop and say, "I don't know."

Ogie: No, no. That's what makes this province! When something is wrong, we don't just leave it there. We say there's gotta be a political solution. That's our way of solving things. Until recently.

Diane: You aren't listening, Ogie. All those things I stood for back when I was a kid? I didn't know if they were right or wrong. I thought they were right because you thought they were right. I never had a chance to find out for myself. And then when I married Allen ... I thought things were right because he thought so.

Ogie: Did you hear what he said?

Diane: Who?

Ogie: Woodsworth. Woodsworth.

Diane: Oh, Ogie.

Announcer: The Riders scrimmaging. ... It is first and ten ...

Ogie: "Yet we are confident that we are in the line of progress — that time and tide are with us. If our movement is to be successful, it must bear — as we think it does — something of the character of a religious crusade. Only thus can we overcome the danger of being swayed by personal ambition or by the hope of immediate success. Only thus can we rally the masses to struggle for a better future for themselves and their children." Isn't that inspiring, Agnes? It may take a long time . . . but it's going succeed one day . . . because it's right. It is. Now if we can just get this statement formulated and satisfy everybody . . .

Diane: I've lost him.

Sharyl: This is such a political place. It's like Quebec . . . worse maybe. Everybody has such convictions. Where I grew up religion and politics were taboo. We thought politics was something cooked up by the government to give us something to do on election day.

Announcer: It's a cross play. . . .

Sharyl: I grew up in Oakville.

Announcer: No it isn't.

Sharyl: I think I like it better this way.

Announcer: Bentrim faked a hand off to both of the halfbacks and now he is running up the centre. . . .

Sharyl: Life has more spice.

Announcer: He's getting good blocking . . . he's up to the twenty-five and he's down . . . with very close to a ten yard gain for Saskatchewan.

Diane: You didn't have to grow up with it.

Announcer: They are calling for a measurement.

Ogie: "The present order is marked by glaring inequalities of wealth and opportunity, by chaotic waste and instability, and in an age of plenty it condemns the great mass of people to poverty and insecurity."

Diane: *To Bill.* Are you all right?

Bill: Of course I'm all right, what do you think?

Diane: I was just asking.

Bill: Anybody want anything else? Here, have some taco chips.

He shoves the bowl across the table somewhat forcefully.

Ogie: "We believe that these evils can be removed only in a planned and socialized economy owned and operated by the people."

Kevin with one eye on the television goes up and pats Ogie gently on the shoulders. Ogie calms down.

Ogie: Yes? Oh. A wonderful document, something to aim at.

Announcer: It's good . . . so it is another Saskatchewan first on the Argo twenty-two.

Ogie: Kevin?

Sharyl: Don't tell Floyd, but I voted socialist in the last election.

Ogie: What's wrong?

Diane: You did?

Kevin: Nothing.

Sharyl: I canceled his vote.

Ogie: Was it me?

Kevin: No, no.

Ogie: I'm sorry.

Floyd: *Showing the effects of a certain amount of alcoholic lubrication.* You know what gets me about these CCF-ers . . . NDPers. . . . They think they own the place. They think there's something just not Saskatchewan about anybody who doesn't think like them. I grew up here. I didn't have it easy. . . . I grew up in East Regina. . . . I was called Bohunk just like the other kids. My parents weren't well-to-do. There were days when they had to scrimp — believe me. I've seen my mother go into other people's houses and do their cleaning. But my parents were thrifty; they were enterprising; they got by . . . better than that. The NDP don't have the monopoly on working class people. And they sound so goddamn righteous about the place. I'm proud of Saskatchewan. I'm proud of the initiative I see in the young people growing up here! Sure I'm a Free Enterpriser . . . sure I'm a right-winger . . . that doesn't make me any less of a Saskatchewan boy. They think that the province was created in their image. Well, I guess we showed 'em didn't we?

Bill: Frankly, I don't care.

Floyd: What? Anyway, I really enjoyed the shock around this place in '82 when we turfed the bastards out.

Sharyl: Floyd...

Floyd: Please, Sharyl. I'm talking. We sent them right into a tailspin. They didn't know what hit them. And then we turned around and did it again! Oh sure we lost support . . . but we held on.

Sharyl: I canceled your vote.

Floyd: In the cities of course . . . but the farmers knew which side their bread was buttered on, eh? They knew.

Sharyl: I canceled your vote.

Floyd: You what?

Sharyl: I voted for the other guys.

Announcer: A short pass to Bender of Saskatchewan. He's round the corner now. He's to the twenty, he's to the fifteen and that's as far as he gets.

Floyd: I don't get it?

Announcer: A seven yard gain on the play by Walter Bender. So it will be second down and three on the Argo fifteen yard line.

Floyd: What other guys?

Ogie: What other guys? That's some lady you've got there.

Floyd: Sharyl, why would you do that?

Ogie: She knew they were right.

Floyd: That's a crock. Sharyl doesn't know anything about politics. She did it to embarrass me. *To Sharyl.* Didn't you?

Sharyl: No.

Floyd: *Genuinely angry.* You're always doing this . . . sneaking around . . . trying to subvert everything I do, undermine every-thing I stand for!

Crowd noised increasing in excitement.

Announcer: Bentrim has the ball. He steps back and then steps for-ward into the pocket. Down field Brown is in the end zone . . . but he's well covered.

Sharyl: Just what do you stand for? I'd really like to know.

Announcer: The pressure is really on / Saskatchewan's rookie quarterback. At the last possible second he gets it away. It looks high. I'm afraid it is going to overshoot the receiver.

Floyd: *Over the announcer at "/".* What's wrong with you? Are you drunk or something? Are you getting your period?

Announcer: No. He shoots straight up into the air and just hauls the ball in.

Kevin: Yea!!!

Announcer: And it is a touchdown. A magnificent catch by Saskatchewan wide receiver Tod Brown. And the Riders are on the score board.

Diane: Who was that?

Kevin: Us.

Diane: Oh.

Announcer: The Western Riders have taken on new life here in this third quarter. Will it be enough to overtake the Boatmen?

Floyd: You know what I stand for.

Sharyl: I haven't the faintest idea.

Floyd: I've never made any bones about what I stand for.

Sharyl: Oh that. All that stuff about free enterprise and how you grew up in the East End of Regina. . . .

Floyd: Yes.

Sharyl: And how your name wasn't always Stark. . . .Once it was Starko . . . and how you're proud of where you came from. . . .

Floyd: All of that, yes.

Sharyl: And how you made it to the top and by the way — if you were so proud — how come you changed your name?

Announcer: And there is the point after.

Floyd: How long have we been married?

Sharyl: Too long.

Floyd: Fifteen years.

Announcer: Seventeen to seven for Toronto.

Floyd: And in all that time you never wondered why I changed my name?

Sharyl: I had more important things to worry about.

Floyd: Like?

Sharyl: I thought.

Floyd: Like?

Sharyl: Like where to get my hair done in Regina. . . .

Floyd: Exactly. It doesn't matter why I changed my name and you know why?

Sharyl: I wasn't thinking.

Floyd: Right . . . because being married to me gives you a nice worry-free life, right? So why can't you appreciate it, for a change?

Sharyl: Who says I want a worry-free life?

Floyd: Then just why did you marry me? Tell me that.

Sharyl: I wanted . . . I wanted . . . I don't know what I wanted.

Floyd: *In triumph, such as it is.* There you go.

Sharyl: "There you go." That's what you're all about, isn't it.

Floyd: Eh?

Sharyl: Getting the last word, right? Getting on top and staying there.

Announcer: Here is Ridgway's kick off. . . . It's Dwight Edwards out to his thirty, his thirty-four, his forty. Ray Elgaard downs him at the forty-one. There's a flag on the field.

Sharyl: *In wonderment.* And yes I do. I do know what I wanted.

Floyd: *Sneering.* What? Everlasting happiness?

Sharyl: Okay, I'll shut up. If that's the way you want it. . . .

Announcer: It is holding against Toronto. So they will be starting at their own twenty-nine yard line.

Sharyl: *Not allowing herself to be stopped.* It wasn't just that you were supposed to be a good catch. I wanted something that I knew for sure was really worthwhile. . . . I'm not explaining this right.

Something *absolutely* worth living for . . . fighting for. I thought that maybe the only place for that to happen was between two human beings.

Floyd: You're talking about sex, aren't you? You're going to tell all these people that I'm no good in bed?

Sharyl: *Shaking her head.* No.

Floyd: Well?

No answer. Somewhat disconcerted he continues on an earlier track.

It's not enough to have the occasional ideal here and there. . . . If you're going to have any impact you *have* to get on top and stay on top. Sure I'm competitive. That's what makes the world go around. But you have to have a level playing field . . . and it doesn't hurt to have a few ideals thrown in for good measure. How can you say I don't stand for anything? *Pause.* Is this about kids again?

Sharyl: *Desperately.* Oh, shut up.

Bill: I'll second that.

Floyd: Maybe we should have had kids.

Announcer: A pass to Ken Joiner. And it's complete!

Floyd: *To Bill.* What do you think?

Announcer: He's at the forty.

Bill: I think he's going all the way.

Announcer: The thirty-five.

Floyd: About us having a kid?

Announcer: He might just make this.

Bill: That would be nice, Floyd.

Announcer: The twenty-five.

Floyd: Not now, though. It's too late now.

Announcer: Joiner has left the field behind!

Kevin: *Weakly.* Oh no.

Bill: Sure is, Floyd.

Announcer: The fifteen. The ten. The five. And touchdown!

Kevin rolls on the floor, pounding the carpet in frustration. Diane gets up and flees from the television set. Bill grabs the taco chips back. Floyd gazes at the screen morosely. Sharyl seems to have gone catatonic.

Announcer: A forty yard run by Ken Joiner of the Toronto Argonauts.

Ogie: More is going on here than I understand . . . but it reminds me . . . it reminds me. If I can keep my thoughts together I should be able to tell you. *Indicating Sharyl.* This girl here, she's been looking for the one thing that's so important there isn't anything beyond it. She thinks it's there, somewhere, bless her. As silly as she seems, she hasn't given up on the universe. I decided long ago that that thing of final importance was to be found in politics. She has decided that it is to be found in love. Which one of us is right? Could we both be right? It makes me remember something I once knew but somehow forgot. My wife, Agnes . . . she was beautiful . . . a beautiful woman. There was a kindness there . . . and a passion in her body — in her will — when she opened herself to me. And she turned me . . . not away . . . not away from her . . . not away from myself . . . but through the love that we had — and this is the point, you see — she turned me toward others. You might say our love got political. We became concerned for everybody. I lost some of that when she . . . it's falling apart now. What was I saying? Is anybody listening to me or am I saying this all to myself?

Kevin: I'm listening, Ogie.

Announcer: The point after is good.

Ogie: Are you?

Kevin: Yes.

Announcer: It is twenty-four to seven for Toronto.

Kevin: I might as well.

Announcer: There are just a few seconds remaining in this third quarter.

Kevin: I'm giving up on the game.

Ogie: Don't do that.

Kevin: Why not? The Riders have. It's hopeless.

Ogie: Is it?

Kevin: It's no fun watching . . . we're being trampled.

Ogie: Did it make sense, what I was saying?

Kevin: I couldn't hear everything. You were kind of mumbling.

Ogie: Was I?

Kevin: I can't understand half of what you say anymore.

Announcer: And that is the end of the third quarter. The Argos outscoring the Saskatchewan Roughriders by seventeen points. We'll return with more CFL action in a moment.

Bill: *Wry.* Some action.

Sound of commercial.

Kevin: It's getting worse, isn't it?

Ogie: How do you mean? You mean my old brain?

Kevin: Yeah.

Ogie: Probably.

Kevin: What are you doing, when you go off like that.

Ogie: I don't know. Thinking about things.

Kevin: Just thinking?

Ogie: Reliving old times.

Kevin: Why?

Ogie: It's comforting.

Kevin: I miss you.

Ogie: But I'm always here.

Kevin: No you're . . . *Breaks off.* It bothers me. More than anything else.

Ogie: What?

Kevin: I don't want you to change.

Ogie: Am I changing? I still feel the same. It's the same old me, Kevin.

Kevin: You really feel the same?

Ogie: Well, I look in the mirror and I haven't always looked this way. . . .

Kevin: Inside.

Ogie: Inside. *Somewhat disgusted.* That can be a problem. I think of a person I should know quite well. . . . I see the face. I don't know who the hell it is. I'll look at somebody and I know that buried under there is a whole host of memories . . . but I can't get at them. . . . Yes . . . my body is changing . . . my brain is getting weird. But it's me that's doing the changing . . . see. I'm still the same. Anyway it's not important. . . .

Kevin: I need you, Ogie. I don't have anybody else.

Ogie: Oh, what about all those good looking girls down at your school . . . that one who's always coming by to see you? . . .

Kevin: The ones I'm interested in aren't interested.

Ogie: And the ones that are interested in you . . .

Kevin: Aren't interesting.

They laugh.

Ogie: I remember the feeling.

Kevin: You too?

Ogie nods.

Kevin: Even back then?

Announcer: Tron Armstrong is receiving for the Riders.

Ogie: Yep.

Kevin: Some things never change?

Ogie: No matter how much you want them to.

Announcer: He's at the thirty, the thirty-five . . .

Ogie: *Glowing.* But Kevin, there are other things that can . . . oh . . . be improved — revolutionized. I've seen it happen. Hell, I've made it happen.

Announcer: He's putting the moves on.

Kevin: I'm just a kid. I don't even know how the world operates yet.

Ogie: The beginning of wisdom . . .

Announcer: The forty-five. He's getting good blocking.

Kevin: It doesn't feel like my problem.

Ogie: The beginning of stupidity.

Announcer: The fifty-five.

Floyd: Go! Go! Go! Go!

Announcer: Argos' fifty.

Kevin: I mainly think about my own problems.

Ogie: Oh well.

Announcer: Armstrong having trouble breaking free.

Kevin: Except remember Michael? No that was before you came to live with us. Michael was this kid I knew in public school . . . and he was never very well dressed or anything. And one day he walked to school without a coat on . . . just in a tee shirt.

Announcer: Armstrong fighting his way down to the thirty.

Kevin: And it was something like thirty below out. I went to his house once. It was really run down. He said he lived with his grandmother . . . but he had to take care of his little brother and sister most of the time. I think of him a lot.

Announcer: The fifteen.

Kevin: He was just a little thin guy. One day I went by his house and there was nobody there. . . . Everything was all black and sooty.

Announcer: The ten.

Kevin: There were a few boards nailed across the window. I found out there'd been a fire there. Kids playing with matches.

Announcer: The five. Touchdown!

Floyd: Yea! Touchdown, Touchdown! We're back in the game. How about that Armstrong, eh?

Diane: *Dull.* Good.

Bill: *Dull.* Wonderful.

Sharyl: *Dull.* Yeah.

Floyd: Well you're really enthusiastic.

Kevin: Who got it?

Floyd: Armstrong.

Kevin: That's his third this season . . . he's caught twenty-three passes so far this year.

Floyd: Really?

Kevin: *To Ogie.* Anyway I didn't ever see him after that. But I thought it shouldn't be like that. That's wrong.

Ogie: Some folk say a society shouldn't twist itself end to end just for a few cases like Michael and his relatives. That's for charity to take care of. Send them to the food bank.

Diane: *Intervening.* Keep it balanced, Ogie. Keep it balanced.

Ogie: What balance? What balance?

Diane: Don't bully us, Ogie.

Ogie: What balance?

Diane: Like a good business climate. . . . More jobs. Poverty disappeared.

Ogie: Do you believe that?

Diane: Maybe.

Ogie: *To Kevin.* Do you?

Kevin: It sort of makes sense.

Diane: There is such a thing as reliance on . . .

Ogie: Yes?

Diane: On yourself.

Kevin: Don't poor people bring it on themselves?

Ogie: Sure, they just love to be poor and hungry. Where did you get that? Did you get that from your stepfather?

Diane: Leave him out of this.

Bill: Might as well.

Kevin: Well, don't they, sometimes?

Diane: Some of them.

Floyd: Sure. They drink their money away . . . or they're lazy. They sit around watching TV all day. . . .

Short pause.

Ogie: What about your friend Michael? Did he bring it on himself?

Kevin: No.

Ogie: No.

Kevin: Oh.

Ogie: Yep.

Kevin: That's what you're getting at.

Bill: What about me? Did I bring it on myself?

Announcer: The point after is good.

Floyd: You? What are you talking about? Come on, Bill. You're not poor!

Announcer: And it is now fourteen: Riders. Twenty-four: Argos.

Floyd: You'll get enough to tide you over, don't worry. And a man of your resources? A man who can put in a fireplace all by himself . . .

Bill: Yeah, right. That's true. But I'm out of a job, right? Right?

Floyd: Yeah.

Bill: And I'm sitting around drinking, right? And watching bloody TV. So I guess I got a little in common with all those lousy welfare bums, right?

Floyd: You're not on welfare.

Bill: Yippy.

Floyd: You're just going through loss-of-job syndrome.

Bill: Yippy.

Floyd: Everybody goes through it. . . . You'll get over it. They'll put you through a seminar on loss-of-job syndrome.

Bill: Yippy.

Floyd: You'll adjust. Stop saying that.

Bill: It's like falling off a tightrope. Only I'm still falling. *Pause.* Maybe we have been playing a little fast and loose with the social programs, Floyd.

Floyd: *Alarmed.* Don't talk like that. Have another drink. You'll feel better tomorrow.

Sharyl: I agree with him.

Floyd: You have another drink, too.

Sharyl: Have another drink? Single mothers who don't have enough money for medicine for their children.

Floyd: Stay out of this, Dear.

Sharyl: What about them?

Floyd: They'll get a refund, sooner or later. . . .

Sharyl: What about legal aid cutting back. I think that's wrong.

Floyd: You do, do you? Pimps and prostitutes can afford a buck or two to defend themselves. . . .

Sharyl: Women who can't afford to sue their husbands for non-payment of alimony. . . . Tell them to have another drink, why don't you?

Floyd: Sharyl . . .

Sharyl: Crippled old people who can't afford bus service . . .

Floyd: That's the City.

Sharyl: Didn't they get cut?

Floyd: Where are you getting this stuff? *To Bill.* She never reads the papers.

Sharyl: Teen-age girls who can't afford birth control pills.

Floyd: They shouldn't have sex.

Sharyl: Easy for you to say.

Floyd: Just because we've cut back here and there . . .

Sharyl: And they took the dental care out of the schools, right?

Floyd: We've still got the best health plan in the country.

Sharyl: Don't they have to take their kids to dentists' offices, now? I don't think some of these parents can even get themselves to dentists. . . .

Floyd: That's their fault. We're spoiled . . . we're spoiled rotten. You go to Ontario. They never had a dental plan, a drug plan. They have to pay huge premiums just for medicare every month . . . and that's the richest province.

Kevin: *To Ogie.* Is this what you've been going on about?

Floyd: You can't have a Cadillac social program when your economy is going down the drain. And even in the best of times that sort of thing saps the energy out of people. No, you have to stimulate big business . . . and little business. Give them the breaks . . . then maybe you can afford — down the road a ways — to help out somebody who may be in trouble . . . temporarily.

Sharyl: It doesn't sound like an improvement.

Floyd: It will be. Dear, you don't know anything about this. Please keep quiet.

Ogie: That's it, all right. Basic capitalist economics.

Floyd: Well how else are you going to do it? Buy some more potash mines? Nationalize Honest Jake's Used Junk? Tax the profit out of the oil companies?

Bill: Slow down, Stark. He's just an old man.

Ogie: We didn't do badly did we?

Floyd: You are the cause of every problem we have today.

Ogie: But you have been the government for the last six years.

Floyd: Lucky for this poor province we have been.

Diane: We go into these things with such blind faith.

Floyd: It's a question of good management.

Diane: I thought the Tories would be good managers. But they did a lot of bumbling around. Ran up the deficit, didn't they?

Announcer: . . . Up to the thirty . . . the thirty-five . . . and Toronto will scrimmage at their own thirty-eight.

Ogie: It's not a question of management. You can always hire good managers. It's a question of what you want for the people.

Floyd: The people. Well tell us, just who are the people?

Ogie: Trust a Tory to ask that question.

Announcer: Renfroe is looking for a receiver.

Bill: Hey look at this, Kevin.

But Kevin is caught up in this other battle.

Announcer: He's still looking.

Floyd: I'll tell you who you socialists think The People are!

Announcer: James Curry is closing in on him.

Floyd: Poor people! Down-and-outers!

Announcer: *Groaning with the impact.* Oooh, he hits him!

Ogie: And you think The People are bankers. . . .

Floyd: We do not.

Ogie: And Corporate magnates and three-piece suits.

Floyd: No. The pioneers and the small businessmen and the farmers and the good solid families.

Ogie: I don't disagree with that.

Kevin: Come on. People are everybody.

Ogie: Well there are them that gets and them that gives.

Floyd: And we want to see that everybody gets and you want to see that everybody gives.

Announcer: Second down for Toronto on their thirty-four yard line. Renfroe still seems a little shaken. He has taken more than his share of punishment in this game.

Kevin: So what do you say to that, Ogie?

Announcer: There's the pass. . . .

Kevin: Ogie?

Announcer: It is knocked down by Joe Fuller, number seven.

Ogie: There's an awful lot of misery out there.

Floyd: There are no free rides.

Ogie: That's all right for you to say. You've gotten your fair share.

Floyd: Worked for every penny. I'm not ashamed of it. We're very comfortable. Very happy.

Announcer: So it is third down and Toronto will be forced to punt.

Ogie: Money buys happiness?

Floyd: You'd better believe it. Ask her. *Meaning Sharyl.*

Sharyl gets up and very slowly and very deliberately begins to rip her sweater to shreds. Floyd tries to stop her.

Floyd: Sharyl!

Sharyl: Don't touch me.

There is something to her voice that causes him to freeze. When she has demolished the sweater she sits down rather demurely.

For fifteen years, Floyd, I have been trying to get your attention. Do I have it now?

Floyd: You sure have, Honey.

Sharyl: Don't call me that. I've been trying to start a relationship with you, Floyd . . . for fifteen years. Don't say anything. Let me finish. So for fifteen years I've been listening to you, trying to appreciate your point of view . . . trying to appreciate your personality . . . trying to appreciate you. I think I'll stop trying now. There may be something to appreciate but I'm not sure it's worth the effort. Because I've just realized — I guess I'm slow at realizing things — that all you do is bury me in words, opinions, orations . . . and that's our relationship. So I am going to take the car and leave. Give me two hours and then come home in a taxi. Or get Bill to drive you if he still wants to have anything to do with you. I'll be packed and gone. After that if you want to try and get my attention for a change, good luck, Honey.

Announcer: The Riders are at their own forty yard line. Tod Brown is going deep. It is a pass to Tod Brown. He has it!

Sharyl: But first I'm going to see who wins the game.

Announcer: Brown at the thirty, the twenty-five, the twenty, the fifteen, the ten, the five, Touchdown! Tod Brown for the Saskatchewan Roughriders.

Diane: That was a nice sweater.

Floyd: See what happens when you vote socialist? You get stupid.

Diane: There are Tories with a sense of humanity. . . .

Ogie bites his lip.

Sharyl: This isn't one of them.

Announcer: Saskatchewan is closing in on Toronto. The score is now twenty to twenty-four. Toronto leading by only four points. However the time remaining in the game is only ninety seconds. That still gives the Riders a chance of coming from behind . . . and they have been known to pull it out of the fire at the last minute. . . . However, somehow I doubt that. . . .

Sharyl: Go Riders.

Announcer: There's the point after. Twenty-one now to twenty-four.

Ogie: We'd better watch. I'll probably get another stroke . . . but we'd better watch.

Diane: Ogie?

He stops.

Diane: I don't know what to do.

Ogie waits.

Diane: Everything feels so shaky all of a sudden.

Ogie: What did you expect? That you'd be safe for the rest of your life.

Diane: I thought I might be. Look at him.

Ogie: Stick with him.

Diane: You don't even like him.

Ogie: He'll come through.

Announcer: Ridgway is teeing up the ball. . . .

Ogie: Stick with him. Both of them. *Meaning Kevin as well.* And stick it to them once in a while. That's what your mother did to me.

Diane: But you were so sure of yourself.

Ogie: You thought that?

Diane: Like a rock.

Ogie: I never was. . . . "Muddle through," she'd say. "What are you, scared?" Yep, I was. So she'd say, "Well it is scary." So then we'd muddle through. But I'm still scared.

Diane: But the Regina Manifesto and all of that.

Ogie: It was a good theory. It should have worked. To establish a co-operative commonwealth. Well, it did work . . . except when we got scared and got away from it a few times. And now — now when what we built is falling apart — it seems to me more than ever like we were on the right track. It is all being torn down, isn't it Diane? It's not just my old brain?

Announcer: The Toronto return is stopped on the Toronto thirty-five.

Diane: We'll see.

Ogie: That's not good enough.

Diane: No it isn't.

Ogie: Well, there'll be time to take care of that . . . but now . . .

Ogie nods towards Bill and Diane goes behind his chair and starts to massage his neck.

Bill: What are you doing?

Diane: Guess.

Bill: Won't do any good. You'll need a jackhammer to break through all that.

Diane: More than likely. You don't have to worry, you know. I'll get a job.

Bill: You?

Diane: Yes me! There was life before Bill, you know.

Bill: Sorry.

Diane: I think I might take a course in welding.

Bill: Welding?

Diane: I'll join the Welders' Union. I'll get active in labor organizing.

Bill: What? You're putting me on.

Diane: It's time Diane the Red Menace made a comeback. . . . Hey, relax.

Bill: Me too. I'll help.

Diane: You?

Bill: Yes me. Why not?

Diane: Why?

Bill: I've gotta get back at those bastards.

Diane: I don't think revenge is good politics.

Ogie: You don't question their motives . . . you need all the help you can get. Didn't I teach you anything? It takes all kinds to make a . . . what? What is that expression?

Floyd: What's going on here?

Bill: Nothing. Watch the game.

Ogie: *To Diane.* So you've become a born again activist.

Diane: I don't know, Ogie. Don't expect it to be anything grandiose. I'll just take it as it comes, okay?

Ogie: Okay. Muddle through. Better.

Kevin: Than what?

Ogie: Than living way back then — all those lost glories.

Announcer: A beautiful catch by Joiner and he is down to the Riders' forty.

Floyd: What are you going to do for money?

Announcer: Toronto at the Riders' forty.

Sharyl: I don't know.

Floyd: That's what I thought.

Sharyl: Maybe I'll go into business. I've been thinking I could open a clothing shop . . . one of those places that remakes women over into new images.

Floyd: Snowball in hell.

Announcer: It's Fenerty and he makes it to the twenty-five before he is pushed out of bounds by James Curry. And there seems to be some objection from the Argo sideline to that move by James Curry.

Sharyl: Who asked you?

Kevin: *To Bill.* Who'd want to work for a geek like that anyway?

Bill: You have a point there.

Floyd: What?

Bill: Watch the game, Floyd. Thanks, Kevin.

Kevin: No charge.

Announcer: It's Joiner again. He makes it down to the Rider fifteen, he's still going, the ten, the five . . .

Ogie *Yelling.* No!

Everybody looks at him.

Ogie: Sorry.

Announcer: And there is a pile up.

Kevin: Where's the ball?

Announcer: Did Ken Joiner manage to get the ball into the end zone? I believe he did . . .

Bill: I believe he didn't.

Announcer: . . . but with the mass of players heaped up on the line . . . it is by no means certain. . . .

Sharyl: Pray everybody.

Announcer: No, the ball is short of a touch down by about a yard.

Sharyl: *Fervently.* Thank you.

Announcer: Renfroe is in and under . . . he has the ball. It is a hand-off to Fenerty. What? Fenerty has lost the ball. The Riders have recovered on their own one yard line. Wait a minute. James Curry is running the ball. I didn't think Curry could hold on to anything except a quarterback. Curry is running the ball. Curry is just ambling all the way down the field. Curry is going all the way! It's Curry for a major score. Nobody can touch him. And he has made it!

The sound of the finishing signal.

Announcer: And there is the gun. The game is over. And what a finish. Nobody could have predicted it but the Saskatchewan Roughriders have come from behind to win this football game with a score of twenty-eight points to the Argos' twenty-four! Fantastic!

Ogie: *After the ruckus has died down.* All right, now that that is over, let us get back to real life.

THE END

Further Reading

About Rex Deverell, the plays, and the Globe Theatre

Ball, Denise. "Globe Theatre's Rex Deverell is kept busy," *Regina Leader Post* (Sept. 14, 1979).

Bessai, Diane. "Drama in Saskatchewan." In E. F. Dyck, ed. *Essays on Saskatchewan Writing* (Regina: Saskatchewan Writers Guild, 1986): 223-47.

_____. "Learning From Play" (review of *Boiler Room Suite*), *NeWest Review* 3. 5 (Jan. 1978): 2.

Blackstone, Mary. "Beyond Batoche," (review), *NeWest Review* 10. 10 (Summer, 1985): 18.

_____. "Quartet one of Deverell's Best" (review of *Quartet for Three Actors*), *NeWest Review* 12. 7 (March 1987): 16.

Burrs, Mick. "In Place: Spiritual Explorations of a Rooted Playwright," *Canadian Theatre Review* 42 (Spring 1985): 41-49.

Filewood, Alan. *Canadian Encounters: Documentary Theatre in English Canada* (Toronto: Univ. of Toronto Press, 1987).

Hillis, Doris. "Rex Deverell." In *Plainspeaking: Interviews with Saskatchewan Writers* (Regina and Moose Jaw: Coteau Books, 1988): 65-80.

Osachoff, Margaret Gail. "Games People Play" (review of *Afternoon of the Big Game*), *NeWest Review* 13. 7 (March 1988): 18.

Salloum, Heather. "A Critical Biography of Rex Deverell: Outlining the Mysteries" (Unpublished Master's Thesis, Carleton University, 1982).

Scholar, Michael. "*Beyond Batoche*: The Playwright in Mid-Career," *Canadian Drama/L'Art dramatique canadien* 11. 2 (1985): 329-339.

Wallace, Robert, and Cynthia Zimmerman, eds. "Rex Deverell." In *The Work: Conversations with English-Canadian Playwrights* (Toronto: Coach House Press, 1982): 127-41.

By Rex Deverell

Plays for adults available in published or acting editions

Quartet For Three Actors (Toronto: Playwrights Union of Canada, 1987).

Righteousness (Toronto: Playwrights Canada, 1983).

Medicare! In *Showing West* (Edmonton: NeWest Press, 1983).

Black Powder: Estevan, 1931 (Moose Jaw: Coteau Press, 1982, and in *Grain*, Feb, 1982).

Drift (Toronto: Playwrights Canada, 1981).

Boiler Room Suite (Vancouver: Talonbooks, 1978).

Miscellanea

"Towards a Significant Children's Theatre." *Canadian Children's Literature* 8/9 (1977).

"A Tribute to Sue Kramer," *Canadian Theatre Review* 21 (Winter, 1979).

UNIVERSITY OF ALBERTA BOOKSTORE

5013 CASH-1   1895 0001 111

DEVERELL OF THE GL   MDS 1   10.95
            SUBTOTAL   10.95
G.S.T. R108102831   .77
               TOTAL   11.72

CASH TENDER   20.00
         CHANGE   8.28
RECEIPT REQUIRED FOR REFUND/EXCHANGE

                        1/28/91 11:18

Prairie Play Series
Diane Bessai, General Editor

Published by NeWest Press:

Blood Relations and Other Plays, by Sharon Pollock
Blood Relations
One Tiger to a Hill
Generations

Showing West: Three Prairie Docu-Dramas, edited by
Diane Bessai and Don Kerr
The West Show, Theatre Passe Muraille
Far as the Eye Can See, Rudy Wiebe and Theatre Passe Muraille
Medicare! Rex Deverell

NeWest Plays by Women, edited by Diane Bessai and Don
Kerr
Whiskey Six Cadenza, Sharon Pollock
Play Memory, Joanna M. Glass
The Occupation of Heather Rose, Wendy Lill
Inside Out, Pamela Boyd

Five from the Fringe, edited by Nancy Bell
Life After Hockey, Kenneth Brown
The Betrayal, Laurier Gareau
One Beautiful Evening, Small Change Theatre
The Land Called Morning, John Selkirk
Cut! Lyle Victor Albert

Eight Plays for Young People, edited by Joyce Doolittle
Tikta'litkak, Brian Paisley
Cornelius Dragon, Jan Truss
More of a Family, Alf Silver
The Other Side of the Pole, Marney Heatley, Stephen Heatley, and
Edward Connell
Dr. Barnardo's Pioneers, Rick McNair
The Day Jake Made Her Rain, W.O. Mitchell
Melody Meets the Bag Lady, Rex Deverell
Vandal, William Horrocks